Anne
Sexton

The Artist and Her Critics

Anne Sexton

The Artist and Her Critics

EDITED BY J. D. McCLATCHY

Indiana University Press

Bloomington and London

Library of Congress Cataloging in Publication Data
Main entry under title:

Anne Sexton: the artist and her critics.

Bibliography: P.
  1. Sexton, Anne—Criticism and interpretation—
Addresses, essays, lectures. I. McClatchy, J. D.,
1945–
PS3537.E915Z57   811'.5'4   77-23646
ISBN 0-253-30748-1   1 2 3 4 5 82 81 80 79 78

Contents

PREFACE

The two aspects of this collection, both its documentary and its interpretive material, are meant to help establish an intelligent critical perspective on Anne Sexton's work. For any poet this is necessary, but for Sexton it seems particularly urgent for two reasons. First, there is the unevenness of her poetry, matched by the erratic estimates of it by others. It is important that her stronger verse be distinguished from her weaker. I suspect there is a similar kind of sentimentality in the responses of either those readers who condescend to Sexton or those who canonize her, the former dismissing her poems as pathological and the latter overvaluing them as prophecy. And this is the second reason for this book: to direct our attention away from the woman and back toward her art. She may hold interest as a cultural phenomenon or "figure"—though, to my mind, the manner of her life and the motive for her suicide resist any effort to make her into a feminist martyr, as has been done with Sylvia Plath. Sexton's importance is and will remain as a poet.

In ways that become increasingly apparent, Sexton has emerged as an especially representative artist for the last two decades of American poetry. The start of her work in an insistent, lyrical formalism and her subsequent shift to more open, dramatic forms rehearse a major trend in our poets' relationship to verse. But beyond such technical matters, her larger methods —as they unfolded, from confessionalism to surrealism—are a part of the most significant and energizing developments in poetry since the decline of modernism, and Sexton's use of these modes extended their authority. In her more mature work, the terms of her "inward argument" changed. Where before she had turned first toward the self and then into its underworld, her middle books turned to myths, traditional or imagined, as instruments of self-interpretation. It is important to remember that these more objective devices, whether tales from the Brothers Grimm or stories from the Bible, were always poised as ladders starting in her own foul rag-and-bone shop of the heart. And always her style was in service to her subjects, two of which

vii

—the limits of sanity, and the nature and roles of womanhood—she explored more effectively than any poet of her generation.

Without question her last few books betray a haste that made for a frequent and unfortunate waste of her powers. But that very haste seems finally symptomatic of a more profound impatience, often with herself and her craft, arising from the difficult spiritual quest she had embarked on at the end. And to match all these demands she made on and with poetry, she varied her tone constantly—now strident or hushed, now declamatory or haunted. Taken as a whole, all of her arts converged finally on the mystery of identity and portrayed what Keats called the purgatorial "World of Pains" necessary to school the self "destined to possess the sense of Identity." The actual pains of experience and the psychological pains of memory are our most precise probes for discovering, and so defining, the contours of the self, and Sexton's plunges into her own depths often risk sensationalism. But her revelations are always forceful because of their intimacy, and valuable because of their authenticity. And their effect is always purposive: to create shocks of recognition in her reader.

A brief explanation of the plan of this book may be useful. Its first half is in three parts. Part I comprises the three best interviews Sexton gave: the first is broad and biographical, the second is thematic in focus, and the third concentrates on technique. Part II reproduces the worksheets for a Sexton poem and is the best sort of evidence—first-hand—of her working methods. Part III is a series of reminiscences by some of those people closest to her career—whether as teacher, colleague, student, or friend. I had asked those who wrote (many others refused to write at all, the subject being still too painful for them) to address themselves primarily to the artist they had worked with rather than to the friend they remembered.

The second half of the book is more distinctly critical. Part IV is an anthology of contemporary reviews of Sexton's various books as they appeared. I have selected pieces—some favorable, some not—which have said things of continuing interest about the poetry. That most of the critics are themselves poets is no accident: neither that they were drawn to Sexton's work nor that their commentary remains vital. Part V is a series of four longer essays, each attempting an overview of Sexton's career by isolating and explaining its strengths. And finally, for the convenience of close students of Sexton, I have included a Chronology and a Selected Bibliography of material other than that contained in this volume (for the original appearances of which the Acknowledgments may serve as a reference guide).

Anne Sexton was my friend, and some of my most vivid memories are of her happily in company, the center of attention, while all sorts of opinions and enthusiasms and disagreements were being shared. This collection was assembled in a similar spirit, and I think there is a good chance she would have liked this format for a discussion of her poetry.

J. D. McC.
June 1977

ACKNOWLEDGMENTS

Barbara Kevles, "The Art of Poetry: Anne Sexton": Reprinted from *Writers at Work: The Paris Review Interviews,* Fourth Series, edited by George Plimpton (New York: Viking Press, 1976), 397–424. Copyright © 1974, 1976 by The Paris Review, Inc. All rights reserved. Used by permission of The Viking Press. Originally appeared as "The Art of Poetry XV: Anne Sexton," *Paris Review,* 52 (Summer 1971), 159–91.

Patricia Marx, "Interview with Anne Sexton": Reprinted by permission from *The Hudson Review,* XVIII.4 (Winter 1965–66), 560–70. Copyright © 1966 by The Hudson Review, Inc.

William Packard, "Craft Interview with Anne Sexton": Reprinted from *The Craft of Poetry,* edited by William Packard (New York: Doubleday, 1974), 19–23. Copyright © 1970 by The New York Quarterly Poetry Review Foundation, Inc. Used by permission of Doubleday & Co., Inc. Originally appeared in *New York Quarterly,* 3 (Summer 1970), 8–12.

Denise Levertov, "Light Up the Cave": Copyright © 1974 by Denise Levertov. Used by permission of the author. Originally appeared in *Ramparts,* 13.5 (December 1974–January 1975), 61–63.

John Malcolm Brinnin, "Offices (Boston University)": Reprinted by permission of the author from *American Poetry Review,* 4.3 (1975), 15.

James Dickey: From "Five First Books," *Poetry,* XCVII.5 (February 1961), 318–19. Reprinted in *Babel to Byzantium* (New York: Farrar, Straus & Giroux, 1968), 133–34. Copyright © 1956, 1957, 1958, 1959, 1960, 1961, 1962, 1963, 1964, 1965, 1966, 1967, 1968 by James Dickey. Used by permission of the author and Farrar, Straus & Giroux, Inc.

Geoffrey Hartman: From "Les Belles Dames Sans Merci," *Kenyon Review,* XXII.4 (Autumn 1960), 696–99. Used by permission of the author.

May Swenson: From "Poetry of Three Women," *The Nation,* 196.8 (February 23, 1963), 165–66. Used by permission of the author and publisher.

Thom Gunn: From "Poems and Books of Poems," *Yale Review,* LIII.1 (Autumn 1963), 140–41. Copyright © 1963 by Yale University. Used by permission of the author and publisher.

Louise Bogan: From "No Poetesses Maudites: May Swenson, Anne Sexton," *A Poet's Alphabet* (New York: McGraw-Hill, 1970), 432. Copyright © 1970 by Ruth Limmer as trustee. Used with permission of McGraw-Hill Book Co. Originally appeared in "Verse," *The New Yorker* XXXIX (April 27, 1963), 176.

Ian Hamilton: From "Poetry," *London Magazine* IV (March 1965), 87–88. Used by permission of *London Magazine*.

Hayden Carruth: From "In Spite of Artifice," *The Hudson Review,* XIX.4 (Winter 1966–67), 698. Copyright © 1967 by The Hudson Review, Inc. Used by permission of the publisher.

Charles Gullans: From "Poetry and Subject Matter: From Hart Crane to Turner Cassity," *The Southern Review,* 7.2 (Spring 1970), 497–98. Used by permission of the publisher.

Thomas P. McDonnell: "Light in a Dark Journey," *America,* 116.19 (May 13, 1967), 729–31. Used by permission of America Press.

Mona Van Duyn: From "Seven Women," *Poetry,* CXV.6 (March 1970), 430–32. Copyright © 1970 by The Modern Poetry Association. Used by permission of the editor of *Poetry.*

Daniel Hughes: From "American Poetry 1969: From B to Z," *Massachusetts Review,* XI.4 (Autumn 1970), 668–71. Copyright © 1970 by The Massachusetts Review, Inc. Used by permission of the publisher.

Joyce Carol Oates: From "Private and Public Lives," *University of Windsor Review,* V.2 (Spring 1970), 107–108. Used by permission of the author.

Christopher Lehmann-Haupt: "Grimms' Fairy Tales Retold," *New York Times* (September 27, 1971), 37. Copyright © 1971 by The New York Times Co. Reprinted by permission.

Vernon Young: From "Lines Written in Rouen," *The Hudson Review,* XXIV.4 (Winter 1971–72), 683–84. Copyright © 1972 by The Hudson Review, Inc. Used by permission of the publisher.

Arthur Oberg: From "The One Flea Which Is Laughing," *Shenandoah,* XXV.1 (Fall 1973), 87–89. Copyright © 1973 by *Shenandoah:* The Washington and Lee University Review. Used by permission of the editor.

Muriel Rukeyser: "Glitter and Wounds, Several Wildernesses," *Parnassus: Poetry in Review,* 2.1 (Fall/Winter 1973), 215–21. Used by permission of the author and publisher.

Sandra M. Gilbert: "Jubilate Anne," *The Nation,* 219.7 (September 14, 1974), 214–16. Used by permission of the author and publisher.

Joyce Carol Oates: "Singing the Pathologies of Our Time," *New York Times Book Review* (March 23, 1975), 3–4. Copyright © 1975 by The New York Times Co. Reprinted by permission.

Robert Mazzocco: From "Matters of Life and Death," *New York Review of Books,* XXII.5 (April 3, 1975), 22–23. Copyright © 1975 by Nyrev, Inc. Reprinted by permission from *The New York Review of Books.*

Patricia Meyer Spacks: "45 Mercy Street," *New York Times Book Review* (May 30, 1976), 6. Copyright © 1976 by The New York Times Co. Used by permission.

Richard Howard, "Anne Sexton: 'Some Tribal Female Who Is Known but Forbidden' ": *Alone With America: Essays on the Art of Poetry in the United States Since 1950* (New York: Atheneum, 1971), 442–50. Copyright © 1965, 1966, 1967, 1968, 1969 by Richard Howard. Used by permission of the author and publisher.

Robert Boyers, "*Live or Die:* The Achievement of Anne Sexton": *Salmagundi,* II.1 (Spring 1967), 41–71. Used by permission of the author.

J. D. McClatchy, "Anne Sexton: Somehow To Endure": An earlier, shorter version of this essay appeared in *The Centennial Review,* XIX.2 (Spring 1975), 1–36.

Worksheets for "Elizabeth Gone" are copyright © 1978 by Linda Gray Sexton and Loring Conant, Jr., executors of the estate of Anne Sexton. Used by permission.

Excerpts from the poetry of Anne Sexton used by permission of Houghton Mifflin Co.

The editor is grateful to Linda Gray Sexton for her support; to Lois Ames, Sexton's designated biographer, for material included in the Chronology; and especially to Polly Connor Williams for her invaluable assistance.

A SEXTON CHRONOLOGY

1928 November 9: Anne Gray Harvey born in Newton, Massachusetts, to Mary Gray Staples Harvey and Ralph Churchill Harvey.

1934–45 Educated in Wellesley public schools.

1945–47 Attended Rogers Hall, a preparatory school for girls in Lowell, Massachusetts. Began writing poetry, published in the school yearbook.

1947 Entered The Garland School, a Boston finishing school for women.

1948 August 16: married to Alfred Muller ("Kayo") Sexton II, with whom she had eloped to North Carolina.

1949 Moved to Cochituate, Massachusetts. Awarded scholarship to a modeling course sponsored by the Hart Agency of Boston.

1950 Moved to Baltimore while her husband was in naval training.

1951 Returned to Massachusetts, employed at Hathaway House bookstore and as Hart model.

1952 Moved to San Francisco.

1953 Returned to Massachusetts. July 21: Linda Gray Sexton born. August: purchased house at 40 Clearwater Road, Newton Lower Falls, Massachusetts.

1954 Hospitalized at Westwood Lodge for emotional disturbance. July 15: Anna Ladd Dingley, her spinster great-aunt and confidante, died at age 86.

1955 August 5: Joyce Ladd Sexton born.

1956 March: admitted to mental hospital, her children sent to relatives. November 9: attempted suicide. December: began writing poetry with encouragement of her second psychiatrist, Dr. Martin.

1957 Enrolled in John Holmes's poetry workshop at Boston Center for Adult Education.

1958 Scholarship to Antioch Writers' Conference; worked with W. D. Snodgrass. Accepted into Robert Lowell's graduate writing seminar at Boston University. Friendships with Sylvia Plath, Maxine Kumin, George Starbuck.

1959 March 10: Mary Gray Staples Harvey died of cancer. June 3: Ralph Churchill Harvey died suddenly of a cerebral hemorrhage. August: received Robert Frost Fellowship to attend Breadloaf Writers' Conference. October: pneumonia, appendectomy, ovarectomy. December 10: delivered the Morris Gray Poetry Lecture at Harvard.

1960 April 22: *To Bedlam and Part Way Back* published. Studied with Philip Rahv and Irving Howe at Brandeis University. Friendship with James Wright.

1961 Appointed with Maxine Kumin to be the first scholars in poetry in the Radcliffe Institute for Independent Study. Taught poetry writing at Harvard and Radcliffe.

1962 June: hospitalized at Westwood Lodge. November: awarded the Levinson Prize from *Poetry*.

1963 January: *All My Pretty Ones* nominated for National Book Award. May 22: awarded the first traveling fellowship of the American Academy of Arts and Letters. August 22–October 27: toured France, Belgium, Holland, Switzerland, Italy, and Germany with her friend Sands Robart. Awarded Ford Foundation grant for residence with the Charles Playhouse, Boston.

1964 June: toured Europe with her husband. July: began seeing new psychiatrist. *Selected Poems* published in England, where it was a Poetry Book Society selection. December: moved to 14 Black Oak Road, Weston, Massachusetts.

1965 Elected a Fellow of The Royal Society of Literature, London. Received the first literary magazine travel award from the International Congress of Cultural Freedom.

1966 Began work on a never-completed novel. July: attempted suicide. August: safari in Africa with her husband. November 9: broke her hip on her thirty-eighth birthday.

1967 May: awarded Pulitzer Prize for *Live or Die*. Received Shelley Award from the Poetry Society of America. July: read at International Poetry Festival in London, then toured England. Taught at Wayland High School.

1968 June 11: awarded honorary Phi Beta Kappa from Harvard. July: the rock group "Anne Sexton and Her Kind" was formed and began touring. Taught poetry class at McLean's Hospital in Belmont, Massachusetts.

1969 Served as editorial consultant to *New York Poetry Quarterly*. April: awarded Guggenheim Fellowship. Began work at American Place Theatre, New York City, on *Mercy Street,* which opened October 8. August: began seeing new psychiatrist. June: awarded honorary Phi Beta Kappa from Radcliffe. Began teaching at Boston University and conducting workshops in her home for Oberlin College Independent Study students.

1970 Served on board of directors of *Audience* magazine. June: made honorary Doctor of Letters, Tufts University. August 10: attempted suicide.

1972 Made full professor at Boston University. Spring: held Crashaw Chair in Literature at Colgate University. Made honorary Doctor of Letters, Fairfield University.

1973 Made honorary Doctor of Letters, Regis College. Served on Pulitzer Prize jury. February: hospitalized at Westwood Lodge. March: asked her husband for a divorce and they separated. May 5: Conrad Susa's operatic adaptation of *Transformations* was given its premiere by the Minneapolis Opera Company. Summer: lectured at Breadloaf Writers' Conference. August: entered McLean's Hospital. November 5: divorce granted. Winter: hospitalized at Human Resources Institute, Brookline, Massachusetts.

1974 October 4: committed suicide by carbon monoxide poisoning at 3:30 P.M. in the garage of her home.

Anne
Sexton

The Artist and Her Critics

PART I

Interviews

BARBARA KEVLES

The Art of Poetry:
Anne Sexton
(1968)

The interview took place over three days in the middle of August, 1968. When asked about dates of publications or other events, Anne Sexton kept saying, "Let me think, I want this to be accurate." And she'd use the births of her children as reference dates to chronicle the event in question. Sometimes her distinctions between real and imagined life blurred, as in scenes from Pirandello. Often, her answers sounded like incantations, repetitious chants which if pared down would lose something of their implications, and so, for the most part, they are preserved in their entirety. Even when replying from written notes, she read with all the inflections and intonations of—as she describes her readings—"an actress in her own autobiographical play."

BK: *You were almost thirty before you began writing poetry. Why?*

AS: Until I was twenty-eight I had a kind of buried self who didn't know she could do anything but make white sauce and diaper babies. I didn't know I had any creative depths. I was a victim of the American Dream, the bourgeois, middle-class dream. All I wanted was a little piece of life, to be married, to have children.

3

I thought the nightmares, the visions, the demons would go away if there was enough love to put them down. I was trying my damnedest to lead a conventional life, for that was how I was brought up, and it was what my husband wanted of me. But one can't build little white picket fences to keep nightmares out. The surface cracked when I was about twenty-eight. I had a psychotic break and tried to kill myself.

BK: *And you began to write after the nervous breakdown?*

AS: It isn't quite as simple as all that. I said to my doctor at the beginning, "I'm no good; I can't do anything; I'm dumb." He suggested I try educating myself by listening to Boston's educational TV station. He said I had a perfectly good mind. As a matter of fact, after he gave me a Rorschach test, he said I had creative talent that I wasn't using. I protested, but I followed his suggestion. One night I saw I. A. Richards on educational television reading a sonnet and explaining its form. I thought to myself, "I could do that, maybe; I could try." So I sat down and wrote a sonnet. The next day I wrote another one, and so forth. My doctor encouraged me to write more. "Don't kill yourself," he said. "Your poems might mean something to someone else someday." That gave me a feeling of purpose, a little cause, something to *do* with my life, no matter how rotten I was.

BK: *Hadn't you written limericks before that?*

AS: I did write some light verse—for birthdays, for anniversaries, sometimes thank-you notes for weekends. Long before, I wrote some serious stuff in high school; however, I hadn't been exposed to any of the major poets, not even the minor ones. No one taught poetry at that school. I read nothing but Sara Teasdale. I might have read other poets but my mother said as I graduated from high school that I had plagiarized Sara Teasdale. Something about a statement of hers . . . I had been writing a poem a day for three months, but when she said that, I stopped.

BK: *Didn't anyone encourage you?*

AS: It wouldn't have mattered. My mother was top billing in our house.

BK: *In the beginning, what was the relationship between your poetry and your therapy?*

AS: Sometimes, my doctors tell me that I understand something in a poem that I haven't integrated into my life. In fact, I may be concealing it from myself, while I was revealing it to the readers. The poetry is often more advanced, in terms of my unconscious, than I am. Poetry, after all, milks the unconscious. The unconscious is there to feed it little images, little symbols, the answers, the insights I know not of. In therapy, one seeks to hide sometimes. I'll give you a rather intimate example of this. About three or four years ago my analyst asked me what I thought of my parents having intercourse when I was young. I couldn't talk. I knew there was suddenly a poem there, and I selfishly guarded it from him. Two days later, I had a poem, entitled, "In the Beach House," which describes overhearing the primal scene. In it I say, "Inside my prison of pine and bedspring,/over my window sill, under my knob,/it is plain they are at/the royal strapping." The point of this little story is the image, "the royal strapping." My analyst was quite impressed with that image and so was I, although I don't remember going any further with it then. About three weeks ago, he said to me, "Were you ever beaten as a child?" I told him that I had been, when I was about nine. I had torn up a five-dollar bill that my father gave to my sister; my father took me into his bedroom, laid me down on his bed, pulled off my pants and beat me with a riding crop. As I related this to my doctor, he said, "See, that was quite a royal strapping," thus revealing to me, by way of my own image, the intensity of that moment, the sexuality of that beating, the little masochistic seizure—it's so classic, it's almost corny. Perhaps it's too intimate an example, but then both poetry and therapy are intimate.

BK: *Are your poems still closely connected to your therapy as in the past?*

AS: No. The subject of therapy was an early theme—the process itself as in "Said the Poet to the Analyst," the people of my past, admitting what my parents were really like, the whole Gothic New England story. I've had about eight doctors, but only two that count. I've written a poem for each of the two—"You, Doctor Martin" and "Cripples and Other Stories." And that will do. Those poems are about the two men as well as the strange process. One can say that my new poems, the love poems, come about as a result of new attitudes, an awareness of the possibly good as well as the possibly rotten. Inherent in the process is a rebirth of a sense of self, each time stripping away a dead self.

BK: *Some critics admire your ability to write about the terror of child- hood guilts, parental deaths, breakdowns, suicides. Do you feel that writing about the dark parts of the human psyche takes a special act of courage?*

AS: Of course, but I'm tired of explaining it. It seems to be self- evident. There are warnings all along the way. "Go—children— slow." "It's dangerous in there." The appalling horror that awaits you in the answer.

BK: *People speak of you as a primitive. Was it so natural for you to dig so deeply into the painful experiences of your life?*

AS: There was a part of me that was horrified, but the gutsy part of me drove on. Still, part of me was appalled by what I was doing. On the one hand I was digging up shit, with the other hand I was covering it with sand. Nevertheless, I went on ahead. I didn't know any better. Sometimes, I felt like a reporter researching himself. Yes, it took a certain courage, but as a writer one has to take the chance on being a fool . . . yes, to be a fool, that perhaps requires the greatest courage.

BK: *Once you began writing, did you attend any formal classes to bone up on technique?*

AS: After I'd been writing about three months, I dared to go into the poetry class at the Boston Center for Adult Education taught by John Holmes. I started in the middle of the term, very shy, writing very bad poems, solemnly handing them in for the eighteen others in the class to hear. The most important aspect of that class was that I felt I belonged somewhere. When I first got sick and became a displaced person, I thought I was quite alone, but when I went into the mental hospital, I found I wasn't, that there were other people like me. It made me feel better—more real, sane. I felt, "These are my people." Well, at the John Holmes class that I attended for two years, I found I belonged to the poets, that I was *real* there, and I had another, "These are my people." I met Maxine Kumin, the poet and novelist, at that class. She is my closest friend. She is part superego, part sister, as well as pal of my desk. It's strange because we're quite different. She is reserved, while I tend to be flamboyant. She is an intellectual, and I seem to be a primitive. That is true about our poetry as well.

BK: *You once told me, "I call Maxine Kumin every other line." Is that a slight exaggeration?*

AS: Yes. But often I call her draft by draft. However, a lot of poems I did without her. The year I was writing my first book, I didn't know her well enough to call that often. Later, when she didn't approve of such poems as "Flee on Your Donkey"—that one took four years to complete—I was on my own. Yet once, she totally saved a poem, "Cripples and Other Stories."

BK: *In the early days, how did your relatives react to the jangling of family skeletons?*

AS: I tried not to show my relatives any of the poems. I do know that my mother snuck into my desk one time and read "The Double Image" before it was printed. She told me just before she died that she liked the poem, and that saved me from some added guilt. My husband liked that poem, too. Ordinarily, if I show him a poem, something I try not to do, he says, "I don't think that's too hotsy-totsy," which puts me off. I try not to do it too often. My in-laws don't approve of the poems at all. My children do—with a little pain, they do.

BK: *In your poems, several family skeletons come out of the camphor balls—your father's alcoholic tendencies, your mother's inability to deal with your suicide attempt, your great-aunt in a straitjacket. Is there any rule you follow as to which skeletons you reveal and which you don't?*

AS: I don't reveal skeletons that would hurt anyone. They may hurt the dead, but the dead belong to me. Only once in a while do they talk back. For instance, I don't write about my husband or his family, although there are some amazing stories there.

BK: *How about Holmes or the poets in your class, what did they say?*

AS: During the years of that class, John Holmes saw me as something evil and warned Maxine to stay away from me. He told me I shouldn't write such personal poems about the madhouse. He said, "That isn't a fit subject for poetry." I knew no one who thought it was; even my doctor clammed up at that time. I was on my own. I tried to mind them. I tried to write the way the others, especially Maxine, wrote, but it didn't work. I always ended up sounding like myself.

BK: *You have said, "If anything influenced me, it was W. D. Snod-grass' "Heart's Needle." Would you comment on that?*

AS: If he had the courage, then I had the courage. That poem about losing his daughter brought me to face some of the facts about my own life. I had lost a daughter, lost her because I was too sick to keep her. After I read the poem, "Heart's Needle," I ran up to my mother-in-law's house and brought my daughter home. That's what a poem should do—move people to action. True, I didn't keep my daughter at the time—I wasn't ready. But I was beginning to be ready. I wrote a disguised poem about it, "Unknown Girl in the Maternity Ward." The pain of the loss . . . .

BK: *Did you ever meet Snodgrass?*

AS: Yes. I'd read "Heart's Needle" in *The New Poets of England and America*. I'd written about three quarters of *To Bedlam and Part Way Back* at the time, and I made a pilgrimage to Antioch Writer's Conference to meet and to learn from Snodgrass. He was a surprising person, surprisingly humble. He encouraged me, he liked what I was doing. He was the first established poet to like my work, and so I was driven to write harder and to allow myself, to dare myself to tell the whole story. He also suggested that I study with Robert Lowell. So I sent Mr. Lowell some of my poems and asked if he would take me into the class. By then I'd had poems published in *The New Yorker* and around a bit. At any rate, the poems seemed good enough for Lowell and I joined the class.

BK: *Which poems did you submit to Lowell?*

AS: As far as I can remember, the poems about madness—"You, Doctor Martin," "Music Swims Back to Me" . . . about ten or fifteen poems from the book.

BK: *Was this before or after Lowell published* Life Studies?

AS: Before. I sent him the poems in the summer; the following spring *Life Studies* came out. Everyone says I was influenced by Robert Lowell's revelation of madness in that book, but I was writing *To Bedlam and Part Way Back,* the story of my madness, before *Life Studies* was published. I showed my poems to Mr. Lowell as he was working on his book. Perhaps I even influenced him. I have never asked him. But stranger things have happened.

BK: *And when was your first book,* To Bedlam and Part Way Back, *published?*

AS: It was accepted that January; it wasn't published for a year and a half after that, I think.

BK: *Where was Lowell teaching then?*

AS: The class met at Boston University on Tuesdays from two to four in a dismal room. It consisted of some twenty students. Seventeen graduates, two other housewives who were graduates or something, and a boy who had snuck over from M.I.T. I was the only one in that room who hadn't read *Lord Weary's Castle.*

BK: *And Lowell, how did he strike you?*

AS: He was formal in a rather awkward New England sense. His voice was soft and slow as he read the students' poems. At first I felt the impatient desire to interrupt his slow, line-by-line readings. He would read the first line, stop, and then discuss it at length. I wanted to go through the whole poem quickly and then go back. I couldn't see any merit in dragging through it until you almost hated the damned thing, even your own poems, especially your own. At that point, I wrote to Snodgrass about my impatience, and his reply went this way, "Frankly, I used to nod my head at his every statement, and he taught me more than a whole gang of scholars could." So I kept my mouth shut, and Snodgrass was right. Robert Lowell's method of teaching is intuitive and open. After he had read a student's poem, he would read another evoked by it. Comparison was often painful. He worked with a cold chisel, with no more mercy than a dentist. He got out the decay, but if he was never kind to the poem, he was kind to the poet.

BK: *Did you consult Robert Lowell on your manuscript of* To Bedlam and Part Way Back *before you submitted it to a publisher?*

AS: Yes. I gave him a manuscript to see if he thought it was a book. He was enthusiastic on the whole, but suggested that I throw out about half of it and write another fifteen or so poems that were better. He pointed out the weak ones, and I nodded and took them out. It sounds simple to say that I merely, as he once said, "jumped the hurdles that he had put up," but it makes a difference who puts up the hurdles. He defined the course, and acted as though, good race horse that I was, I would just naturally run it.

BK: *Ultimately, what can a teacher give a writer in a creative-writing class?*

AS: Courage, of course. That's the most important ingredient. Then, in a rather plain way, Lowell helped me to distrust the easy musical phrase and to look for the frankness of ordinary speech. Lowell is never impressed with a display of images or sounds—those things that a poet is born with anyhow. If you have enough natural imagery, he can show you how to chain it in. He didn't teach me what to put into a poem, but what to leave out. What he taught me was taste—perhaps that's the only thing a poet can be taught.

BK: *Sylvia Plath was a member of Lowell's class also, wasn't she?*

AS: Yes. She and George Starbuck heard that I was auditing Lowell's class. They kind of joined me there for the second term. After the class, we would pile in the front seat of my old Ford and I would drive quickly through the traffic to the Ritz. I would always park illegally in a "Loading Only Zone," telling them gaily, "It's O.K., we're only going to get loaded." Off we'd go, each on George's arm, into the Ritz to drink three or four martinis. George even has a line about this in his first book of poems, *Bone Thoughts*. After the Ritz, we would spend our last pennies at the Waldorf Cafeteria—a dinner for seventy cents—George was in no hurry. He was separated from his wife; Sylvia's Ted [Hughes] was busy with his own work; and I had to stay in the city for a seven P.M. appointment with my psychiatrist . . . a funny three.

BK: *In Sylvia Plath's last book, written just before her suicide, she was submerged by the theme of death, as you are in your book* Live or Die. *Did you ever get around to talking about death or your suicides at the Ritz?*

AS: Often, very often, Sylvia and I would talk at length about our first suicide, in detail and in depth—between the free potato chips. Suicide is, after all, the opposite of the poem. Sylvia and I often talked opposites. We talked death with burned-up intensity, both of us drawn to it like moths to an electric light bulb, sucking on it. She told the story of her first suicide in sweet and loving detail, and her description in *The Bell Jar* is just that same story. It is a wonder we didn't depress George with our egocentricity; instead, I think, we three were stimulated by it—even George—as if death made each of us a little more real at the moment.

BK: *In a BBC interview, Sylvia Plath said, "I've been very excited by what I feel is the new breakthrough that came with, say, Robert Lowell's* Life Studies *... This intense breakthrough into very serious, very personal emotional experience, which I feel has been partly taboo ... I think particularly of the poetess Anne Sexton, who writes also about her experiences as a mother; as a mother who's had a nervous breakdown, as an extremely emotional and feeling young woman. And her poems are wonderfully craftsman-like poems, and yet they have a kind of emotional psychological depth, which I think is something perhaps quite new and exciting." Do you agree that you influenced her?*

AS: Maybe. I did give her a sort of daring, but that's all she should have said. I remember writing to Sylvia in England after her first book, *The Colossus,* came out and saying something like, "If you're not careful, Sylvia, you will out-Roethke Roethke." She replied that I had guessed accurately. But maybe she buried her so-called influences deeper than that, deeper than any one of us would think to look, and if she did, I say, "Good luck to her!" Her poems do their own work. I don't need to sniff them for distant relatives: I'm against it.

BK: *Did Sylvia Plath influence your writing?*

AS: Her first book didn't interest me at all. I was doing my own thing. But after her death, with the appearance of *Ariel,* I think I was influenced and I don't mind saying it. In a special sort of way, it was daring again. She had dared to do something quite differ- ent. She had dared to write hate poems, the one thing I had never dared to write. I'd always been afraid, even in my life, to express anger. I think the poem "Cripples and Other Stories" is evidence of a hate poem somehow, though no one could ever write a poem to compare to her "Daddy." There was a kind of insolence in them, saying, "Daddy, you bastard, I'm through." I think the poem "The Addict" has some of her speech rhythms in it. She had very open speech rhythms, something that I didn't always have.

BK: *You have said, "I think the second book lacks some of the impact and honesty of the first, which I wrote when I was so raw that I didn't know any better." Would you describe your development from the second book to the third and from your third to the fourth?*

AS: Well, in the first book, I was giving the experience of madness; in the second book, the causes of madness; and in the third book, finally, I find that I was deciding whether to live or to die. In the third I was daring to be a fool again—raw, "uncooked," as Lowell calls it, with a little camouflage. In the fourth book, I not only have lived, come on to the scene, but loved, that sometime miracle.

BK: *What would you say about the technical development from book to book?*

AS: In *Bedlam,* I used very tight form in most cases, feeling that I could express myself better. I take a kind of pleasure, even now, but more especially in *Bedlam,* in forming a stanza, a verse, making it an entity, and then coming to a little conclusion at the end of it, of a little shock, a little double-rhyme shock. In my second book, *All My Pretty Ones,* I loosened up and in the last section didn't use any form at all. I found myself to be surprisingly free without the form which had worked as a kind of superego for me. The third book I used less form. In *Love Poems,* I had one long poem, eighteen sections, that is in form and I enjoyed doing it in that way. With the exception of that and a few other poems, all of the book is in free verse, and I feel at this point comfortable to use either, depending on what the poem requires.

BK: *Is there any particular subject which you'd rather deal with in form than in free verse?*

AS: Probably madness. I've noticed that Robert Lowell felt freer to write about madness in free verse, whereas it was the opposite for me. Only after I had set up large structures that were almost impossible to deal with did I think I was free to allow myself to express what had really happened. However in *Live or Die,* I wrote "Flee on Your Donkey" without that form and found that I could do it just as easily in free verse. That's perhaps something to do with my development as a human being and understanding of myself, besides as a poet.

BK: *In* Live or Die, *the whole book has a marvelous structured tension—simply by the sequence of the poems which pits the wish to live against the death instinct. Did you plan the book this way? Lois Ames speaks of you as wishing to write more "live" poems because the "die" poems outnumbered them.*

AS: I didn't plan the book any way. In January of 1962, I started collecting new poems the way you do when a book is over. I didn't know where they would go or that they would go anywhere, even into a book. Then at some point, as I was collecting these poems, I was rereading *Henderson the Rain King* by Saul Bellow. I had met Saul Bellow at a cocktail party about a year before and I had been carrying *Henderson the Rain King* around in my suitcase everywhere I traveled. Suddenly there I was meeting Saul Bellow, and I was overenthusiastic. I said, "Oh, oh, you're Saul Bellow, I've wanted to meet you," and he ran from the room. Very afraid. I was quite ashamed of my exuberance and then sometime, a year later, reading *Henderson the Rain King* over again, at three in the morning, I wrote Saul Bellow a fan letter about Henderson, saying that he was a monster of despair, that I understood his position because Henderson was the one who had ruined life, who had blown up the frogs, made a mess of everything. I drove to the mailbox then and there! The next morning I wrote him a letter of apology.

Saul Bellow wrote me back on the back of a manuscript. He said to me, "Luckily, I have a message to you from the book I am writing [which was *Herzog*]. I have both your letters—the good one which was written that night at three A.M. and then the contrite one, the next day. One's best things are always followed by apoleptic, apologetic seizure. Monster of despair could be *Henderson*'s subtitle." The message that he had encircled went this way, "With one long breath caught and held in his chest, he fought his sadness over his solitary life. Don't cry you idiot, live or die, but don't poison everything." And in circling that and in sending it to me, Saul Bellow had given me a message about my whole life. That I didn't want to poison the world, that I didn't want to be the killer; I wanted to be the one who gave birth, who encouraged things to grow and to flower, not the poisoner. So I stuck that message up over my desk and it was a kind of hidden message. You don't know what these messages mean to you, yet you stick them up over your desk or remember them or write them down and put them in your wallet. One day I was reading a quote from Rimbaud that said, "Anne, Anne, flee on your donkey," and I typed it out because it had my name in it and because I wanted to flee. I put it in my wallet, went to see my doctor, and at that point was committed to a hospital for about the seventh or eighth time. In the hospital, I started to write the poem "Flee on Your Donkey," as though the message had come to me at just the right moment. Well, this was true with Bellow's quote from his book. I kept it over my desk and when I went to

Europe, I pasted it in the front of my manuscript. I kept it there as a quotation with which to preface my book. It must have just hit me one day that *Live or Die* was a damn good title for the book I was working on. And that's what it was all about, what all those poems were about. You say there's a tension there and a structure, but it was an unconscious tension and an unconscious structure that I didn't know was going on when I was doing it.

BK: *Once you knew the title of the book, did you count up the "live" poems and count up the "die" poems and then write any more poems because of an imbalance?*

AS: No, no, that's far too rigid. You can't write a poem because of an imbalance. After that I wrote "Little Girl, My Stringbean, My Lovely Woman." Then I wrote a play, then "A Little Uncomplicated Hymn" and other poems. Some were negative and some were positive. At this time I knew that I was trying to get a book together. I had more than enough for a book, but I knew I hadn't written out the live or die question. I hadn't written the poem "Live." This was bothering me because it wasn't coming to me. Instead of that, "Cripples and Other Stories" and "The Addict" were appearing, and I knew that I wasn't finishing the book, that I hadn't come to the cycle, I hadn't given a reason. There's nothing I could do about this and then suddenly our dog was pregnant. I was supposed to kill all the puppies when they came; instead, I let them live and I realized that if I let *them* live, that I could let *me* live, too, that after all I wasn't a killer, that the poison just didn't take.

BK: *Although you received a European traveling fellowship from the American Academy of Arts and Letters, there are, to date, very few poems published about your European experience. Why?*

AS: First of all poems aren't postcards to send home. Secondly I went to Europe with a purpose as well as with a grant. My great-aunt, who was really my best childhood friend, had sent letters home from Europe the three years that she lived there. I had written about this in a poem called "Some Foreign Letters." I had her letters with me as I left for Europe and I was going to walk her walks, and go to her places, live her life over again, and write letters back to her. The two poems that I did write about Europe mention the letters. In "Crossing the Atlantic," I mention that I have read my grandmother's letters, and my mother's letters. I had swallowed their words like Dickens, thinking of Dickens' journals in America. The second poem, "Walking in Paris," was written about my great-aunt, how she used to walk fourteen or fifteen miles a day in Paris, and I call her Nana. Some critics have thought I meant Zola's Nana, but I didn't any more than I meant the Nana in Peter Pan. However, the letters were stolen from my car in Belgium. When I lost the letters in Brussels, that was the end of that kind of poem that I had gone over there to write.

BK: *You were to go abroad for a year, but you only stayed two months. Do you want to comment on that?*

AS: Two and a half months. I got sick over there; I lost my sense of self. I had, as my psychiatrist said, "a leaky ego" and I had to come home. I was in the hospital for a while and then I returned to my normal life. I had to come home because I need my husband and my therapist and my children to tell me who I am. I remember, I was talking with Elizabeth Hardwick on the phone and saying, "Oh, I feel so guilty. I couldn't get along without my husband. It's a terrible thing, really, a modern woman should be able to do it." Although I may be misquoting her, I may have remembered it the way I needed to hear it, she said to me, "If I were in Paris without my husband, I'd hide in a hotel room all day." And I said, "Well, think of Mary McCarthy." And Elizabeth Hardwick said, "Mary McCarthy, she's never been without a man for a day in her life."

BK: *From 1964 to 1965, you held a Ford Foundation Grant in playwriting and worked at Boston's Charles Street Playhouse. How did you feel writing something that had to be staged?*

AS: I felt great! I used to pace up and down the living room shouting out the lines, and what do they call it . . . for walking around the stage . . . *blocking* out the play as I would go along.

BK: *Was the play* [Mercy Street] *ever performed?*

AS: There were little working performances at the Charles Playhouse when we had time. It was pretty busy there. Now and then they would play out a scene for me, and then I would rewrite it and send it in to the director special delivery. He would call me up the next morning and say, "It's not right," and then I would work on it again, send it to him that evening, and then the next morning, he'd call, and so on it went. I found that I had one whole character in the play who was unnecessary because, as they acted it, the director had that person be quiet and say nothing. I realized that that dialogue was totally unnecessary, so I cut out that character.

BK: *Did you find that the themes in your poetry overlapped into your play? Was your play an extension of your poetry?*

AS: Yes. Completely. The play was about a girl shuffling between her psychiatrist and a priest. It was the priest I cut out, realizing that she really wasn't having a dialogue with him at all. The play was about all the subjects that my poems are about—my mother, my great-aunt, my father, and the girl who wants to kill herself. A little bit about her husband, but not much. The play is really a morality play. The second act takes place after death.

BK: *Many of your poems are dramatic narratives. Because you're accustomed to handling a plot, was it easy for you to switch from verse to scene writing?*

AS: I don't see the difference. In both cases, the character is confronting himself and his destiny. I didn't know I was writing scenes; I thought I was writing about people. In another context—helping Maxine Kumin with her novel—I gave her a bit of advice. I told her, "Fuck structure and grab your characters by the time balls." Each one of us sits in our time; we're born, live and die. She was thinking this and that and I was telling her to get inside her characters' lives—which she finally did.

BK: *What were your feelings when you received the Pulitzer Prize for Poetry for* Live or Die *in 1967?*

AS: Of course, I was delighted. It had been a bad time for me. I had a broken hip and I was just starting to get well, still crippled, but functioning a little bit. After I received the prize, it gave me added incentive to write more. In the months following, I managed to write a poem, "Eighteen Days Without You," in fourteen days—an eighteen-section poem. I was inspired by the recognition that the Pulitzer gave me, even though I was aware that it didn't mean all that much. After all, they have to give a Pulitzer Prize every year and I was just one in a long line.

BK: *Do you write a spate of poems at one time or are you disciplined by a writing schedule?*

AS: Well, I'm very dissatisfied with the amount I write. My first book —although it took three years to complete—was really written in one year. Sometimes ten poems were written in two weeks. When I was going at that rate, I found that I could really work well. Now I tend to become dissatisfied with the fact that I write poems so slowly, that they come to me so slowly. When they come, I write them; when they don't come, I don't. There's certainly no disciplined writing schedule except for the fact that when a poem comes a person must be disciplined and ready flexing his muscles. That is, they burst forth and you must put everything else aside. Ideally it doesn't matter what it is, unless your husband has double pneumonia or the child breaks his leg. Otherwise, you don't tear yourself away from the typewriter until you must sleep.

BK: *Do the responsibilities of wife and mother interfere with your writing?*

AS: Well, when my children were younger, they interfered all the time. It was just my stubbornness that let me get through with it at all, because here were these young children saying, "Momma, Momma," and there I was getting the images, structuring the poem. Now my children are older and creep around the house saying, "Shh, Mother is writing a poem." But then again, as I was writing the poem "Eighteen Days Without You"—the last poem in *Love Poems*—my husband said to me, "I can't stand it any longer, you haven't been with me for days." That poem originally was "Twenty-one Days Without You" and it became "Eighteen Days" because he had cut into the inspiration; he demanded my presence back again, into his life, and I couldn't take that much from him.

BK: *When writing, what part of the poem is the prickliest part?*

AS: Punctuation, sometimes. The punctuating can change the whole meaning, and my life is full of little dots and dashes. Therefore, I have to let the editors help me punctuate. And, probably the rhythm. It's the thing I have to work hardest to get in the beginning—the feeling, the voice of the poem, and how it will come across, how it will feel to the reader, how it feels to me as it comes out. Images are probably the most important part of the poem. First of all, you want to tell a story, but images are what are going to shore it up and get to the heart of the matter—but I don't have to work too hard for the images—they have to come —if they're not coming, I'm not even writing a poem, it's pointless. So I work hardest to get the rhythm, because each poem should have its own rhythm, its own structure. Each poem has its own life, each one is different.

BK: *How do you decide a length of line? Does it have something to do with the way it looks on a page as well as how many beats there are to a line?*

AS: How it looks on a page. I don't give a damn about the beats in a line, unless I want them and need them. These are just tricks that you use when you need them. It's a very simple thing to write with rhyme and with rhythmic beat—those things anyone can do nowadays; everyone is quite accomplished at that. The point, the hard thing, is to get the true voice of the poem, to make each poem an individual thing, give it the stamp of your own voice, and at the same time to make it singular.

BK: *Do you ever find yourself saying, "Oh, yes, I've explored that in another poem," and discarding a poem?*

AS: No, because I might want to explore it in a new way . . . I might have a new realization, a new truth about it. Recently I noticed in "Flee on Your Donkey" that I had used some of the same facts in *To Bedlam and Part Way Back,* but I hadn't realized them in their total ugliness. I'd hidden from them. This time was really raw and really ugly and it was all involved with my own madness. It was all like a great involuted web, and I presented it the way it really was.

BK: *Do you revise a great deal?*

AS: Constantly.

BK: *Do you have any ritual which gets you set for writing?*

AS: I might, if I felt the poem come on, put on a certain record, sometimes the "Bachianas Brasileiras" by Villa-Lobos. I wrote to that for about three or four years. It's my magic tune.

BK: *Is there any time of day, any particular mood that is better for writing?*

AS: No. Those moments before a poem comes, when the heightened awareness comes over you and you realize a poem is buried there somewhere, you prepare yourself. I run around, you know, kind of skipping around the house, marvelous elation. It's as though I could fly, almost, and I get very tense before I've told the truth —hard. Then I sit down at the desk and get going with it.

BK: *What is the quality of feeling when you're writing?*

AS: Well, it's a beautiful feeling, even if it's hard work. When I'm writing, I know I'm doing the thing I was born to do.

BK: *Do you have any standard by which you judge whether to let an image remain in a poem, or be cut?*

AS: It's done with my unconscious. May it do me no ill.

BK: *You've said, "When I'm working away on a poem, I hunt for the truth . . . It might be a poetic truth, and not just a factual one." Can you comment on that?*

AS: Many of my poems are true, line by line, altering a few facts to get the story at its heart. In "The Double Image," the poem about my mother's death from cancer and the loss of my daughter, I don't mention that I had another child. Each poem has its own truth. Furthermore, in that poem, I only say that I was hospitalized twice, when, in fact, I was hospitalized five times in that span of time. But then, poetic truth is not necessarily autobiographical. It is truth that goes beyond the immediate self, another life. I don't adhere to literal facts all the time; I make them up whenever needed. Concrete examples give a verisimilitude. I want the reader to feel, "Yes, yes, that's the way it is." I want them to feel as if they were touching me. I would alter any word, attitude, image or persona for the sake of a poem. As Yeats said, "I have lived many lives, I have been a slave and a prince. Many a beloved has sat upon my knee, and I have sat upon the knee of many a beloved. Everything that has been shall be again."

BK: *There Yeats is talking about reincarnation.*

AS: So am I. It's a little mad, but I believe I am many people. When I am writing a poem, I feel I am the person who should have written it. Many times I assume these guises; I attack it the way a novelist might. Sometimes I become someone else and when I do, I believe, even in moments when I'm not writing the poem, that I am that person. When I wrote about the farmer's wife, I lived in my mind in Illinois; when I had the illegitimate child, I nursed it—in my mind—and gave it back and traded life. When I gave my lover back to his wife, in my mind, I grieved and saw how ethereal and unneccessary I had been. When I was Christ, I felt like Christ. My arms hurt, I desperately wanted to pull them in off the Cross. When I was taken down off the Cross, and buried alive, I sought solutions; I hoped they were Christian solutions.

BK: *What prompted you to write "In the Deep Museum," which re-counts what Christ could have felt if he were still alive in the tomb? What led you to even deal with such a subject?*

AS: I'm not sure. I think it was an unconscious thing. I think I had a kind of feeling Christ was speaking to me and telling me to write that story . . . the story he hadn't written. I thought to myself, this would be the most awful death. The Cross, the Crucifixion which I so deeply believe in has almost become trite, and that there was a more humble death that he might have had to seek for love's sake, because his love was the greatest thing about him—not his death.

BK: *Are you a believing nonbeliever? Your poems, such as "The Division of Parts" and "With Mercy for the Greedy," suggest you would like to believe, indeed struggle to believe, but can't.*

AS: Yes. I fight my own impulse. There is a hard-core part of me that believes, and there's this little critic in me that believes nothing. Some people think I'm a lapsed Catholic.

BK: *What was your early religious training?*

AS: Half-assed Protestant. My Nana came from a Protestant background with a very stern patriarchal father who had twelve children. He often traveled in Europe, and when he came back and brought nude statues into his house, the minister came to call and said, "You can't come to church if you keep these nude statues." So he said, "All right, I'll never come again." Every Sunday morning he read the Bible to his twelve children for two hours, and they had to sit up straight and perfect. He never went to church again.

BK: *Where do you get the "juice" for your religious poetry?*

AS: I found when I was bringing up my children, that I could answer questions about sex easily. But I had a very hard time with the questions about God and death. It isn't resolved in my mind to this day.

BK: *Are you saying then that questions from your children are what prompted you to think about these poems—that doesn't sound quite right.*

AS: It isn't. I have visions—sometimes ritualized visions—that come to me of God, or of Christ, or of the saints, and I feel that I can touch them almost . . . that they are part of me. It's the same "Everything that has been shall be again." It's reincarnation, speaking with another voice . . . or else with the devil. If you want to know the truth, the leaves talk to me every June.

BK: *How long do your visions last? What are they like?*

AS: That's impossible to describe. They could last for six months, six minutes, or six hours. I feel very much in touch with things after I've had a vision. It's somewhat like the beginning of writing a poem; the whole world is very sharp and well-defined, and I'm intensely alive, like I've been shot full of electric volts.

BK: *Do you try to communicate this to other people when you feel it?*

AS: Only through the poems, no other way. I refuse to talk about it, which is why I'm having a hard time now.

BK: *Is there any real difference between a religious vision and a vision when you're mad?*

AS: Sometimes, when you're mad, the vision—I don't call them visions really—when you're mad, they're silly and out of place,
whereas if it's a so-called mystical experience, you've put everything in its proper place. I've never talked about my religious
experiences with anyone, not a psychiatrist, not a friend, not a
priest, not anyone. I've kept it very much to myself—and I find
this very difficult, and I'd just as soon leave it, if you please.

BK: *A poem like "The Division of Parts" has direct reference to your
mother's dying. Did those excruciating experiences of watching
someone close to you disintegrate from cancer force you to confront
your own belief in God or religion?*

AS: Yes, I think so. The dying are slowly being rocked away from us
and wrapped up into death, the eternal place. And one looks for
answers and is faced with demons and visions. Then one comes
up with God. I don't mean the ritualized Protestant God, who
is such a goody-goody . . . but the martyred saints, the crucified
man. . . .

BK: *Are you saying that when confronted with the ultimate question,
death, that your comfort comes, even though watered-down, from
the myths and fables of religion?*

AS: No myth or fable ever gave me any solace, but my own inner
contact with the heroes of the fables, as you put it, my very
closeness to Christ. In one poem about the Virgin Mary, "For the
Year of the Insane," I believed that I was talking to Mary, that
her lips were upon my lips; it's almost physical . . . as in many
of my poems. I become that person.

BK: *But is it the fact in your life of someone you know dying that forces
you into a vision?*

AS: No, I think it's my own madness.

BK: *Are you more lucid, in the sense of understanding life, when you
are mad?*

AS: Yes.

BK: *Why do you think that's so?*

AS: Pure gift.

BK: *I asked you, are you a believing disbeliever. When something happens like a death, are you pushed over the brink of disbelieving into believing?*

AS: For a while, but it can happen without a death. There are little deaths in life, too—in your own life—and at that point, sometimes you are in touch with strange things, otherworldly things.

BK: *You have received a great deal of fan mail from Jesuits and other clergy. Do any of them interpret what you write as blasphemy?*

AS: No. They find my work very religious, and take my books on retreats, and teach my poems in classes.

BK: *Why do you feel that most of your critics ignore this strain of religious experience in your poetry?*

AS: I think they tackle the obvious things, without delving deeper. They are more shocked by the other, whereas I think in time to come people will be more shocked by my mystical poetry than by my so-called confessional poetry.

BK: *Perhaps your critics, in time to come, will associate the suffering in your confessional poetry with the kind of sufferers you take on in your religious poetry.*

AS: You've summed it up perfectly. Thank you for saying that. That ragged Christ, that sufferer, performed the greatest act of confession, and I mean with his body. And I try to do that with words.

BK: *Many of your poems deal with memories of suffering. Very few of them deal with memories that are happy ones. Why do you feel driven to write more about pain?*

AS: That's not true about my last book, which deals with joy. I think I've dealt with unhappy themes because I've lived them. If I haven't lived them, I've invented them.

BK: *But surely there were also happy moments, joyous, euphoric moments in those times as well.*

AS: Pain engraves a deeper memory.

BK: *Are there any poems you wouldn't read in public?*

AS: No. As a matter of fact, I sing "Cripples and Other Stories" with my combo to a Nashville rhythm.

BK: *What is your combo?*

AS: It's called "Her Kind"—after one of my poems. One of my students started putting my poems to music—he's a guitarist and then we got an organist, a flutist, and a drummer. We call our music "Chamber Rock." We've been working on it and giving performances for about a year. It opens up my poems in a new way, by involving them in the sound of rock music, letting my words open up to sound that can be actually heard, giving a new dimension. And it's quite exciting for me to hear them that way.

BK: *Do you enjoy giving a reading?*

AS: It takes three weeks out of your life. A week before it happens, the nervousness begins and it builds up to the night of the reading, when the poet in you changes into a performer. Readings take so much out of you, because they are a reliving of the experience, that is, they are happening all over again. I am an actress in my own autobiographical play. Then there is the love. . . . When there is a coupling of the audience and myself, when they are really with me, and the Muse is with me, I'm not coming alone.

BK: *Can you ever imagine America as a place where thousands of fans flock to a stadium to hear a poet, as they do in Russia?*

AS: Someday, perhaps. But our poets seem to be losing touch. People flock to Bob Dylan, Janis Joplin, the Beatles—these are the popular poets of the English-speaking world. But I don't worry about popularity; I'm too busy.

BK: *At first your poetry was a therapeutic device. Why do you write now?*

AS: I write because I'm driven to—it's my bag. Though after every book, I think there'll never be another one. That's the end of that. Good-by, good-by.

BK: *And what advice would you give to a young poet?*

AS: Be careful who your critics are. Be specific. Tell almost the whole story. Put your ear close down to your soul and listen hard.

BK: *Louis Simpson criticized your poetry, saying, "A poem titled 'Menstruation at Forty' was the straw that broke this camel's back." Is it only male critics who balk at your use of the biological facts of womanhood?*

AS: I haven't added up all the critics and put them on different teams. I haven't noticed the gender of the critic espcially. I talk of the life–death cycle of the body. Well, women tell time by the body. They are like clocks. They are always fastened to the earth, listening for its small animal noises. Sexuality is one of the most normal parts of life. True, I get a little uptight when Norman Mailer writes that he screws a woman anally. I like Allen Ginsberg very much and when he writes about the ugly vagina, I feel awful. That kind of thing doesn't appeal to me. So I have my limitations, too. Homosexuality is all right with me. Sappho was beautiful. But when someone hates another person's body and somehow violates it—that's the kind of thing I mind.

BK: *What do you feel is the purpose of poetry?*

AS: As Kafka said about prose, "A book should serve as the ax for the frozen sea within us." And that's what I want from a poem. A poem should serve as the ax for the frozen sea within us.

BK: *How would you apply the Kafka quote to your new book,* Love Poems?

AS: Well, have you ever seen a sixteen-year-old fall in love? The ax for the frozen sea becomes imbedded in her. Or have you ever seen a woman get to be forty and never have any love in her life? What happens to her when she falls in love? The ax for the frozen sea.

BK: *Some people wonder how you can write about yourself, completely ignoring the great issues of the times, like the Vietnam War or the civil rights crisis.*

AS: People have to find out who they are before they can confront national issues. The fact that I seldom write about public issues in no way reflects my personal opinion. I am a pacifist. I sign petitions, etc. However, I am not a polemicist. "The Fire Bombers"—that's a new poem—is about wanton destruction, not about Vietnam, specifically; when Robert Kennedy was killed, I wrote about an assassin. I write about human emotions; I write about interior events, not historical ones. In one of my love poems, I say that my lover is unloading bodies from Vietnam. If that poem is read in a hundred years, people will have to look up the war in Vietnam. They will have mixed it up with the Korean or God knows what else. One hopes it will be history very soon. Of course, I may change. I could use the specifics of the war for a backdrop against which to reveal experience, and it would be just as valid as the details I am known by. As for the civil rights issue, I mentioned that casually in a poem, but I don't go into it. I think it's a major issue. I think many of my poems about the individual who is dispossessed, who must play slave, who cries "Freedom Now," "Power Now," are about the human experience of being black in this world. A black emotion can be a white emotion. It is a crisis for the individual as well as the nation. I think I've been writing black poems all along, wearing my white mask. I'm always the victim . . . but no longer!

Interview with
Anne Sexton

(1965)

PM: *I understand that you started writing poetry only in 1957. What made you begin at such a late date?*

AS: Well, it was actually personal experience, because I had had a nervous breakdown, and as I was recovering I started to write, and I got more and more serious about it, and I started out writing almost a poem a day. It was a kind of rebirth at twenty-nine.

PM: *What do you think caused you to write poetry after a breakdown? What was the impetus?*

AS: It's too strange. It's just a matter of coincidence. I think probably I'm an artist at heart, and I've found my own form, which I think is poetry. I was looking at educational television in Boston, and I. A. Richards was explaining the form of a sonnet, and I thought, "Well, so that's a sonnet." Although I had learned it in high school, I hadn't ever done anything about it. And so I thought, "I'll try that, too. I think maybe I could." So I sat down and wrote in the form of the sonnet. I was so pleased with myself that for about three months I wrote a sonnet every day. There are no sonnets in my book. They have since been discarded. But that's the way I started.

PM: *When did you start taking yourself seriously as a poet?*

AS: I think when I was published. After I'd been writing about a year and a half I started sending things to magazines, and collecting rejection slips. I wasted a lot of time on it. There were kind of two sides of me. One part was writing poems very seriously and the other was running this little fool's business, which meant I will send out my poems today to four magazines, and the mail will bring five or six poems back.

PM: *You often mention your experience in an asylum where you wrote poetry. Did you write when you were very disturbed, or afterwards? Did you find writing had a beneficial effect on your health?*

AS: I don't think so particularly. It certainly did not create mental health. It isn't as simple as my poetry makes it, because I simplified everything to make it more dramatic. I have written poems in a mental institution, but only later, not at the beginning.

PM: *There is a popular notion that creative genius is very close to insanity. Many of our major poets now, such as Robert Lowell and Theodore Roethke before he died, often had mental breakdowns. Do you feel there's truth in this notion?*

AS: Well, their genius is more important than their disease. I think there are so many people who are mentally disturbed who are not writers, or artists, or painters or whatever, that I don't think genius and insanity grow in the same bed. I think the artist must have a heightened awareness. It is only seldom this sprouts from mental illness alone. However, there *is* this great feeling of heightened awareness that all artists must have.

PM: *In your book* All My Pretty Ones, *you quote this part of a letter written by Franz Kafka: "The books we need are the kind that act*

*upon us like a misfortune, that make us suffer like the death of
someone we love more than ourselves. A book should serve as the
ax for the frozen sea within us." Is this the purpose you want your
poetry to serve?*

AS: Absolutely. I feel it should do that. I think it should be a shock
to the senses. It should almost hurt.

PM: *Do you find that all poetry does this when you read it? Do you
admire certain poetry more for doing this?*

AS: No, not necessarily. I think it's just my little declaration to
myself. I put it in the book to show the reader what I felt, but
Kafka's work certainly works upon me as an ax upon a frozen
sea. But I admire many poets, many writers who don't do this.

PM: *I wonder if you would further explain that metaphor.*

AS: I see it very literally as an ax, cutting right through a slab of ice.
I think we go along very complacently and are brainwashed with
all kinds of pablum, advertisements every minute, the sameness
of supermarkets, everything—it's not only the modern world,
even trees become trite—and we need something to shock us, to
make us become more aware. It doesn't need to happen in such
a shocking way, perhaps, as in my poetry. I think of the poetry
of Elizabeth Bishop, which seems to have beautiful ordered clarity. Her fish hurts as much as Randall Jarrell's speaking people.
They are two of my favorite poets. Their work shocks me into
being more alive, and that's maybe what I mean. The poet
doesn't have to use my method to have that happen to me. And
Rilke, think of Rilke with his depth, his terrible pain!—

PM: *Do you find that the writing of poetry achieves this for you as well
as the reading of it?*

AS: No, the writing actually puts things back in place. I mean, things
are more chaotic, and if I can write a poem, I come into order
again, and the world is again a little more sensible, and real. I'm
more in touch with things.

PM: *How does a poem come into being?*

AS: Oh, that's a terrible question! I don't know. Sometimes you get a line, a phrase, sometimes you're crying, or it's the curve of a chair that hurts you and you don't know why, or sometimes you just want to write a poem, and you don't know what it's about. I will fool around on the typewriter. It might take me ten pages of nothing, of terrible writing, and then I'll get a line, and I'll think, "That's what I mean!" What you're doing is hunting for what you mean, what you're trying to say. You don't know when you start.

PM: *Do you work on it a long time?*

AS: I work on it a very long time. For one lyric poem I rewrote about three hundred typewritten pages. Often I keep my worksheets, so that once in a while when I get depressed and think that I'll never write again, I can go back and see how that poem came into being. You watch the work and you watch the miracle. You have to look back at all those bad words, bad metaphors, everything started wrong, and then see how it came into being, the slow progress of it, because you're always fighting to find out what it is that you want to say. You have to go deeper and deeper each time. You wonder why you didn't drown at the time—deeper and deeper.

PM: *Is it a struggle or pleasure?*

AS: Oh, it's a wonderful pleasure. It's a struggle, but there's great happiness in working. As anyone knows, if you're doing something that you love and you're struggling with it, there's happiness there, particularly if you can get it in the end. And I'm pretty stubborn. I need to keep after it, until I get it. Or I keep after it until I kill it.

PM: *Do you discard many poems that you write?*

AS: Well, now I think I prediscard them. I don't write them, which is one reason why I write less than I did in the beginning. I wrote

a lot of unimportant poems, and now when I look at a poem, I
always wonder why was this written. There should be a reason
for it. It should do something to me. It should move me. I have
some poems that have haunted me for four or five years, and
they're unfinished and maybe they'll never be finished. I know
they're not right, but it hurts not to write them. I have this great
need somehow to keep that time of my life, that feeling. I want
to imprison it in a poem, to keep it. It's almost in a way like
keeping a scrapbook to make life mean something as it goes by,
to rescue it from chaos—to make "now" last.

PM: *In your first volume of poetry,* To Bedlam and Part Way Back,
*you quote another passage from a letter, this time from Schopen-
hauer to Goethe, and it says, "It is the courage to make a clean
breast of it in the face of every question that makes a philosopher."
I take it that you mean this courage also makes a poet.*

AS: Yes, exactly. It's very hard to reveal yourself. Frankly, anything
I say to you is useless and probably more deceiving than revealing. I tell so much truth in my poetry that I'm a fool if I say any
more. To really get at the truth of something is the poem, not the
poet.

PM: *Do you find that you are more truthful in your poetry than you
are to yourself?*

AS: Yes, I think so. That's what I'm hunting for when I'm working
away there in the poem. I'm hunting for the truth. It might be
a kind of poetic truth, and not just a factual one, because behind
everything that happens to you, every act, there is another truth,
a secret life.

PM: *You wrote for the Poetry Book Society, "All poets lie. As I said once
in a poem, a writer is essentially a crook. With used furniture he
makes a tree." Now how do you reconcile that with your remark
about poetry being the truth?*

AS: I think maybe it's an evasion of mine. It's a very easy thing to say, "All poets lie." It depends on what you want to call the truth, you see, and it's also a way of getting out of the literal fact of a poem. You can say there is truth in this, but it might not be the truth of my experience. Then again, if you say that you lie, you can get away with telling the awful truth. That's why it's an evasion. The poem counts for more than your life.

PM: *Do you find that you often distort the literal facts of your life to present the emotional truth that lies under them?*

AS: Well, I think this is necessary. It's something that an artist must do to make it clear and dramatic and to have the effect of the ax. To have that effect you must distort some of these facts to give them their own clarity. As an easy example, in my long poem to my daughter and about my mental illness, I don't imply that I was ever in an institution more than once, but that was the dramatic truth. The actual truth was something quite different. I returned quite a few times, and the fact that I have two children was not mentioned in this, because the dramatic point was I had one child, and was writing to her. It made a better poem to distort it this way. I just don't mention it. So you don't have to include everything to tell the truth. You can exclude many things. You can even lie (one can confess and lie forever) as I did in the poem of the illegitimate child that the girl had to give up. It hadn't happened to me. It wasn't true, and yet it was indeed the truth.

PM: *Are you the ultimate judge of what the truth is?*

AS: No. There's the trouble. No, I'm not.

PM: *What is the criterion?*

AS: I don't think there is one. I mean, people lie to themselves so much—postmarks lie, even gravestones lie. The effort is to try to get to some form of integrity when you write a poem, some whole life lived, to try to present it now, to give the impact. It's the same as with a novelist, only it's in little sections.

PM: *Are you ever influenced, or do you ever learn anything from critics?*

AS: Oh, they're very disturbing. I don't know what I learn. I just want to say, "Gee whiz, kids, that's the best way I could do it," something like that. One prolific poet whom I greatly admire can hardly write a damning review without mentioning my name in connection with "mechanically bad writing." What should I do? Send him a telegram? I carried one very bad review in my wallet all over Europe. The good reviews I left at home. But even over there I was still Anne. I couldn't change her. I think mostly reviewers are upsetting. You just love the praise, and you try to shut out the criticism. I don't know how much they can influence you. I don't think they always read you correctly, but you always think the ones that like you are reading you pretty well.

PM: *Very few women have been great poets. Do you find that there's a difficulty in being a woman and a creative artist?*

AS: I think they are really very closely allied. I don't think it's that difficult at all. It's within a woman to create, to make order, to be an emotional, full human being, I think; perhaps men are better because they are denied this in their lives. Therefore they put more of it into a poem, and maybe if you are born with an extra amount, as a woman, it works out all right. You have enough for life itself, you have a family, and then you have some left over. It always seems to me I have too much left over. Maybe that's an ingredient.

PM: *In one of your poems, "The Black Art," you wrote, "A woman who writes feels too much those fancies and portents," and then in another stanza, "A man who writes knows too much of spells and fetishes." Do you think there is this distinction between the woman being the feeling creature and the man being the rational?*

AS: I don't think so, really. I think I was lying a little bit. It is in that same poem I said a writer is essentially a crook, and we're quite together in that, the male and female. I don't think that man is the rational being, and there are some marvelous women poets who are very rational: Marianne Moore, Elizabeth Bishop. May Swenson is a very good poet and certainly not overemotional in any way. She knows just when to hold back and when to give forth. Then there are male poets who are so emotional that I don't think this holds true. Great poets know both.

PM: *You were mentioning that perhaps the reason that more men have been great poets is that they are denied the creativity that comes naturally to women, through having children. Do you think then that some kind of channeling or denial is important?*

AS: Well, it hasn't been for me. I think that it might be so. Sometimes I think, "Oh, I'm so lonely." This is the curse of being a writer or an artist, but then I think that great artists such as Rilke have treasured this, worshipped this. And then sometimes I think I'd give it all up if I could just be comfortable and with things. I think women are essentially *with* things. They're part of the earth, and perhaps it's my own peculiar trait that I feel not part of the earth. Therefore I look at it a little more sharply. I feel a little more outcast, and it perhaps makes me more of a writer.

PM: *That may be the dilemma of the modern woman, though—*

AS: Oh, I don't know! Poor modern woman!

PM: *What is your feeling about the "feminine mystique"? One is always hearing of the problems of modern woman. Do you think it's any worse now?*

AS: Maybe modern woman is more conscious now, more thinking. I can't tell. Sometimes I feel like another creature, hardly a woman, although I certainly am, in my life. I can't be a modern woman. I'm a Victorian teenager—at heart. I noticed in Europe that women are not complaining as much, and their lives are certainly not as good as ours. We have much more freedom, and we can speak up, and I like that. I like to speak up.

PM: *You mentioned before that as a writer you feel alone and not part of the earth.*

AS: It isn't as a writer. It's as a human being.

PM: *Do you feel you are associated with any other poets?*

AS: I am often likened to Robert Lowell or W. D. Snodgrass, and I think we all kind of got born into this about the same time, writing in a certain frank style. I do find that perhaps I'm drawn to women poets because some of them have some quality that I lack. I often find myself liking a poet, for example, May Swenson or Elizabeth Bishop, who does something that I can't do at all, and I admire it for being so clear and true and having a beauty that doesn't seem to shine from my poetry at all. I don't feel as though I'm part of any group, because I'm too much off by myself, and not in the academic world, except that I did study with Robert Lowell for a while.

PM: *I wonder in what way you feel his poetry influenced your work?*

AS: Actually, this is a terrible thing to admit, but I had not read any of his poetry when I studied with him. I did not go to college, and when I was studying with him I was so innocent as not to have read any of his poems, and his *Life Studies* had not come out at the time. They came out after I had finished studying with him. So they didn't influence me at all, because I hadn't seen them. If anything influenced me it was W. D. Snodgrass' *Heart's Needle.* I had written about half of my first book when I read that poem, and it moved me to such an extent—it's about a child, and he has to give up his child, which seems to be one of my themes, and I didn't have my own daughter at that time—that I ran up to my mother-in-law's where she was living and got her back. I could only keep her at that time for a week, but the poem moved me to *action.* It so changed me, and undoubtedly it must have influenced my own poetry. At the time everyone said, "You can't write this way. It's too personal; it's confessional; you can't write this, Anne," and everyone was discouraging me. But then I saw Snodgrass doing what I was doing, and it kind of gave me permission.

PM: *I wonder what is the relationship between form and making a poem function like an ax. In what way do you approach a poem stylistically and in what way does content dominate?*

AS: Content dominates, but style is the master. I think that's what makes a poet. The form is always important. To me there's something about fiction that is too large to hold. I can see a poem, even my long ones, as something you could hold, like a piece of something. It isn't that I care about the shape of it on the page, but the line must look right to me. About half of my poems are in some sort of form. The poems that aren't in form have a shape, just the same, even if it isn't a vase or anything that simple, but they have a kind of shape, a body of their own. There are some stories that are long and thin. They should be. There's a reason for it. I don't decide this. The story writes itself and must find its right form. I'm not talking about something that's particularly academic, or perhaps it is. It's just a little trick that I have of my own.

PM: *Do you mean by form just the physical look of the poem?*

AS: Yes, sometimes, but also the sound. But I think of it as something you can hold. I think of it with my hands to begin with. I don't know what the poem will be and I start out writing and it looks wrong. I start a long line and that looks wrong, and a short line, and I play around with rhyme, and then I sometimes make a kind of impossible syllabic count, and if I can get the first verse and it's right, then I might keep on with that for four more verses, and then I might change it because I felt that it needed a new rhythm. It has as much to do with speech as it does with the way it will look on the page, because it will change speech—it's a kind of compression. I used to describe it this way; that if you used form it was like letting a lot of wild animals out in the arena, but enclosing them in a cage, and you could let some extraordinary animals out if you had the right cage, and that cage would be form.

PM: *In the same article that you wrote for the Poetry Book Society you said, "Form for me is a trick to deceive myself, not you, but me."*

AS: I can explain that exactly. I think all form is a trick in order to get at the truth. Sometimes in my hardest poems, the ones that are difficult to write, I might make an impossible scheme, a syllabic count that is so involved that it then allows me to be truthful. It works as a kind of superego. It says, "You may now face it, because it will be impossible ever to get out." Almost any accomplished poet can do this. The point is can you get to the real, the sharp edge of the poem? But you see how I say this not to deceive you, but to deceive me. I deceive myself, saying to myself you can't do it, and then if I can get it, then I have deceived myself, then I can change it and do what I want. I can even change and rearrange it so no one can see my trick. It won't change what's real. It's there on paper.

PM: *Do you really set the rules to begin with?*

AS: I don't set the rules. I don't sit down and say, "I'm going to have *a, b, c, d, e* and fourteen syllables." I work and work for the first stanza, and if it looks right and if it feels right, then I cement it. I say, "Okay, here it is." I have done this with some poems. The syllabic count is this, the rhyme goes *a, b, c, a, b, c,* or however, and I follow that, and then after I've done it, and it's sometimes very hard, I may change it so that no one could look back over it and see that I had made this small conceit. Better to hide conceits like this and leave it raw. Take our rules and leave the instant.

PM: *And this works in your best poems?*

AS: Well, perhaps my hardest. I must say I don't do it as often now. In my newer poems I'm not using form half as much, and I don't know to what to attribute this. I don't know what it is.

PM: *By form then you really mean the physical shape of the poem and how it sounds?*

AS: And how it rhymes and the length of the lines. Sometimes a short line is a very sharp thing, and the breaking of a line, the breaking of the rhythm is a very important thing. I think of all these things quite magically, and not in some academic way, because I don't really know what my form is. With old poems I have to go back and study it like a graduate student, because I forget it, suppress it. I forget what I did, and that's why sometimes I keep these worksheets to look back and see what kind of little magical tricks I use to get to it.

PM: *Over the seven or eight years you have been writing poetry, do you feel you've developed in terms of form or style?*

AS: Well, perhaps, I would say I think the second book better written than the first and yet, in a way, I think the second lacks some of the impact and honesty of the first, which I wrote when I saw so raw that I didn't know any better. In the second book I knew a little bit more about how to write, and sometimes, perhaps, I cooled it too much. I didn't let myself go enough. I think maybe this will happen in a third book, which is not finished; that there are too many poems I'm not writing, that in a way I know too much. The first book was just kind of a miracle. I don't know how it came to be. There is some very bad writing in some of my best poems, and yet those flaws seem to me to make them even better. A little more honest in their own kind of silly way. There they are with all their flaws, a little more human, you might say.

PM: *Do you find that you deal very much with the same themes? There do seem to be recurring themes throughout.*

AS: Yes, there's the mother–child theme, and death very much, although, I think maybe a little less. Any writer, any artist I'm sure, is obsessed with death, a prerequisite for life. I'm afraid they are quite repetitive, but I think that's all right. I don't think you need too many different themes. I could defend this, not just because it seems to be what I'm doing, but in other writers that I've loved. I could defend their repetition of a theme. I would say to have written this is a wonderful thing, about some other writer, and then I try not to condemn myself for not changing a little more, although my critics like it if I change. They want to see me broaden my scope and do something different.

PM: *Do you find you come to an understanding or a peace with the problems that you're dealing with, through writing about them all the time?*

AS: Just in a very small way, a very qualified way. There is a big change after you write a poem. It's a marvelous feeling, and there's a big change in the psyche, but I think you really go into great chaos just before you write a poem, and during it, and then to have come out of that whole, somehow is a small miracle, which lasts for a couple of days. Then on to the next.

WILLIAM PACKARD

Craft Interview
with Anne Sexton

(1970)

AS: I have a terrible memory—it's all a mystery to me, it all just happens.

WP: *Do you revise much?*

AS: Yes, I've revised as much as three hundred times on one lyric poem. The title of that poem was "The Truth the Dead Know." I showed it to Robert Lowell after I'd rewritten it fifty times. He said the ending wasn't right. I don't remember—I ended it with the dead saying something. He said the dead don't speak. The more I thought about it the more I agreed with him, and that's when I turned them into stone.

WP: *How long did you work on that poem?*

AS: I don't remember how many months it took—maybe two. The poem "Flee on Your Donkey"—I rewrote that for four years. I hung onto it and revised it every six months. Everyone said it was a useless poem; even my best friend said, "It embarrasses me," and Cal Lowell said it was better to be a short story. I fussed with it and I played with it and I worked with it.

43

WP: *What physical conditions do you find best for revision?*

AS: I think that would depend on the physical conditions of the first writing. My play was written to music by Villa-Lobos, and I put it on tape so I could play it all the while I was writing. When the kids were young, I would turn on a symphony to make a constant noise to drown them out so I could work. I wrote the poem "Vision Apart" to *Swan Lake.* I often write in silence, too. I can't just have the radio on. Any talking distracts me. I like quiet. Once I tried to write a poem a day. I wrote for eighteen days. The kids would walk by my room and say, "Shhh, Mommy's writing a poem!"

WP: *What do you think is valuable about poetry workshops?*

AS: They were very valuable to me. It's where I started. All you need is one friend to tell you to write a poem a day. It's not the criticism—it's the stimulation, the countered interest. It's a time to grow. My first workshop was with John Holmes in Boston, with George Starbuck and Maxine Kumin. If I'd gone to a real poetry workshop I'd have been scared. As it was, this was a friendly group. You'd always have enough ego to bring two poems. We all met once a month. We missed it very much when it ended.

WP: *Then you went on to study with Robert Lowell. Was it the beginning of your confessional poetry?*

AS: At that time Lowell had not revealed what he was doing. He was very stern. He went line by line. Sometimes he would spend five minutes on a first line. It was line dissection. What was inspiring was that he would take a poem by a great poet and relate it to the workshop poem.

WP: *That must have been stimulation in an advanced sense.*

AS: It was. Lowell introduced me to Lawrence, and to his own poetry. I came there at just the right time. I had *To Bedlam and Part Way Back* almost finished, and he helped me to hold it down.

WP: *Why did you choose to write poetry?*

AS: I haven't got the slightest idea. When I was eighteen or nineteen I wrote for half a year. One time I tried painting, but I wasn't good. When I was twenty-eight, I saw I. A. Richards on television. He was talking about the form of the sonnet, its images, and I thought, I can do that. I would like to be a photographer if the camera could work the way fingers work. I like to capture an instant. A picture is a one-second thing—it's a fragile moment in time. I try to do it with words.

WP: *Do you ever play craft games with your poetry?*

AS: I always call it tricks, not craft. Craft is a trick you make up to let you write the poem. The only game I ever played was with the word "star." I did everything I could with the arrangement of s-t-a-r. Conrad Aiken once saw a palindrome on the side of a barn: Rats Live On No Evil Star (and I want that to be on my gravestone, because I see myself as a rat, but I live on no evil star). Rats and star: I wrote a list of all the words I could make out of those letters. Then I sat down with the words and made up a poem. The game I do play is I say to myself, This poem is too hard to write. It is impossible for me, I can't do it. Then I start fooling around with some stanzas, running a syllable count. I use syllabics and rhyme. I get a good beginning to the poem. Then I say to myself, But I can't do the poem, it's too hard. I use this as a kind of superego. Then I proceed to do the poem. I make up the game, and then I don't follow it too carefully. Games don't get me involved. It's always the content that gets me involved. I make up the game to go along with the content. I start every poem with a powerful emotion. I write in the morning. I use yellow paper, sometimes lined school paper. I write at the typewriter and make extensive corrections. I sit at a desk, my feet up on a bookcase. I have cigarettes, naturally, burned down to one long gray ash. How do I write? Expand, expand, cut, cut, expand, expand, cut, cut. Do not trust spontaneous first drafts. You can always write more fully. The beautiful feeling after writing a poem is on the whole better even than after sex, and that's saying a lot.

WP: *How would you define confessional poetry?*

AS: How would *you* define confessional poetry?

WP: *We'd probably say it was autobiographical—associated with a certain purgation, and sometimes classified as therapy.*

AS: Was Thomas Wolfe confessional or not? Any poem is therapy. The art of writing is therapy. You don't solve problems in writing. They're still there. I've heard psychiatrists say, "See, you've forgiven your father. There it is in your poem." But I haven't forgiven my father. I just wrote that I did.

WP: *Do you feel a tension between the narrative impulse and the lyric impulse?*

AS: I'm too rhythmic. You fight what you've got. I can't bear to be too rhythmical if I'm going to be confessional. I'm very fond of rhymes. I don't feel that off rhymes have the slam-it-home feeling of an on rhyme. Once in a while I use an off rhyme. I like double rhyme. Driving once into Boston, I suddenly thought that "cancer" rhymes with "answer." And so I wrote some lines. They are macabre, and yet it's an honest way of saying it. It makes it more real.

WP: *What do you do with lines that you can't use?*

AS: I put them all on paper, and then I put them in my rejection drawer. It's usually a set of lines, not just one.

WP: *Does anything keep you away from poetry?*

AS: Talking. Talking keeps you away from poetry. Not teaching, teaching keeps you close. I think I teach by instinct. I'm getting more vulgar in my old age. Now, what do I mean by "vulgar"? Not tasteless. Of the people. Common, is that it? Vernacular. A little less effete. Writing in the vulgate, but that sounds effete. We are being influenced now by South American poets, Spanish poets, French poets. We are much more image-driven as a result. Neruda is the great image-maker. The greatest colorist. Rilke is marvelous, but Neruda springs me loose, also Roethke. Images are the heart of poetry. And this is not tricks. Images come from the unconscious. Imagination and the unconscious are one and the same. You're not a poet without imagery.

WP: *To get images out of yourself you have to have a good relationship with yourself.*

AS: Yes—no, look at Hart Crane. He didn't have a very good relationship with himself, but look at his images. That's why I say you have to start with Neruda. Literal translation is best. When I am translated I want just the images, never mind the syllables and the rhymes. I'm proud of them, of my images.

WP: *Since, for you, images are the most vital part of poetry, what painters do you feel closest to?*

AS: I suppose Van Gogh, although that's sentimental to say—all the impressionists. Who was that wonderful man who painted all the jungle scenes? Rousseau.

WP: *How do you feel about concrete poetry?*

AS: What is concrete poetry?

WP: *Poems that are reduced to basic elements, as letters, letters as pictorial symbols.*

AS: A poem is spoken. A poem has to be spoken. I like it on the page, I like to see the stops of the lines.

WP: *How do you feel about public readings?*

AS: I care very much about my audiences. They are very dear to me, but I hate giving readings. I feel I've revealed so much of myself anyway, in the language. People always say, "You do it all so gracefully," and so forth. I can just see myself retreating, wearing a big hat and hiding behind dark glasses.

PART II

Revisions

Worksheets for "Elizabeth Gone"

One of Anne Sexton's best known and most effective poems, "Elizabeth Gone," is a moving elegy for her great-aunt Anna Ladd Dingley, a figure crucial in her life and, as "Nana," recurrent in her work. The following worksheets, dated ("5–6 hours—Jan 19th 1958") and numbered by the poet, are a representative display of Sexton's compositional methods. Other poems, begun as random words on a shopping list or torn envelope, were accumulated in similar ways: expansion, deletion, formal experiments, rhythmical adjustments, endless revision. These worksheets are evidence, too, of the intensity and concentration with which Sexton wrote. The poem, first published in the Spring 1959 issue of *The Hudson Review* and later collected in *To Bedlam and Part Way Back,* has not yet been "finished" in the drafts reproduced here, but the ways she would have gone about completing the poem are clear enough from what has been preserved.

The series of false starts on the opening pages seem a nervous anticipation of the actual poem, but by page 4 Sexton seems to have established, at least in her mind's ear and eye, the seven-line stanza she wanted, with its almost incantatory echoes and refrain. Slowly she includes more of her imagistic memories, trying to balance her focus between the experience and its effect, between the older woman and herself. By page 6, when the determining aspects and feelings are out and down, she begins to sense the poem as a more formal unit, and so tries on the first of several titles, numbers its sections, and tinkers with a rhyme scheme. In the second stanza, for instance, both "Elizabeth" and "shibboleth" are penciled in as possible rhymes to use with "death"—the substitute name providing a convenient example of how a confessional poet changes "real" facts to suit a poem's formal needs.

As more is added, the opening stanzas are gradually perfected—the changes always in service to a more precise and vivid emotional dramatization. At this point in her work on the poem, Sexton has trouble with the later stanzas: as so often with confessional poetry, the difficulties lie not in exposition but in resolution. Only in some later (and unavailable) draft did she condense the last two stanzas here into one, and realign the poem from its tripartite structure here into the doubled meditation on leaving and loss which is the poem's final form and triumph.

I have walked three years in country of death

I held you then in

You lay in the nest of death,
beyond my nervous fingers,
you skin puckered, your breath
uneven like a new babies

You lay in the nest of death,
neyond my nevous fingers where they touched your head
your skin puckered, your breath
                    up from the human bed
baby short as youlooked and said,

"let me go"
and breathed "let me go"

You lay in the nest of death,
byond my nervous fingers where they touched your head,
your skin puckering, your breath
baby short as you looked up from the human bed
and breathed," let me go¢"

You lay in the crate of death,

                    beyond the fumbled prayer I said,
This is not her. They have stuffed her cheeks I said,
            has clay skin and no breath
this body is

You lay in the nest of death

beyond my nervous fingers where they touched your head

your skin puckering, your breath......
grew
baby short as you looked at me for the human bed
    somehow
and cried, "let me go"

You lay in the crate of death

but were not you. They have stuffed her cheeks, I said,
            this
this body is a clay of flesh
            Down in the satin
is not her. And from within the satin and swude of th
            And from the satin and suade of the inhuman bed

something cried... let me go

You lay in the nest of your death

beyond my nervous fingers where they touched your head
                                    Lung
your skin puckering, your breath

growing baby short as you looked at me from the human bed

and shmehow cried... let me go

You lay in the crate of your death
                                            said
but were not you. They have stuffed her cheeks, I cried,
                                    from
this body, this clay of flesh

is not her. Down in stain and suade of the inhuman bed

something cried... let me go

                 of   shell
Your dust ash and fired bone chip

they gave to me

                      ly
They gave me your bone shell

and ash in a cardobard container, rattling like gourds. thrice bles

They gave me your ash bone shells
                                   and
in a carboard container, ratlling like gours, thric blest.

I searched the country of spells,

walked the earth of the livngs, your urn hacught at my breat

when something cried... <u>let me go</u>

I walked
I walked a ye

I waited in cathedral of spells
                               with this urn at my breast
and then walked the country of living, th

when something cried... <u>let me go</u>

You lay in the nest of your death,

beyond my nervous fingers

where they touched your moving head;

your skin puckering, your breath

grown baby short as you looked at me

from the human bed

and somehow cried... <u>let me go</u>

You lay in the crate of your death,

but were not you.

They have stuffed her cheeks, I said,

this body, the clay form of flesh

is not her. And from within the satin

and swaude of the inhuman bed

something cried... <u>let me go</u>

They gave me your ash bonely shells

in a cardboard container,

ratling like gourds and ʄʀɪɢɢ blest.

I waited in the cathedral of spells

and waited in the country of the living

with this urn caught at my breast

when something cried... <u>let me go</u>

I flung out the powder

I flung out your last bonely shells
    the
upon summer ground

returned to the house we had possesed.

buried my face in your lotion smells,
framed the rooms in your snapshot
framed in yoru snapshot
sat always in the cahir you knew best,

when something cried... <u>let me go</u>

propped up my room in your photograph

sat always in the chair you knew best

when something cried... <u>let me go</u>

THE THREE LIVES OF MOURNING

1.

You lay in the nest of your death
beyond my nervous fingers
where they touched your moving head;
you skin puckering, your breath
grown baby short as you look up
at me from the human bed
and somehow cried... <u>let me go</u>

You lay in the crate of your death
but were not you.
They have stuffed her cheeks, I said,
this body, this caly formed flesh
is not her. And from within the satin
and swede of the inhuman bed
something cried... <u>let me go</u>

2.

They gave me you ash bonely shells
in a cardboard container,
rattling like gourds and oven blest.
I waited in the cathedral of spells
and waiting in the country of living
with this urn caught at my breast,
when something cried... <u>let me go</u>

I flung out your last bonely shells
upon the summer ground,

folded into the house we had possessed,

buried my face in your lotion smells,

propped my room in your photograph,
clutched the coat that had clutched your breast
sat always in the chair you knew best,

when something cired... let me go

go tenderly go

So I wove my sense into a mesh

and forgot your apple face

So I wove my day with an iron mesh

grew straight and

                              an
So I wove my day with iron mesh
              shieled
that blocked out your apple face

from me; that

So I wove my days, like an iron mesh

to shield you apple face,

and grieve you   forgot the cry of your caress,
  fresh-
                  spoke name, but no word your flesh,

So I wove my day with iron mesh

that removed your apple face,

forgot the cry of your caress,

spoke name, but no word your flesh,

hard on each numbered day, I strained,

to chisel you out, to gofet, to forget,

sharp on each numbered ay, I cut,
         grain
to chisel youout, to forget you fresh,

wehn something cried... let me go

So I lifted the mark of the irnon mesh

and cried for the sight of you,

your apple face, the hilliness

of your body holding me, the creche,
                          lullaby
and carale of your voice.   touched your going

And I grieved your going, and missed you fresh,

and spoke after you... go tenderly go

and spoke after tears... and tenderly let go

    and as I cred... I let you go
    and then I cried... and let you go
    3.

So I wove my day onto iron mesh

that romoved your apple face,

that forgot the cry of your caress,

and spoke name but no wood your flesh.

Hard on each numbered day, I strained

to grain you out, to forget you fresh,

when something cried... let me go

    So I lifted the mark of the iron mesh

    and screamed for the sight of you,

    your apple face, the hilliness

    of your body holding me, the creche
                          grieved your going
    of your greeting; and sorted your things

    and sorted your things,, losing you fresh,

    and then I cried... and let you go

            let you go

propped my view in your photographs,

clutched the coat that had clutched your breast,

when something cried..<u>let me go</u> <u>let me go</u>

3.

So I ~~wove my day onto an iron~~ mesh

that removed your apple face,

that forgot the cry of your caress,

and spoke name but no word your flesh.

Hard on each numbered day, I pared,

to grain you out, to forget you fresh,

when something ~~creid~~... <u>let me go</u> <u>let me go</u>

So I lifted the mark of the ~~iron~~ mesh

and heard me scream for the sight of you,

your apple face, the hilliness

of your body holding mine, the creche

of your gretting; There, I grieved your going,

sorted your things and lost you fresh.

~~Then I cried~~... <u>and let you go</u> <u>let you go</u>

[handwritten annotations: "ng day", "slanned", "though rigid", "cheek", "cried", "positive", "netd", "so I strand you mind / though a mush", "A + B", "A + B", "A MISTAKE", "a + somehow out", "I strand you out, like though a mush"]

THREE LIVES OF MOURING

The three Petals of Mour...

1.

You lay in the nest of your real death,

beyond the print of my nervous fingers

where they touched your moving head;

your skin puckering, your lung breath

grown baby short as you looked up
at my face hovering
at me from this   this human bed,
            cried
and somehow you ... <u>let me go</u>   <u>let me go</u>

You lay in the crate of your last death

but were not you, were not you.

They have stuffed her cheeks, I said,

this clay hand, this mask of Elizabeth,

is not real. And from within the satin

 and suede of this inhuman bed,

something cried... <u>let me go</u>   <u>let me go.</u>

2.

They gave me your ash and bonely shells,
            rattling in a
within a tall cradboard container,

rattling like gourds and over blest.

I waited in the cathedral of spells,

and I waited in the country of the living,

still with this urn caught to my chest,

when something cried... <u>let me go</u>   <u>let me go</u>

I flung out your last bonely shells
and turned from the public sound,
upon
folded my face to room you possessed,
                  smell s,
buried my face in your lotion sem

So I strained you out, my mind in a press

that smashed out apple cheek face,

that spoke name but no word your flesh,

that forgot the cry of your caress.

Hard on each numbered day, I fought

to grain you out, to forget you fresh,

when something cried... <u>let me go</u> <u>let me go</u>

So I lifted memory, and the mind from the press

and heard me scream for the sight of you,

your apple face, the lullaby creche
                    the rounded hilliness
of your greeting, your body's hilliness

of you. And there I did grieve your going,

sorted your things and lost you fresh,

when somehow I cried... <u>and let you go</u> <u>let you go</u>

THREE PETALS OF MOURNING

1.

You lay in the nest of your real death,

beyond the print of my nervous fingers

where they touched your moving head;

your old skin puckering, your lung breath

grown baby short as you looked up last

at my face hovering this human bed,

and somehow cried... <u>let me go</u>   <u>let me go</u>

You lay in the crate of your last death

but were not you, were not you.

They have stuffed her cheeks, I said,

this clay hand, this mask of flesh,

are not real. From the satin

and suede of this inhuman bed,

something cried... <u>let me go</u>   <u>let me go</u>

2.

They gave me your ash and boney shells,

rattling in a cardboard container,

rattling like gourds the over blest.

And I waited in the cathedral of spells

and waited in the counrty of the living,

still with this urn caught to my breast,

when something cried... <u>let me go</u>   <u>let me go</u>

3.

Then I flung out your last boney shells

and turned from the public pry and sound,

folded my face to the room you possessed,

buried my face in your lotion smells,

propped my view in your photographs,

clutched the coat that had cloutched your breast,.

when somehing cried... <u>let me go</u>   <u>let me go</u>

3.

So I strained you out, my mind a press

that smashed your apple cheek face,

that spoke name but no word your flesh,

that forgot the cry of your caress.

Hard on each numbered day, I fought

to grain you out, to forget you fresh,

when something said   <u>let me go</u>   <u>let me go</u>

So I lifted memory, and the mind from the press

and heard me scream for the sight of you,

your apple face, the lullaby creche

of your greeting, the round hilliness

of you. And there I did grieve your going,

did sort your things and hurt for you fresh,

when somehow I cried..<u>and let you go</u>   <u>let you go</u>

                                        January 19th, 1958

Elizabeth Howard (handwritten)

THREE LIVES FOR LOSING

1.

You lay in the nest of your real death,
Beyond the print of my nervous fingers
Where they touched your moving head;
Your old skin puckering, your lung breath
Grown baby short as you look up last ,
At my face swinging over the human bed,
And somehow you cried... <u>let me go</u>   <u>let me go</u>

You lay in the crate of your last death
But were not you, not finally you.
They have stuffed her cheeks, I said,
This clay hand, this rubber of flesh
Are not true. From within the satin
And the suede of this inhuman bed,
Something cried... <u>let me go</u>   <u>let me go</u>

2.

They gave me your ash and boney shells,
Rattling like gourds in the cardboard urn,
Rattling like stone that their over had blest.
I waited you in the cathedral of spells
And I waited you in the country of the living,
Still with this urn crooned to my breast,
When something cried... <u>let me go</u>   <u>let me go</u>

I flung out those last bony shells

And turned from the public swoops and sound,

Turned my face to the room you possessed,

Left my face in your lotion smells,

Left my eyes in your photographs,

      coat

Clutched the ~~coat~~ that had clutched your breast,

When something cried... <u>let me go</u> <u>let me go</u>

3.

I strained you out, my mind was a press

      out

That pushed ~~ye~~ the way of your apple cheek face,

        for

That spoke name, but no word your flesh,

That forgot the cry of your palm's caress.

Hard on each numbered day I fought

To grain you out, to shun you fresh,

When something cried... <u>let me go</u> <u>let me go</u>

I lifted the memory, the mind from its press,

And heard me scream for the look of you,

Your apple face, that simple creche

Of your arms, that round hilliness

Of your arms; and heard me break at your going,

As I sorted your clothes and grew from you fresh,

And somewhere I cried... <u>and let you go</u> <u>let you go</u>

ELIZABETH GONE

1.

You lay in the nest of your real death,
Beyond the print of my nervous fingers
Where they touched your moving head;
Your old skin puckering, your lungs' breath
Grown baby short as you looked up last
At my face swinging over the human bed,
And somewhere you cried, *let me go let me go.*

You lay in the crate of your last death,
But were not you, not finally you.
They have stuffed her cheeks, I said;
This clay hand, this mask of Elizabeth
Are not true. From within the satin
And the suede of this inhuman bed,
Something cried, *let me go let me go.*

2.

They gave me your ash and bony shells,
Rattling like gourds in the cardboard urn,
Rattling like stones that their oven had blest.
I waited you in the cathedral of spells
And I waited you in the country of the living,
Still with the urn crooned to my breast,
When something cried, *let me go let me go.*

So I threw out your last bony shells
And heard me scream for the look of you,
Your apple face, the simple crèche
Of your arms, the August smells
Of your skin. Then I sorted your clothes
And the loves you had left, Elizabeth,
Elizabeth, until you were gone.

68

PART III

Reflections

Anne Sexton

I met Anne Sexton in 1957, and at a moment to be impressed, because I was writing my first autobiographical poems and was carried away by Snodgrass's marvelous *Heart's Needle* sequence. Anne was lean-faced, white-armed, thirty, and a poet for only a few months. She had met Snodgrass that summer and become a "confessional" poet overnight. How many laborious, often useless, steps of apprenticeship she had bypassed. Unlike Snodgrass and Sylvia Plath, she was an amateur. I am not sure I know what I mean by this. In my writing class, which she attended for a year or so, her comments and questions were more to the point than the more studious. In the beginning, her lines were overpoetic; she gave promise of becoming a fifties Edna Millay. Yet on her own, she developed a more sensitive, realistic idiom. Her gift was to grip, to give words to the drama of her personality. She did what few did, cut a figure. What went wrong? For a book or two, she grew more powerful. Then writing was too easy or too hard for her. She became meager and exaggerated. Many of her most embarrassing poems would have been fascinating if someone had put them in quotes, as the presentation of some character, not the author.

At a time when poetry readings were expected to be boring, no one ever fell asleep at Anne's. I see her as having the large, transparent, breakable, and increasingly ragged wings of a dragonfly—her poor, shy, driven life, the blind terror behind her bravado, her deadly increasing pace . . . her bravery while she lasted. For relief, I quote one of her finest and quieter poems.

> I knew you forever and you were always old,
> soft white lady of my heart. Surely you would scold
> me for sitting up late, reading your letters,
> as if these foreign postmarks were meant for me.
> You posted them first in London, wearing furs
> and a new dress in the winter of eighteen-ninety.
> I read how London is dull on Lord Mayor's Day,
> where you guided past groups of robbers, the sad holes
> of Whitechapel, clutching your pocketbook, on the way
> to Jack the Ripper dissecting his famous bones.
> This Wednesday in Berlin, you say, you will
> go to a bazaar at Bismarck's house. And I
> see you as a young girl in a good world still,
> writing three generations before mine. I try
> to reach into your page and breathe it back . . .
> but life is a trick, life is a kitten in a sack.
>
> This is Italy. You learn its mother tongue.
> I read how you walked on the Palatine among
> the ruins of the palaces of the Caesars;
> alone in the Roman autumn, alone since July.
> When you were mine they wrapped you out of here
> with your best hat over your face. I cried
> because I was seventeen. I am older now.
> I read how your student ticket admitted you
> into the private chapel of the Vatican and how
> you cheered with the others, as we used to do
> on the Fourth of July. One Wednesday in November
> you watched a balloon, painted like a silver ball,
> float up over the Forum, up over the lost emperors,
> to shiver its little modern cage in an occasional
> breeze. You worked your New England conscience out
> beside artisans, chestnut vendors and the devout.
>
> Tonight I will learn to love you twice;
> learn your first days, your mid-Victorian face.
> Tonight I will speak up and interrupt
> your letters, warning you that wars are coming,

that the Count will die, that you will accept
your America back to live like a prim thing
on the farm in Maine. I tell you, you will come
here, to the suburbs of Boston, to see the blue-nose
world go drunk each night, to see the handsome
children jitterbug, to feel your left ear close
one Friday at Symphony. And I tell you,
you will tip your boot feet out of that hall,
rocking from its sour sound, out onto
the crowded street, letting your spectacles fall
and your hair net tangle as you stop passers-by
to mumble your guilty love while your ears die.

(from "Some Foreign Letters")

DENISE LEVERTOV

Light Up the Cave

The news of Anne Sexton's death saddened a great many people, and startled those who had assumed that, despite all the troubles of which her poetry told, she had come to the long stretch of middle age with some reserves of strength; though—I am told—the friends who knew her best were confirmed in their fear that her determination towards suicide had not really been deflected. My own sadness at the death of a fellow poet is compounded by the sense of how likely it is that Anne Sexton's tragedy will not be without influence in the tragedies of other lives.

She herself was, obviously, too intensely troubled to be fully aware of her influence or to take on its responsibility. Therefore it seems to me that we who are alive must make clear, as she could not, the distinction between creativity and self-destruction. The tendency to confuse the two has claimed too many victims. Anne Sexton herself seems to have suffered deeply from this confusion, and I surmise that her friendship with Sylvia Plath had in it an element of identification which added powerfully to her malaise. Across the country, at different colleges, I have heard many stories of attempted—and sometimes successful—suicides by young students who loved the poetry of Plath and who supposed that somehow, in order to become poets themselves, they had to act out in their own lives the events of hers. I don't want to see a new epidemic of the same syndrome occurring as a response to Anne Sexton's death.

74

The problem is not, however, related only to suicide *per se*. When Robert Lowell was at the height of his fame among student readers (his audience nowadays is largely an older one) many of them seemed to think a nervous breakdown was, if not imperative, at least an invaluable shortcut to artistry. When W. D. Snodgrass's *Heart's Needle* won the Pulitzer Prize, young couples married and divorced, it seemed, especially in order to have the correct material to write about.

I am not being flippant. Innumerable young poets have drunk themselves into stupidity and cirrhosis because they admired John Berryman or Dylan Thomas and came to think they must drink like them to write like them. At the very least it is assumed that creativity and hangups are inevitably inseparable. One student (male) said to me recently, "I was amazed when the first poet I met seemed to be a cheerful person and not any more fucked up than anyone else. When I was in high school I got the idea you *had* to be fucked up to be a real artist!" And a young English teacher in a community college told me she had given up writing poetry because she believed there were unavoidable links between depression and anxiety and the making of art. "Don't you feel terrible when you write poems?"

What exactly is the nature of the confusion, and how has it come about? The mistake itself lies in taking what may possibly be an occupational hazard as a prescriptive stimulus to artistic activity. Whether artists as a class are in fact more vulnerable than other people, or whether their problems merely have more visibility, a serious and intelligent statistical study might perhaps tell us. It makes no difference: the point is that while the creative impulse and the self-destructive impulse can, and often do, coexist, their relationship is distinctly acausal; self-destructiveness is a handicap to the life of art, not the reverse.

Yet it is the handicaps themselves that so often allure the young and untried. The long lives of so many of the greatest artists, sometimes apparently uneventful, sometimes full of passion and suffering, but full too of endurance, and always dominated by love of their work, seem not to attract as models. Picasso, Matisse, Monet, Cezanne,

Pissarro, Corot, Rembrandt, Titian, J. S. Bach, Stravinsky, Goethe, William Carlos Williams, Stevens, Pound, Neruda, Machado, Yeats, Shakespeare, Whitman, Tolstoi, Melville.... There is romance in their tenacity, their devotion, but it is overlooked. Why is this? There are topical reasons, but their roots are in the past, their nature historical and political.

In summary, Western culture began, during the Renaissance—only recently, that is to say, in the calendar of human history—to emphasize individuality to a degree merely foreshadowed in Greece and Rome or in the theological dramas of the Old Testament. Geographical and scientific discoveries spurred the sense of what humanity on its own could do. The "Elizabethan world picture" had wholeness and consistency; but it held the seeds of an expanded view of things. And as feudal social systems underwent economic changes with the rise of the merchant class and the growth of banking procedures, so, too, the social and economic circumstances in which art was produced underwent changes that heightened the new sense of individuality.

The relationship of the artist to other people rapidly altered. The people began to become "the public," "the audience," and the poet, set aside from that "public," began to become more private, more introspective. When his work (or hers—but it was a long time before there were women poets in any numbers) was printed it was increasingly a revelation to the public of the highly personal, rather than being to a large degree the voice of the people itself which it had been the bard's task, in earlier times, to sound forth. The value put on individual expression, the concept of "originality," and untimately even upon individualism as a creed, had been pushed further by the time we reach the period of Romanticism, which developed alongside the Industrial Revolution and was in part reactive to the prospect of facelessness presented to the prophetic eye by that phenomenon.

Twentieth-century alienation is another phase of the reaction. What began as a realization of human potential, a growth of *individuated* consciousness (to use Jung's useful term) out of the unconscious collective, became first a glorification of willful, essentially optimistic individualism, echoing the ambitious, optimistic individualism of its capitalist context, and then, as that turned sour and revealed more and more of greed in its operations, led to the setting of a high esthetic and moral value upon alienation itself.

But alienation is of ethical value, is life-affirmative and conducive to creativity only when it is accompanied by a political consciousness that imagines and affirms (and works toward) an alternative to the society from which it turns away in disgust. Lacking this, the alienated person, if he or she is gifted, becomes especially a prey to the exploitation that characterizes capitalism and is its underlying principle. The manifestations—in words, music, paint, or what have you—of private anguish are exploited by a greedy public, a public greedy for emotion at second hand because starved of the experience of community. Concurrently, for the same reasons, a creative person —whether a pop star or a Sylvia Plath, a John Berryman, an Anne Sexton—internalizes the exploitive, unwittingly becoming *self*-exploitive.

And if the public is greedy, the critics, at their worst, are positively ghoulish, or at the least, irresponsible. I feel, for instance, that it is irresponsible for one local columnist, in a memorial eulogy, to have written of Anne Sexton, "The manner of her death is at once frightening and fascinating to those who responded to her poetry, sharing as they do many of the same fears and insecurities she articulated so well. Her death awakens those fears and insecurities, the way some of her poems did, it raises them up from where they hide, buried by ordinary, everyday things." It is irresponsible because it is a statement made without qualification or development in a context of praise, and without, therefore, helping readers to see (as I suppose the writer herself does not see) that to raise our fears and insecurities into consciousness in order to confront them, to deal with them, is good; but that if the pain is confused with art itself, then people at the receiving end of a poem describing a pain and insecurity they share are not really brought to confront and deal with their problems, but are instead led into a false acceptance of them as signs or precursors of art, marks of kinship with the admired artist, symptoms of what used to be called "the artistic temperament."

Again, when I read the blurbs on the back of the late John Berryman's prizewinning *Delusions, etc.,* and see what A. Alvarez wrote of Berryman's work and death, I feel that a poisonous misapprehension of the nature of poetry is being furthered. "For years," Alvarez says, "I have been extolling the virtues of what I call extremist poetry, in which the artists deliberately push their perceptions to the very edge of the tolerable. Both Berryman and Plath were masters of the style. But knowing now how they both died I no longer believe that any art—even that as fine as they produced at their best—is worth the terrible cost."

At first glance this statement might be taken as being in accord with my own viewpoint; but its effect (since it is obvious that Alvarez believes their art to have been of the highest possible quality, perhaps the best poetry of their time) is still to extol the pursuit of the almost intolerable, the deliberate driving of the self to extremes which are not the unavoidable, universal extremes imposed by the human condition, but—insofar as they are deliberately sought—are luxuries, or which, if part and parcel of individual mental illness, should rather be *resisted* than encouraged in the name of art. In assuming that the disasters of those writers' lives were a form of payment for the virtues of their art, Alvarez, even while he says he has come to feel it is not worth the cost, perpetuates the myth that confounds a love-affair with death with a love-affair with art.

Thus it is that long lives devoted to the practice of art seem lacking in allure, and young would-be artists, encouraged by people older than themselves but equally confused, equally apt to mistake handicap for power, model their lives on the lives of those who, however gifted, were vanquished by their sorrows. It is not understood that the greatest heroes and heroines are truly those who hold out the longest, or, if they do die young, do so unwillingly, resisting to the last.

An instance would be the young guerrilla poets of Latin America, so many of whom have been killed so young. (At least one of them, Javier Heraud, of Peru, would surely have been a major poet. He was shot down at the age of twenty-three.) They were not flirting with death, any more than Victor Jara, the extraordinary and beloved

Chilean musician and poet who was murdered in the Stadium in Santiago just over a year ago. They died politically conscious deaths, struggling for a better life, not just for themselves but for their people, for The People. Their tragedy is very different from the tragedy of suicide; they were conscious actors in dramas of revolutionary effort, not helpless victims.

Anne Sexton's struggle has its political dimensions too—but hers is the story of a victim, not a conscious participant. Anne Sexton the well-to-do suburban housewife, Anne Sexton in Bedlam, Anne Sexton "halfway back," Anne Sexton the glamorous performer, Anne Sexton: timid and insecure, Anne Sexton saying she had always hoped to publish a posthumous volume, Anne Sexton in her garage breathing in the deadly fumes, was—whatever the clinical description of her depression—"caught in history's crossfire." Not because she was a woman—the problem is not essentially related to gender or to sexual stance. Not because she didn't have radical politics—god knows they are not a recipe for great art or for long life (though I can't help feeling that a little more comprehension of the relation of politics to her own life might have helped her). But because she herself was unable to separate her depression and her obsession with death from poetry itself, and because precisely her most enthusiastic readers and critics encouraged that inability.

The artist, the poet (like Hokusai, who called himself "the old man mad about painting" and felt that at seventy he had begun to learn, at ninety would have some command of his powers, and at one hundred would begin to do justice to what he saw in Nature) needs the stamina of an astronaut and the energy derived only from being passionately in love with life and with art. "This is this world, the kingdom I was looking for!" wrote John Holmes. And "You must love the crust of the earth on which you dwell. You must be able to extract nutriment out of sand heap. Else you will have lived in vain," wrote Thoreau.

Such purity, integrity, love, and energy—rarely fully attained but surely to be striven for—are undermined by our exploitive society, which romanticizes its victims when they are of a certain kind (thus distracting us from the unromanticizable lives of the suffering multitude). It romanticizes gifted individuals who have been distorted into an alienated individualism, a self-preoccupation, that is *not* individuation, *not* maturation.

Anne Sexton wrote in "Wanting To Die":

> Suicides have already betrayed the body.
> Stillborn, they don't always die,
> but dazzled, they can't forget a drug so sweet . . .
> To thrust all that life under your tongue!—
> that, all by itself, becomes a passion.

Too many readers, with a perversity that, yes, really does seem to me to be bound up with white middle-class privilege and all its moral disadvantages, would sooner remember, and identify with, lines like those than with these, which (in *The Death Notebooks*) she also wrote:

> Depression is boring, I think
> and I would do better to make
> some soup and light up the cave.

To recognize that for a few years of her life Anne Sexton was an artist *even though* she had so hard a struggle against her desire of death is to fittingly honor her memory. To identify her love of death with her love of poetry is to insult that struggle.

BARBARA   SWAN

A Reminiscence

Anne Sexton and I met as recipients of grants from the Radcliffe Institute during its first year of existence in 1961. The application form had clearly stated that a candidate must have a Ph.D. or the equivalent. Both Anne and I shared a certain awe at those with a Ph.D. and were uncertain about what an equivalent might be. The creative mind deals with a world of the imagination. The artist and the poet carry this world around in their heads. They inhabit it. The scholar with a Ph.D. can study this world, analyze it, criticize it, even try to recreate it in biography, but the scholar can never really know the crazy, intuitive nonsense that whirls around in the mind of an artist.

During out years of friendship Anne moved into my world and I had the lovely privilege of moving into hers. We shared on an intuitive level knowing instinctively the kind of thing that would spark a creative idea. I could open up my book on Edvard Munch, show her the lithograph titled *The Scream,* and know it would fascinate her. It did. Later in the poem "Briar Rose" from *Transformations* she was to use this line:

> The court fell silent.
> The king looked like Munch's Scream.

81

Early in our friendship Anne acquired my lithograph called "The Musicians." It was framed and hung in her study. My lithograph has a flute player, a figure playing a recorder, and a great deal of murk that could be anything. Frankly, I was experimenting with the newly discovered possibilities of texture in lithography and wanted an aura of mystery, but beyond that I had nothing specific in mind.

One day there was a phone call and an excited Anne said, "Barbara, I've written a poem about your lithograph!" She sent me a copy and at that stage it had the title "The Musicians." Later the title was changed to "To Lose the Earth." How could I be prepared for what she saw in my lithograph? I was astonished!

> He plays his flute in a cave
> that a pharaoh built by the sea.
> He is blowing on light,
> each time for the first time.
> His fingers cover the mouths of all the sopranos,
> each a princess in an exact position.

And on it went, images building on images. My harmless fellow playing the recorder became:

> At the far right,
> rising from an underground sea,
> his toes curled on a black wave,
> stands the dwarf,
> his instrument is an extension of his tongue.

Anne had moved into my world like a tornado. She shook it up, rattled it, possessed it like a demon. Naturally, I adored the poem. I had had no idea at all what lurked beneath my murky textures.

Some years later Anne again used a work of mine as inspiration for a poem. It was a large drawing called "Man Carrying a Man," inspired by a fifteenth-century German sculpture of Christ being carried on the back of a man. We were then in the throes of the Vietnam War and I wanted the drawing to express universal compassion for man's fate, the way we all share in it. Anne's poem "Jesus Walking" expresses exactly what I wanted my drawing to say and in the last line she used my title.

> To pray, Jesus knew
> is to be a man carrying a man.

One other poem deals with me and not my work. In "Hurry Up Please It's Time" she describes a day spent in Rockport when we drank vodka and ginger beer and I drew a line drawing, and she says, "Of such moments is happiness made."

It *was* a happy day. I did two line drawings and one appeared on the back of the cover for *The Book of Folly*. Line drawings go very quickly and I drew while we talked. Later we all had drinks with my friends, Professor Edwin Miller and Roz Miller. Then there was seafood at a rather primitive lobster place with an open porch and a Munch-like view of the setting sun across the water. Anne loved it— the mess of the seafood (steamers and lobster), the dramatic sky over Folly Cove. We all said that we must do it again, but of course nothing is ever the same and we never did.

Anne and I collaborated in three areas concerning her work—a broadside, book covers, and the drawings for *Transformations*. At the Impressions Workshop where I was learning lithography the owner, George Lockwood, decided to launch a series of broadsides with various artists doing prints in collaboration with contemporary poets. It was obvious that I should work with Anne. She chose the poem "For the Year of the Insane." Because it was so autobiographical I felt I should use her face, and this resulted in a number of working drawings from life. I think it was around this time that I did a portrait drawing for my own pleasure. As an artist, I loved to draw her. Anne was a beauty and the challenge was to go beyond that beautiful face to what lay beneath. Also, when I draw someone I like to explore who the person really is, and these sittings further deepened our friendship. In the broadside I tried to show the outer Anne Sexton, fingering rosary beads, and in the background the darker side, the side that perhaps no one ever really understood.

As for book covers, Anne and I suffered together when dealing with the production department of her publisher. The book itself is designed by one person but the cover is controlled by a different department and our views and the views of the person in charge of book covers did not always converge. It was with *Live or Die* that Anne called me in despair to say, "They've sent me a terrible book cover with pink and blue flowers and green frogs. It looks like a children's book. Have you anything I can use?" I found a drawing called *Gothic Heads,* and since Anne did have some control over her book covers it was offered and accepted. It was a delicate drawing and the heads were supposed to be diagonal but the book cover designer made them vertical and then plastered thick black letters across the top of the drawing. Later, after the book came out the person in charge of book covers said that even she was offended by the lettering. I still shudder when I look at it.

When Anne asked me to do a drawing for *The Book of Folly* cover I decided to control the lettering by incorporating my images within the letters as in medieval manuscripts. Anne had sent me the entire manuscript of her book, so my letters became inhabited by the girl with the chair, the girl with long hair, Lazarus, an angel. Folly became half skeleton, half a masked costume figure. Jesus nailed to the cross fitted within the confines of a Y. It was not easy to draw in this way and I suffered more with those letters than if I had done a simple drawing. For this cover it was I who said the border should be red, a bloody red. As I read the poems I was struck by such lines as "Tonight all the red dogs lie down in fear" or "Once there was blood as in a murder" or "and the vibrating red muscle of my mouth." I could go on. The color red seemed to me pervasive.

Anne and I corresponded about the cover for *The Death Notebooks.* On July 26, 1973, I received this letter from Anne in Pigeon Cove, where I spend the summer:

Dear, dear Barbara

I am interested in what you say about the "underbelly" of our lives. The color blue sounds right to me. At least I trust you more than I trust myself. As a matter of fact, those poems were always kept in a blue notebook. All of your ideas and your miniature drawing appeal, but that is not surprising, for you are very sensitive to the poet's word —at least *your* two poets.

I am interested in what you said about the nine psalms at the end. I worry about them. I'm afraid they are excessive or maybe just plain bad writing. Of course, they involve life's stages as well as praising many of life's or God's objects.

Do write again when you get back from Maine. I would love to hear from you.

Love,
A.

My idea for a cover drawing was to create the look of a crack opening across the cover revealing what I referred to as the "under-belly" of our lives. The eye peering out at the bottom is, of course, Anne's. Again I was struck by a dominant color . . . "expecting a large white angel, with a blue crotch" . . . "The shocking blue sky" . . . "Take the blue eyes of my mother" . . . "The autumn sky, Mary blue."

I also pointed out to Anne that she seemed to like the word "belly" and I would love to draw a fat belly and also a rounded rear end. I said that any book calling itself *The Death Notebooks* had to have at least two nudes on the cover to boost sales. Besides, the poems had a great deal to do with life. Because my drawing zoomed across the cover, the lettering was forced to behave itself.

Our collaboration with *Transformations,* based on *Grimms' Fairy Tales,* was the most sustained and the most rewarding for me. It all began when Anne asked me if I knew a woodcut artist who could illustrate these poems. She had in mind a kind of Gothic, slightly expressionist style. We went together to the print department of the Boston Public Library, but what we saw seemed suitable only for children's books. Then, over lunch at Joseph's, a favorite restaurant of Anne's, she said, "Barbara, would you consider it?" I had never done a book but my reply was, "Send me a poem." In the mail came "Snow White" and I loved it. Immediately I was on the phone. "Anne, I don't know about you but I identify with the poor old queen." "So do I," said Anne. I made a drawing that portrays the universal problem of the aging beauty, needing every beauty prop available, and the young girl, smug and indifferent, temporarily secure in her glorious youth. In the last lines of the poem Snow White begins to look in her mirror and you know that twenty years later, she, too, will face a middle-age crisis.

After that, poem after poem came to me in the mail. Anne and I agreed that I should absorb each poem individually, do a drawing, and then await the next poem. Between the poem and the drawing there would be a phone call and I would tell Anne my visual reaction to the poem, what I felt I could express. Always my reactions intrigued her. When it came to the poem "Iron Hans" what I wanted to draw surprised her because it was not her vision. She had imagined a drawing with Iron Hans battling around in a cage as a wild man. My drawing showed the young prince being carried into the woods on the shoulders of Iron Hans because the prince saw through his wildness and trusted him. "The poem has to do with compassion," I said. Anne had identified with the wild man in a cage, like a madwoman trapped in an asylum. But for me in Anne's poems there is a cry for compassion. As for my drawing, Anne said, "You're right."

Two of my drawings are in the style of Edvard Munch because it seemed appropriate. In the poem "Briar Rose" Anne even refers to Munch's "The Scream," and the tormented incestuous relationship seemed best served by stark curves of black and white. In "The Wonderful Musician" I was influenced by the way Munch's lines seem to give out the sound of a scream, and so I curved and twisted the lines from the violin to give the sound and the shape of a death dance. Even skulls emerge.

Cinderella and her prince are a dull pair and I had to do a dull drawing.

> Regular Bobbsey twins.
> That story.

Rapunzel was a pleasure for me because of the relationship of Mother Gothel to the beautiful Rapunzel.

A woman
who loves a woman
is forever young.

I don't think anyone had ever before thought of the lesbian aspect in Mother Gothel's isolation of Rapunzel in a tower. I tried to show the possessive love of Mother Gothel and I turned Rapunzel into a Victorian beauty perhaps like the heroine of John Fowles's novel *The French Lieutenant's Woman.*

What a good time we had with "The Twelve Dancing Princesses." In Anne's poem there is no doubt they are freaked out. In my drawing I came up with a combination of Busby Berkeley and Isadora Duncan. Anne and I laughed over that, the chorus line and the free spirit.

In "Red Riding Hood" Anne enjoyed my idea that the hunter should be listening for the fetal heartbeat in the wolf who had just eaten Red Riding Hood and the grandmother. As Anne wrote, "He appeared to be in his ninth month."

As for Hansel and Gretel," I felt it would be an ironic touch to put BLESS THIS HOME over the kitchen stove as the witch is about to be baked.

> Gretel,
> seeing her moment in history,
> shut fast the oven,
> locked fast the door,
> fast as Houdini,
> and turned the oven on to bake.

I would also like to say that any little girl who bakes an old lady is not a dear little girl. She is a rather nasty little girl.

My drawing for "The Frog Prince" has a great deal that is phallic going on behind the plate of liver and bacon that the frog is sitting on. I was not certain that the publisher would be comfortable with it so I pointed it out. The editor smiled and said, "We've grown up quite a bit here at Houghton Mifflin."

When *Transformations* was published Anne inscribed a book to me, writing "with love and with awe at your genius." It was typical of her generous spirit that she could write exactly what might please my ego. Who ever knows what genius is? I prefer to turn the compliment her way. She and I tilted at windmills together. It was exhilarating.

CHARLES MARYAN

The Poet on Stage

I'm not a playwright. I just wrote this on a grant. I like
to read my poems. I don't know anything about the theater. I got this grant.

—*Anne Sexton to Charles Maryan*

In 1969 I was sent two plays by a literary agent. One play was called
Tell Me Your Answer True. The agent said that she did not think that
it was commercial but she wanted me to read it and perhaps I would
be able to get the play on. "The author," she said, "is a poet and won
a Pulitzer Prize." The author she referred to was Anne Sexton, and
the play was to be retitled *Mercy Street* and presented ten months
later at The American Place Theatre.

I kept no journal or notes on *Mercy Street,* so I must depend totally
on recall. Also Anne and I never corresponded during our collaboration. We either worked together or talked on the telephone.

The impact of reading Anne's play for the first time was not immediate. The first version was set in a dreamlike carnival atmosphere
with a ringmaster who called people from their seats on stage into a
center ring to act out their lives. It seemed to me Dantesque in
atmosphere, but the actual scenes were very realistic within this amorphous structure.

At various times after I had read the play I would find myself
thinking about it quite unconsciously. I read it again and decided I

89

had to see the play staged. I called the agent and said that I was interested in doing the play and that I wanted to show it to The American Place. She said okay but they had already seen it; however, if I wanted to try again, go ahead.

I called Wynn Handman, the artistic director of The American Place, who said, "We've read it," and I said, "Read it again," and he did. Wynn called a couple of weeks later to say that he was interested. Now, to this point I had never met Anne Sexton. I am not sure that I had ever read her poetry, and so at Wynn's suggestion Anne was asked to come in from Boston to meet with us and talk about doing a two-week work-in-progress on the play—that is, if Anne approved of me as the director. By the time the meeting occurred I had reread the play several times and felt that the limbo atmosphere and carnival idiom had to be either reinforced or changed, but I was convinced that what was there was a very gifted first play by a writer who could and should write plays. That feeling never changed.

We met in Wynn's office around noon. Anne did not say much except that she would like to see her play done. Wynn and I exchanged ideas and then Anne and I went off to lunch. There may have been a phone call before this but this was our first real meeting. What we actually talked about I don't remember, but what was established at this first meeting was that we could talk. Anne would listen; she listened as well as anyone I've ever known and permitted me to say whatever I needed to say and responded simply and directly. She expressed then and maintained always that she knew little about the theater but liked it and invested us theater people with special knowledge that she did not have. We agreed to work on the play for two weeks and see what would happen. She left the casting to me and so in the spring we began.

We did not touch the script before we gave it to the actors. The main character of *Mercy Street* is a woman named Daisy, and the play follows her odyssey through her recollections and immediate problems. My first choice for the part was Marian Seldes, and I spoke with her even before I had met Anne. Marian and I had worked together before and I thought that she was just what the role needed. She also is very sensitive to poetry and is often asked to read on television. Her reaction was, "I'll do it." I said I would send her a script as soon as I had one to give out, and she replied that she would trust me and that she loved Anne's poetry so that I could count on her.

The rest of the cast for the reading was assembled in much the same way—actors whom I knew and who for the most part knew each other. The most remarkable thing about the casting was the resemblance between Marian and Anne. They actually looked like sisters and their relationship was always, even from the first, one of real understanding and caring.

We read the play through and I remember Anne saying that until she heard the actors, especially Marian, she thought she read her own work very well but now she had doubts that she should do it. She was excited and concerned and totally open to what the actors said. We read the play frequently. We worked on scenes; however, getting a handle on the play was hard. Again the problem was connecting the scenes: where are we? Which event follows which?—it wasn't clear. Also, there seemed to be a climax to the play in the first part rather than the second. We were working against a deadline and in two weeks we had to show Wynn Handman and his staff a staged reading that they would want to produce fully for their next season. At one point during a rehearsal Anne and I were discussing a scene and the problem of where it was placed, when Marian looked at us from the stage and said, "Why don't you just reverse the acts?" Neither Anne nor I had thought of the solution, but we agreed with Marian and that began the form of the play that we finally presented.

No one committed the script to memory and I staged the play with a minimum of movement. The actors sat in chairs and moved only to play a scene with the scripts in their hands. There were about six of us in the theater for the presentation. Anne and I thought it went very well, and we began the waiting period to hear if The American Place would do it.

Anne wanted the play done. She was excited. She liked what we did and enjoyed the few rehearsals she attended. She fit in easily and we loved her. Exactly how long we had to wait I can't remember. Wynn

Handman and I spoke several times. The problem was how to present the material. By doing a reading we could ignore where the play actually took place, but with a full production the individual scenes had to be dealt with physically; therefore a literal setting representing the many locales would be too expensive and too boring. The American Place was then housed in an actual church and I suggested that the whole play could happen in a church within a mass. Daisy could come to this church to decide whether to live or die—the priest could be transformed into the psychiatrist and by rebuilding St. Clement's into a theatrical church setting we could make the physical transformations in and out of the mass.

I called Anne. She was receptive. The reality of having to come up with a satisfactory concept for a producer was not hard for her to grasp, and thematically she thought it would work since Daisy spoke about Christ and the religious imagery was constant in the play, but we would have to work the mechanics out together.

I then went to Wynn and gave him the entire play in the concept; there were a series of phone calls—Wynn to Anne, Anne to Chuck, Chuck to Wynn—and finally silence. I would call Anne and started feeling the burden of not hearing. We were like two kids waiting to hear—conspiring—angry that we had to wait so long, but hopeful. Then it came. The word that we would open the season with Anne's play, still called, at this time, *Tell Me Your Answer True.*

It was now June—we started rehearsal September 2 and we had to fit the play with a concept. My knowledge of a High Episcopal Mass —that was the one we picked and Anne thought it best—was zero. Anne's actual knowledge of religious practices was not much better, so my first trip to Weston was for a weekend so that we could go to church and start our collaboration.

She made me feel very comfortable in her house, as did the whole family; we drank a lot, talked a lot, and Sunday morning we drove into Boston to the one High Episcopal Church. Anne and I tried to follow the service—in order to see how the play would fit. I was to learn the mass and write a plan of how the scenes would fit. She would work on the timing, the clarification of the scenes, and write connecting material, but she was adamant. I had to know the mass. We worked that weekend in the kitchen and in her study, but somehow the kitchen was the place where we could spread out and drink coffee. It was the right room for us. Anne's dog, a Dalmatian, took some getting used to. The dog was not used to me and was very protective of Anne and guarded her study. We had some visitors, usually late in the afternoon—Lois Ames, Maxine Kumin and her children. We would work from 9:00 A.M. to 4:00 P.M. and then break entirely.

Our next meeting was for a longer period of time. I think four or five days. By then, I had a better grasp of the mass. Scenes needed work—clarity was our objective—and at one point we were stuck. I was convinced that one scene was not right. Anne wrote, rewrote, and finally, after several attempts, she said to me, "You write it." I protested but Anne said, "No, you write it and I'll get some idea, maybe." I sat down in the kitchen and wrote the scene. Anne worked on something else. When I had finished she read it and said, "This is terrible but I think I know now what you mean." It worked. She rewrote the scene and it was excellent.

The late summer and early fall were devoted to going to church, studying the mass, casting, and getting a design for the show. We were complete by September 2. Two actors had changed because the originals were not available. It was hot. The American Place was not air-conditioned. Anne came to New York with Lois Ames, and took up residence at the Algonquin. She, like most people new to New York, was not used to walking, so at the first rehearsal she noticed that Marian Seldes was wearing slippers. Marian gave Anne her slippers to wear, which she kept, and she would sit, cigarette, a can of beer, wearing gold slippers, and watch us work. Again she fit in beautifully.

We had to change the great-aunt. That was a must. We could not find an older woman who would say the text; it was filled with sexual fantasy, and so we found a young woman who could play it, Me'l Dowd, and the family became complete again. There were two characters in the play who were merely voices—demons really of the characters' madness. They were difficult to integrate into the play due to the new concept of the mass, but I loved them. I had a long talk with Anne about these voices, because she actually had experienced a good deal of hallucinating that she could recall and discuss. She could and would talk to me and the cast about her madness, her experiences, her feelings at various times as casually and as cheerfully as one would remember an incident from one's past. There was no hesitation in her attitude about revealing herself. Any autobiographical reference was always explained, talked about calmly, "Yes, sometimes they took shapes and then sometimes they were just voices. They can be whatever you want them to be, Chuck."

Wynn wanted them out; I wanted them in; Anne had to decide. Anne respected Wynn a great deal. The implications of producers are obvious and he *had* produced Robert Lowell—the voices were cut and I was not able to stop it. It was the beginning of doubts that, for Anne, kept growing, if only because the incident had fed her lack of self-confidence. The play was taking real shape, and Wynn again wanted cuts. The amorphous quality of the atmosphere, which I believed helped the play, and the set-ups for the voices that made transitions possible that Anne knew instinctively were right, were cut. It was always me saying no, Wynn saying cut, and Anne having to decide, and as we approached the opening the strain began to show. I was not experienced to know how to keep this from happening. The culmination came in Wynn's office after a rehearsal before we were to play to our first audience. Wynn was after clarification about the great-aunt. I thought we had clarified too much and Anne froze. She kept repeating one phrase over and over. She had come to the realization that her living, breathing work was going to be shown. There was not a consensus of positive opinion and theater critics are scary enough for the toughest author. I finally saw that Wynn had not a clue about Anne's condition. She was, to use her phrase, doubling off, and so I said let's go home, Anne, you're getting nutty, and we left.

All this time our work was done very joyfully. Before we opened we were told that we were extended a week because there was so much interest in the play. Anne became more tentative and withdrawn but the spirit of the production was very positive, unlike most shows at

The American Place. The night we opened we never changed or rewrote—we let it stand. We, the cast and I, were happy with what we had. Anne approved and said she liked it. Wynn and his staff were enthusiastic. The critics were positive, for the most part, but no "money" notices. We played our six weeks and closed. The spirit of the actors was that of being in a hit. We were page one four weeks in a row in the *New York Times* entertainment section. After the experience of going through a New York opening, Anne never seemed as excited about her work and we hardly ever spoke of it. She smiled, but the acceptance of her play was not like that of her books and she was more convinced than ever that she was not a playwright.

Anne, Marian, and I stayed in touch. Marian and I were invited to her book party for *Transformations* at Sardi's, and Anne and I continued to talk every few months. I would try to prod her for a new play and she would suggest that I adapt one of her books of poems and laugh. She and Maxine Kumin drove to Beverly, Massachusetts, to see a summer show. Her enjoyment of the theater never left, and for me the hope of another Sexton play never came to an end. It has been seven years since *Mercy Street*. At least twenty times a year people mention the play to me and Marian in very complimentary terms. I am constantly asked about it by theater people all over the country. All these questions over an off-Broadway play that ran six weeks seven years ago? I think Anne was a playwright, and that was our only real disagreement.

POLLY C. WILLIAMS

Sexton in the Classroom

In the last ten years of her life, Anne Sexton taught several poetry workshops. Whether at Wayland High School, McLean Hospital, Boston University, or at her home, each workshop was representative of the others. In these workshops, which met for two hours once a week, there were usually ten to twenty members who were chosen from a larger group of young poets who had submitted their work for consideration.

In the early fall of 1974, I was one of the eight Boston University students admitted to Anne Sexton's last workshop. Because she had been publicly categorized a "confessional poet," I approached this workshop with the preconceived notion that all of the people involved would be writing in the "confessional" vein. To my surprise, an array of young poets with varying styles had been chosen. We met in the B.U. English Department's library, a dismal Victorian room with several easy chairs and no books. Half an hour later Anne Sexton arrived with a briefcase overflowing with papers, and after apologizing for being late she kicked off her sandals and lit a cigarette.

Immediately one was aware of the immense power behind her presence. She was much more stunning than her photographs—much more intimate than her reputation would suggest. She was not called "Mrs. Sexton" or "Ms. Sexton," simply "Anne" for she treated her students as her peers. The purpose of the first meeting was not to criticize or dwell on individual poems and attitudes but simply to get to know each member of the group. One by one we gave our names, ages, favorite poets, reasons for writing, and then read a few of our own poems. In the past Anne had commenced most of her workshops in this same manner. Those at Boston University (which began in January of 1970) were taped by or for her biographer and friend Lois Ames. Anne felt that the endeavor might be humorous because a tape recorder could eventually become an "omniscient" extra member of the group.

When the actual "workshopping" began the following week, Anne's first requirement was that a poem should be able to stand alone —no explanations and certainly no apologies. Proceeding alphabetically, we read and marked our own copies of the poem to be discussed, it was read aloud, and finally Anne made a few comments before asking for the group's general criticism. She never hesitated to say, "Wrong word," "NO! NO! NO!," "I won't stand for this," or simply "I love it," "You're all better than I am, goddammit."

Although Anne occasionally examined the form and technique in her students' work, an Anne Sexton Workshop could not truly be labeled academic. Thought-provoking, stimulating, candid, supportive—but *not* academic. This did not minimize the amount of information a student was able to acquire, but the core of knowledge that one gained was based on ideas and feelings—not forms and techniques. By fostering self-confidence, she assured the young poet *why* he or she should continue writing. Although Anne shared many of her own writing theories, she never fully assisted with the *how* to write poetry. For that reason the class was more an idea-shop than a form-shop.

If the class was stimulated by a certain idea, an assignment often developed. Participation was optional but Anne urged her students to experiment with new poem ideas. As she said, "It will be fun if it doesn't come out, and we'll all show our failures." One assignment, that Anne also wrote a poem for, was to write a love letter in a burning building (an idea we stole from a creative writing class also held at

B.U.). A few weeks later Anne introduced another assignment: "Emily's Dreams."

> Poets come to no good end, we all know that. Except some do—Emily
> [Dickinson], she seemed to take care of herself didn't she? . . . She must
> not have talked to herself—of course her poems were a talking—but
> her father, you see, always was there. Wonder what her dreams were.
> There's a good assignment.

To further motivate a student into writing for an assignment, Anne periodically shared her writing methods and theories. One of her fundamental approaches to writing was that one should expand for the sake of expansion. Only when the pages were overflowing with ideas and images should one go back and slice, cut, alter, and delete. If the poem or story still was not right, one should again expand, expand, expand. It is the process itself, not the motivation or ultimate objective, that enables one to discover the stimulating image and correct line.

When a student was unable to find the perfect image, Anne felt that a barrier was blocking the student's unconscious. Anne's job was to evoke or draw out the image and she did so by trying to break down that barrier. "I'm casting out, baiting the hook and casting out." In most of her workshops, Anne utilized an image-provoking technique, similar to brainstorming, which revolved around the idea of approaching the image from the back door. Anne would take an object and say "What is this *not*?" In the course of picturing what an object was *not*, one would often discover an unusual image that the object actually was. The image does not necessarily have to be accurate, indeed there would be a danger if it was too accurate. But the image must be clear, for a poem must create a vivid image in the mind of the reader. A poet must paint a picture and not simply explain what it means to look at one. Referring to a line in one of our poems, "The poem becomes the conscience of the street," Anne said it was "an intellectual pompous line—sealed off in a tomb." Anne praised images such as "bubble gum breath" but criticized the over-explanatory, unoriginal image (such as "enormous rat" or "gorgeous mist"). One of our poems ended with the line "bloody delicious casserole." Anne's reaction: "'Delicious'—no. You implied it, don't tell us about it."

Just as Anne felt the image or simile should be original and therefore a little off-beat, she felt the form within a poem should have the same qualities. Her students were usually young poets and Anne was often confronted with the student who was intimidated or overly influenced by past masters of form. Replying to a student who had once been required to write in iambic pentameter, Anne said:

> Well, I wouldn't give that until I felt someone was such a master at, um, at the good line, the everything, the right ending—they're ready to attack form and I feel that you should do it secretly, sneakedly. Go to the people that write in good tight form and study them. First of all, iambic pentameter, kept, is the most boring thing in the world, in my opinion. It should be broken. . . . It is a very strange creepy-crawlly art.

Form was one of the essential ingredients of a short poem I presented in class. In its entirety the poem read:

> Once through time with no end to come
> there shown the two in hand who solved
> the query never while together raised:
> the why of yes we can.

Anne criticized the ending of the poem, saying it was too predictable and boring because of the completed rhythm. Insisting that the poem would be improved if the last two words were omitted, Anne said:

> It's so nice to break it. Kind of Molly Bloomish . . . Will you please, for me, take out "we can?" Or are you in love with it? You understand, this poem is yours. Anything anyone says, you can just say, to yourself, "Shit on them, I'm keeping it."

Omitting "we can" would be "Molly Bloomish"—daring and interesting to change form like breaking iambic pentameter or twisting the usual. For Anne, nursery rhymes were potentially powerful; to alter them would shock the reader versus lulling him or her to sleep. "They hit you—they give you low blows 'cause you see, you learn them as a kid." Anne had utilized this same technique with fairy tales in her fifth book, *Transformations.*

If an impasse was reached over one of Anne's suggestions, the class would occasionally vote on it. Anne realized that the writing or polishing of a poem was a long process: first the "kernel of a poem," then the poem, finally the endless workshopping. Even after her poetry was published, Anne found lines she would have changed. After reading us "Gods" from *The Death Notebooks,* she felt that the "Mrs. Sexton" in the first line should actually read "Ms. Sexton." Anne herself wrote several versions and drafts of most of her poems, often relying on the help of close friends, fellow poets, and her students. One of the virtues of the class structure was that communal workshopping offered more feedback, thereby speeding up the rewriting process.

No matter how young or inexperienced a poet might be, if the poem was good, Anne felt it should be published. Her highest praise, never falsely given, was "Send it to *The New Yorker!*" Believing that it was a satisfying feeling to see one's own work in print, Anne explained her own submission method. Before sending a poem out, one should address and stamp the envelope to the next place. One must assume the poem will be returned, thereby avoiding the agony of rejection. The system worked for Anne and she encouraged her students to use it.

Perhaps the major concept that Anne installed in her students was the idea that every poem was part of one great poem. And because every poet was similar to every other in sensibility and motivation, she demanded that her students involve themselves in the class. In her attempts to make workshopping a communal effort, Anne often minimized her own importance and role as teacher. Referring to herself as just another member of the group, she demanded that we challenge anything we did not agree with.

> I get these lines and they're all stinky and you don't even boo. Now wait a minute, have I told you the whole, I mean, that you're supposed to boo me and hiss me at some point in the class ... ? That's when you've won. You've won your good marks. You've, you've gone way beyond me, you've already said, "Look, she's a fake, she doesn't know anything. Ah, I know better." And it's a mutual thing and you'll find

that I'll say something and you'll go "Boo. Hiss." Right? And I like it. I'm happy. Then I'm proud, then I think I've done my job and they don't really need me—not that you need me anyway.

Our last workshop with Anne was on October 2, two days before she died. She remarked that she certainly was making a mess of this particular class, which she attributed to exhaustion and the mood she was in (which she described as both "cryie" and "drifty as hell"). But Anne pulled all her fragmented comments together by saying:

> I have to play the fool. I don't know, I got to get, you know, I got to get your unconsciouses moving and I have to do it with all these mistakes. I mean I have to let myself be a fool, and say any damn thing that, you know, appears and blurt it out. You should be doing the same thing. Are you too proud or something? Ashamed to be a fool? Look, the bravest thing a poet can be is a fool. I mean, that's the toughest thing. You're going to find out 'cause that's what you end up being half the time. That's the hardest thing—a fool. I said that in *The Paris Review* and I still maintain it. That's the hardest thing: to be a fool. You can be anything; you can be stinking, no good, a rotten poet—but to be a fool—nobody wants to be a fool.

Throughout the class Anne had said whatever she genuinely felt regardless of how people would react. She had to gamble that others would consider her a fool, but the risk was worth the satisfaction of expressing her true feelings. Anne had played the fool, which had shown us that it was tough but that it was also possible to be tough enough. She, being someone we respected and admired, also allowed herself to be a fool, which was something we had never realized or been willing to notice before. Her explanation showed us that the awareness and expression of this role was absolutely essential to the understanding of one's own identity as a poet.

As a teacher, Anne was both sensitive and wise. During the two hours of class or times we met afterward for a drink, she was receptive and always, always a great deal of fun. Her humor was classic. One day after workshopping three different poems she said, "That's enough emotionally. So let's get good and dirty now." One was always aware of her passion for laughter, for teaching, indeed, her passion for life. Her company alone was an "excitable gift."

JOHN MALCOLM BRINNIN

Offices
(Boston University)

What words will do. *"In search,"* I start, *"of her
identity..."* I bite my pencil end
and pip it out, *"she found her character."*
True? Or is it the other way around?
The celebration, as they call it, 's on
at four. Time's up. After the folk-song bit,
I'll say my piece, then wind up with John Clare:
I long for scenes where man has never trod,
  A place where woman never smiled or wept;
There to dwell with my Creator, God,
  And sleep as I in childhood sweetly slept.

Extreme unction. (While that garage stayed shut
to the print of holy thumbs and scatted prayer,
did crankcase rainbows make their own anointment?)
Unction! I catch her metal echo. "Christ, John,"
as, years ago, it whanged the arbored night
of some Sicilian part of Somerville,
"it's not the talk, let's face it, my big mouth ...
it's simple fact: I am the living Plath."
I walk down the dead hall, no one in sight.
The framed card on the white door says it all.
(God rest Ms. Dog.) *Anne Sexton: By Appointment.*

102

MAXINE KUMIN

A Friendship
Remembered

As the world knows, we were intimate friends and professional allies. Early on in our friendship, indeed almost as soon as we began to share poems, we began to share them on the telephone. Since we lived initially in the same Boston suburb and later in contiguous ones (Ma Bell's unlimited contiguous service be praised!), there were no message units to reckon with, which surely would have inhibited me, though probably not Annie, whose long-distance phone bills were monumental down the years. It was her habit when alone at night (and alone at night meant depressed always, sometimes anxious to the point of pain as well) to call on old friends. But that's a digression. What I wanted to say was I don't know what year, but fairly early on, we both installed second phone lines in our houses so that the rest of each of our families—the two husbands, the five children—could have equal access to a phone and we could talk privately for as long as we wanted. I confess we sometimes connected with a phone call and kept that line linked for hours at a stretch, interrupting poem-talk to stir the spaghetti sauce, switch the laundry, or try out a new image on the typewriter; we whistled into the receiver for each other when we were ready to resume. It worked wonders. And to think that it only cost seven or eight bucks a month!

How different from January and February of 1973, when I went to Centre College in Danville, Kentucky, as a writer-in-residence. We

103

agreed ahead of time to divide the phone bill we would incur. Anne called me every afternoon at five; she was then writing *The Awful Rowing Toward God* at white heat—two, three, even four poems a day. I tried hard to retard the process for I felt it was all happening too fast and it scared me. It was too much like Plath spewing out those last poems. Nevertheless, I listened, commented, helped, tried to provide some sort of organizational focus. We averaged one hour a day on the phone, only because I was too cheap to talk longer. My share of the bill came to about $300, which was pretty liberated for me. I am descended from a lineage that panicks as soon as the three-minute mark is passed.

Writing poems and bouncing them off each other by phone does develop the ear. You learn to hear line-breaks, to pick up and be critical of unintended internal rhyme, or intended slant rhyme or whatever. We did this so comfortably and over such an extended period of time that indeed when we met—usually over lunch at my house, for Anne almost always stopped off to lunch with me after seeing whichever of her infamously inept psychiatrists—we were somewhat shy of each other's poem there on the page. I can remember so often saying, "Oh, so *that's* what it looks like" of a poem I had heard and visualized through half a dozen revisions.

Over the years, her lines shortened and the line-breaks grew, I think, more unexpected. In the early days we were both working quite strictly in form. We measured and cut and pasted and reworked arduously, with an intense sense of purpose, both of us believing in the rigors of form as a forcing agent, that the hardest truths would come right if they were hammered to fit (see the title poem, "All My Pretty Ones"). I confess we both had rhyming dictionaries and we both used them. Typically, we had totally different kinds. Anne's grouped rhyme-words according to their common endings—all the one-syllable words, for example, followed by the two-syllable ones, and so on—whereas mine worked by orthography, which made it quirkier because it went not by sound but by spelling. It was Anne's aim to use rhyme unexpectedly, brilliantly but aptly; even the most unusual rhyme, she felt, must never obtrude on the sense of the line, nor must the normal word order, the easy tone of natural vernacular usage, be wrenched to save a rhyme. She would willingly push a poem through twenty or more drafts; she had an unparalleled tenacity and abandoned a "failed" poem only with regret if not downright anger after dozens of sessions.

Nevertheless, I would say that Anne's poems were frequently "given" ones. "Riding the Elevator Into the Sky" (in *The Awful Rowing Toward God*) is an example. The newspaper article mentioned in its first stanza gave rise to the poem and the poem itself came quite easily and cleanly, as if written out beforehand in the clean air and then transcribed onto the page with very few alterations. "Letter Written on a Ferry While Crossing Long Island Sound" (in *All My Pretty Ones*) was a "given" poem, too; given by the fortuitous sight of the nuns. As I remember it, the poem was written much as it now appears on the printed page, except for the minor skirmishes required to effect that marvelous closure in each stanza where the fourth from the last and the last lines rhyme (save for the first stanza, and "cup" and "up" in the middle of the last stanza). Also, it was originally called "Letter Written on the Long Island Ferry" and was made more specific on the advice of Howard Moss. "Young" and "I Remember" (both also in *All My Pretty Ones*) required very little revision, as my memory serves, whereas "The Truth the Dead Know" went through innumerable workings to arrive at its final form. In this poem, the poet is locked into an *a b a b* rhyme-scheme with little room for pyrotechnics. The language is purified to an amazing degree, I think, reflecting Anne's wish to open *All My Pretty Ones* with a spare, terse, tough elegy for her parents, one without biographical detail, the very detail she would get into later, in the title poem or in "The House." That title poem was one which underwent many revisions to force it into the exigency of an *a b a b, c d c d, e e* stanza. We both admired the multi-syllabic rhymes of "slumber"/"disencumber" and "navigator"/"later," to say nothing of the *tour de force* final couplet.

The initial impetus for her poems usually came as a direct visitation to the cave of her desk. She invoked the muse by reading other poets and playing her favorite records over and over. The background of music acted in some way to free her to create, which always astonished me, for whom it is an intrusion. Often with the volume turned up loud, loud enough to drown out all other sounds, she could pull an intricate rhyme-scheme out of the air. Is it worth noting that massed orchestral strings, full volume, served too as a device for her to cover and block out the bad voices? (The time before the time she killed herself, it was with music at crescendo: a scream, I thought when I got there. I don't know if the radio was playing that last time; I think so.) As for her subject matter, we all know it came for the most part directly out of her own life and times, with little if any psychological distance on the trauma or pleasure that gave rise to the poem. Still, she transmuted the events. She was able to take the rawest facts —her mother's agonizingly slow death from cancer, her father's stroke, her entire wretched childhood experience as what was undoubtedly an undiagnosed hyperkinetic youngster, kept behind a gate in her own room—and to make of them a whole.

Someone once said that we have art in order not to die of the truth. Not only did Sexton's confessional poems most vividly and truly keep her alive, but they sustained and spoke to a vast audience. I would say that she drew great sustenance and comfort from the knowledge that her work reached out to and beyond the normal sensitive reader of poetry (though, for god's sake, what is "normal" or "sensitive"?) and touched the minds of many deeply troubled people. For a while it seemed that psychiatrists all over the country were referring their patients to Anne's work, as if it were the balm in Gilead. At the same time that it comforted and fed her to know that she mattered as a poet beyond the usual sphere of self-congratulating, self-adulating bards, she had considerable ambivalence about her work. Accused of exhibitionism, she was determined only to be more flamboyant; nevertheless, the large Puritan hiding inside suffered and grieved over the label "confessional" poet. For instance, when she wrote "Cripples and Other Stories" (in *Live or Die*), a poem that almost totally "occurred" on the page, she crumpled it up, as if in embarrassment, and tossed it into the wastebasket. We fished it out and saved it; I thought it then and think it now a remarkable document.

The "saving" of that poem was to make the tone consistent and to smoothe out some of the cruder rhythmical spots. This was the sort of mechanical task Anne could fling herself into gladly. The results were often doubly effective. In "The Operation" (a key poem in *All My Pretty Ones*), for example, the experience—awesome and painful —is hammered into art by way of form and rhyme. Both squeeze the raw event until the juice runs in the reader, I think. I do not mean to downplay the force of metaphor in the poem—the "historic thief," the "humpty-dumpty," etc.—but it is the impact of rhyme and the shape of the poem's three parts (its form) that bring it off. For instance, the retardation of the rhyming sounds at the end of the first section—"leaf"/"straw"/"lawn"/"car"/"thief"/"house"/"upon"— in those short, fairly sharply end-stopped lines, build to the impact. Or, to take yet another poem, I remember "Faustus and I" (in *The Death Notebooks*) was headed for the discard pile; it was then a free-verse poem and as such had, for me, an evilly flippant tone. I seem to remember that I often helplessly suggested, "Why don't you pound it into form?" and often it worked. In the case of "Faustus and I" the suggestion worked because the rhyme scheme gave the poem a dignity and nobility it deserved. It worked because the pounding elicited a level of language, a level of metaphor she hadn't quite reached in the early versions.

Anne also had an almost mystical faith in the "found" word or image, as well as in metaphor by mistake, by typo or misapprehension. She would fight hard to keep an image, a line, a word usage, but if you were just as dogged in your conviction that the line didn't work, was sentimental or mawkish, that the word usage was ill-suited or trite, she would capitulate—unless she was totally convinced of her own rightness. Then there was no shaking her. We learned somehow, from each other and from trusting each other's critical sense, not to go past the unshakable core, not to trespass on style or voice. Perhaps we learned this in the early years of our student workshops, first at the Boston Center in classes with John Holmes, and later in our own house-by-house workshops with John Holmes and George Starbuck and Sam Albert. These were often real encounters, real square-offs, but we all respected and admired one another—an idea that seems terribly old-fashioned somehow today, that poets could be competitive and full of ego but genuinely care for one another's well-being. That was a good group, now that I think back on it; we all wrote at white heat and many of the best poems any of us ever wrote were tested in that crucible. Anne, in fact, as a result of this experience, came to believe in the value of workshops. She loved growing this way herself, and she urged the technique on her students. Her whole *Bedlam* book grew during her workshop years and virtually every one of those poems was scrutinized across the table. We were still at it when *All My Pretty Ones* was in process. It was awesome the way Anne could come to the workshop biweekly with three, four, five new and complicated poems. She was never meek about it, but she did listen and she did care. She gave generous help and she required, demanded, insisted on generous response.

We might talk for a moment about *Transformations.* Anne was fascinated by fairy tales. They were for her what the Greek myths had been, perhaps, for others. Since she had not had—and she was grim about this—the advantage of a higher education (by which she meant *Beowulf,* the Norse eddas, Homer, Milton, etc.—all denied her), she lapsed back to what must have been a halcyon time in her life, the time when her great-aunt, the colossal mother figure of her past, had read German fairy tales to her. Now she reread them all and scoured the libraries for more, even asking my daughter Judy to translate and retranslate some tales from the German so that she could be sure she had gotten every final variant on the story. The wonderful self-mocking, society-mocking wit of *Transformations* is entirely her own; she was a very funny person, quick to satirize a given situation. The book more or less evolved; she had no thought of a collection at first, and I must immodestly state that I urged and bullied her to go on after the first few poems to think in terms of a whole book of them. I also take outright credit for the title. We had been talking about the way many contemporary poets translated from languages they did not themselves read, but used trots or had the poems filtered through an interpreter, and that these poems were *adaptations*. It struck me then that Anne's poems about the fairy tales went one step further and were *transformations*. And for the record let me state that in that same conversation Annie was urging me to collect the "pastoral" poems I'd written, and I said, "But what will I call it?" and she said, "*Up Country,* of course."

The Book of Folly gives further evidence of Anne's interest in myth-making. Whether or not they succeed, she has written three myths of her own and she labored strenuously in the vineyard of prose, finding it foreign and harsh work. But it is true that the story-teller inside the poet sometimes yearns desperately to be let out. Anne's storyteller burst out in these tales and in the Daisy play she wrote early in her career on a Ford grant. (*Tell Me Your Answer True* was its original title, though it ended up as *Mercy Street*—an image that turned up in a dream, the dream a plea for mercy from some-where, anywhere, from Life.) It wasn't the first verbalization of her Christ fascination, nor was it destined to be the last. Christ as Prime Sufferer and God (any kind of god who'd be there) became her final obsessions, perhaps because as her life deteriorated, people were less dependable. But Jesus figured prominently from the very beginning. But what I chiefly remember is how much fun Anne had working on the play, how richly she enjoyed working in dialogue, for which she had a considerable talent. Her ear was quick and true; I always trusted implicitly her criticism of the dialogue in my fiction, and could point to dozens of lines—responses, usually—in my own work which came pure out of Sexton's mouth. She also loved the excitement of being in the theater and being in New York and staying at the Algonquin. She adored her leading actress Marian Seldes (as who would not!), and loved most of all the late late nights after a rehearsal when she would sit up till dawn reworking a speech here, a phrase there, loving the tinkering even more than the glamor of actually having her play produced.

Anne's way of working, whether with a poem or the play or an attempted story, was to try out the draft on as many listeners as she could amass. I felt sometimes that she was putting the matter to a vote, and indeed in her classes at Boston University she fell into the always amusing pattern of inviting the students to vote for or against an image, a line-break, an ending. But she invited and needed the interchange of ideas and attitudes, something that is anathema to most writers who cannot brook outside interference or involvement in an unfinished piece. Anne took strength from outside reactions, as much strength from the negative as from the positive remarks (I am not now speaking of reviewers!), and she genuinely felt that there was always something to be gained in this sharing process. It was her conviction that the least-experienced student could bring something to bear on a worksheet; she weighed and evaluated opinions, keeping some, discarding others, but using them all as a kind of emotional ballast for going on with her work. And she was equally willing to bring her own energy to bear on the meanest poem. She was generous, yes; but it transcends generosity, really. It was evangelical, it was for Poetry, the Higher Good. She lived her poetry, poetry was her life. It had saved her life in a real sense when, in the mid-1950s, she began to write poems as a therapeutic act urged on her by her current psychiatrist. The clear thread that runs through all the books of poems is how tenuous that life was. She was on loan to poetry, as it were. We always knew it would end. We just didn't know when or exactly how.

LOIS AMES

Remembering Anne

Anne and I were first friends. Then, on December 24, 1966, at half after eleven in the evening, she telephoned me and with her usual exuberance said, "My Christmas gift to you is to make you my biographer." I replied only half-jokingly, "I'm not sure this is a present."

From then on I began to observe Anne with a second pair of eyes; listened to her with a third ear; and followed her activities with a tape recorder. We traveled to readings in dreary college towns. We crisscrossed England. We telephoned each other from a dozen different states, and wrote and cabled when short of funds. In 1968 I moved to a town near her home and our visits became more frequent and more intense.

To be close to Anne frequently meant being pierced by her pain and witness to her terrifying hunger which in the end none of us could assuage. Her words secure her immortality: in these notes I'm remembering Anne the woman we all loved—the teacher, the colleague, our remarkable friend.

Anne could be wry, caustic, funny, warm, tender, efficient, insistent, demanding, but, above all, giving. After her death I shook out a kaleidoscope of vivid memories and with other friends and her family mounted a verbal collage of stories.

Even now, each time we meet we extract comfort in our grief from a quickly told tale and a belly laugh and shaking of our heads. Anne would have appreciated that. She set the example. Once she shouted to me by way of admonition, "You should use your grief. No matter what happens, you should swim out of the pain with a finished book held high in your hands!"

I remember Anne the teacher who taught with her whole being. She began with Wayland high school students for the Teachers' and Writers' Collaborative. She was tentative, diffident, and insecure.

Next we slogged through the blizzardy snows of 1968 to a poetry class held with the patients of McLean Hospital, a private mental institution in Belmont, Massachusetts. Here she was consistently sensitive and healing, and learned to be a skillful teacher. Then in early 1969 she held a seminar for Antioch College students in her study at home during the winter interim. Finally, she was appointed professor at Boston University, where she had once been a student in a class with Robert Lowell. Now, instead of Anne Sexton, George Starbuck, Kathleen Spivak, and Sylvia Plath, there sat a new generation of poets. She took their measure and at these classes at B.U. she came into her own: brilliant, incisive, pushing, prodding, cajoling—she lured her students into better poetry than they had known they could make. After the class she retired to the local student hangout to drink beer, smoke cigarettes, and argue. At her home she spent endless, exhausting hours working with these same students on their single poems or gigantic books. Now they are coming into their own: Eric Edwards, Suzanne Rioff, Anne Hussey, Celia Gilbert, Joan Norris, Arlene Stone.

I remember Anne the impractical gift-giver. When my jewelry was stolen she gave me tiny diamond earrings and said, "Don't worry about burglars any more. If they take them, I'll get you another pair. They didn't cost much. And don't worry about losing them either."

I remember Anne who loved God's simple gifts: fishing, the sun, littleneck clams, daisies; and Anne who loved the world's extravagances: mink, diamonds, superior champagne, fresh caviar, and yellow roses. Anne invited poor writers to lunch at the Algonquin, where they could be fussed over by the waiters. But she had a sense of proportion: if someone rich asked her to dinner she also went to the Algonquin, and ordered *double* portions of caviar.

Anne and I exchanged gold talismans against the forces in life that grind you down: the broken fingernail, the broken promise, the broken life. Superstitiously, we always wore the gold discs we'd had engraved with "Don't let the bastards win!"

I remember Anne in the heat of August calling the president of TWA and cajoling him into personally locating my baggage lost in a flight from Europe.

Anne had contempt for inferior poets, but praised and helped the careers of those she held in high regard. She worked hard: writing, rewriting, asking for "crits" from anyone whose help was sensitive and acute, reading her poems to old friends and new. She liked to explore possibilities: her play *Mercy Street,* which she reworked on a Guggenheim at The American Place Theatre in 1969; her rock group, *Anne Sexton and Her Kind,* which was created in 1968, a marriage of her poetry with music; *Transformations,* her rewording of the Brothers Grimm which became an opera, a particular delight to her when it opened to cheers and ovations in Minneapolis in 1972.

I remember Anne in England in 1967. She opened the door of the aged inn in the Cotswolds with awe. She was to sleep in the room where Rilke slept! Anne insisted on an introduction to Pablo Neruda, her hero, whom she approached with respect, enthusiasm, and modesty. At the International Poetry Festival in London, she stood up to W.H. Auden and WON! It was a cutthroat evening. Poets from the world over competed for two minutes of reading time: Anne and Anthony Hecht conferred on how to extend their odd-minute (nine and eleven) allotments. Then Mr. Auden sent an emissary to Ms. Sexton. Auden, in his wrinkles and carpet slippers, held the honored anchor-end of the evening. Mr. Auden requested that Ms. Sexton cut short her reading of *The Double Image* so that Mr. Auden might be at home at 10:00 P.M., as was his custom. Ms. Sexton sent back word that she would be pleased to assist Mr. Auden by exchanging places on the program so that Mr. Auden could be at home according to his custom. Ms. Sexton read *The Double Image* and Mr. Auden left for home at 10:45 P.M.

On a warm July afternoon Anne clutched me in terror at an English country house. "Did you hear what I heard?"

"Yes."

"I think it's a ghost."

"So do I."

"What did you hear?"

"A woman sighing in great ecstasy."

"No, no, Lois. A woman sighing in great sorrow—that's the difference between you and me."

I remember Anne who responded to love and to need with such appreciation. We went to visit Olive Higgins Prouty, the author of *Stella Dallas,* who was then in her eighties. In a desperate attempt to convince Mrs. Prouty that we were genuine, Anne had brought her poetry books with her. She pulled out *All My Pretty Ones* and read "Old" by the muted light under a rose silk lampshade. The suspicious dowager, jaded by her years, relaxed into tears, whispering, "How could you know, how could you possibly know what it means to grow old?"

"I know. I know, and now you know that I know," said Anne.

With a child Anne talked as if to a contemporary. When I turned from the telephone to tell my young son that Anne had killed herself, he swallowed hard and said, "Aw, why did she have to go and do that? She was so nice." That's how we all felt that October night.

For some of us it will take years, perhaps our own lifetimes, to complete our farewells to Anne. She was so filled with exuberance and warmth. Her blue-green eyes were so luminous, like those of a sea witch. She had such wit, intellect, and profound sense of symbol and imagery. She sought so far for so long for a sign of God's favor.

I wrote my own epitaph for Anne when we worked on *Mercy Street* in New York in 1969. It was used as the ending to the play:

> Daisy, you have been brought forth
> from a stiff necked people.
> The Zeal of your house
> doth eat you up.
> O, Daisy, O daughter of Jerusalem,
> there is an enormous hunger in Zion.

PART IV

Reviews

On *To Bedlam and*
Part Way Back
(1960)

JAMES DICKEY

Anne Sexton's poems so obviously come out of deep, painful sections
of the author's life that one's literary opinions scarcely seem to matter;
one feels tempted to drop them furtively into the nearest ashcan,
rather than be caught with them in the presence of so much naked
suffering. The experiences she recounts are among the most harrow-
ing that human beings can undergo: those of madness and near-
madness, of the pathetic, well-meaning, necessarily tentative and
perilous attempts at cure, and of the patient's slow coming back into
the human associations and responsibilities which the old, previous
self still demands. In addition to being an extremely painful subject,
this is perhaps a major one for poetry, with a sickeningly frightening
appropriateness to our time. But I am afraid that in my opinion the
poems fail to do their subject the kind of justice which I should like
to see done. Perhaps no poems could. Yet I am sure that Mrs. Sexton
herself could come closer than she does here, did she not make entirely unnecessary concessions to the conventions of her literary gen-

eration and the one just before it. One can gather much of her tone
and procedure from quotations like "You, Doctor Martin, walk/from
breakfast to madness," and "All day we watched the gulls/striking
the top of the sky/and riding the blown roller coaster." "Riding the
blown roller coaster" is a kind of writing I dislike to such an extent
that I feel, perhaps irrationally, that everyone else including Mrs.
Sexton ought to dislike it, too, for its easy, A-student, superficially
exact "differentness" and its straining to make contrivance and artifi-
ciality appear natural. One would hope that a writer of Mrs. Sexton's
seriousness, and with her terrible story to tell, would avoid this kind
of thing at any price. Yet a large part of her book is composed of such
figures. In the end, one comes to the conclusion that if there were
some way to relieve these poems of the obvious effort of trying to be
poems, something very good would emerge. I think they would make
far better short stories, and probably in Mrs. Sexton's hands, too, than
they do poems. As they are, they lack concentration, and above all
the profound, individual linguistic suggestibility and accuracy that
poems must have to be good. As D. H. Lawrence once remarked in
another connection, they don't "say the real say." But Mrs. Sexton's
candor, her courage, and her story are worth anyone's three dollars.

GEOFFREY HARTMAN

For Denise Levertov and Jean Garrigue poetry is largely an attitude
of mind, a song gradually finding its words and even its experience.
But Anne Sexton, like Ruth Stone, knows her experience, knows it
almost too well. Her poetry is, in consequence, less a means to self-
knowledge than a form of courage—a means to face self-knowledge.
To Bedlam and Part Way Back is a remarkable book (the only volume
here truly a *book*), in which we feel not only the poet's experience but
also something of the morality behind recalling and recording it.
There is more here than a case-history or a "cruel glass."

The experience itself, though involving a stay in an asylum, is simple, moving, and universal. Miss Sexton describes the loss of a child, or rather the *estrangement* of a mother from her child. Hardly born it reminds the mother unbearably of her own childhood, and continues to do so after the asylum:

> And you came each
> weekend. But I lie.
> You seldom came. I just pretended
> you, small piglet, butterfly
> girl with jelly bean cheeks,
> disobedient three, my splendid
> stranger. And I had to learn
> why I would rather
> die than love, how your innocence
> would hurt and how I gather
> guilt like a young intern
> his symptoms, his certain evidence.
>   ("The Double Image")

It is the womb of self-knowledge the child has opened: named Joyce in order to be nicknamed Joy—"Pretty Joy!/Sweet joy but two days old./ Sweet joy I call thee . . ." [Blake, *Songs of Innocence,* "Infant Joy"]—she is the fruit of an entanglement in which every birth signifies a death. The estrangement between mother and child is equally present in the previous generation.

With such a theme, developed not paradigmatically in the manner of Yeats, but directly in the manner of Lowell's life studies, did the poet have to exploit the more sensational aspect of her experience? The opening lines of the book

> You, Doctor Martin, walk
> from breakfast to madness . . .

may show what I mean. This walker is "metaphysical"; his stride is made to yoke disparate things too obviously. Compare such expressions as "the frozen gates/of dinner" or the self-conscious naïveté of "What large children we are/Here [in Bedlam]." Miss Sexton can be so much subtler and gain the same end, as when, also in the opening poem, she rimes "sins" and "moccasins," "myself" and "shelf," when she uses "hotel" indifferently for asylum and summer refuge, or when in "Ringing the Bell" she adapts a nursery rime to describe the "large children." A traditional poem like "Torn Down from Glory Daily," which depicts the tempting down of "king" gulls by crusts of bread, is by its mere obliquity a more powerful picture of the human conditions than her efficiently icy vignettes of the asylum. Only in the latter part of the book, and especially its major poem "The Double Image," do I feel the experience on the mad heath properly subsumed in the action of the whole. It is not that the subject is unpalatable, but that in the minor space of a lyric over-condensations are hard to avoid and strike us coldly. The crudities of "The Double Image," on the other hand, are not compelled by the form but by her genius (the poet is talking of her mother):

> On the first of September she looked at me
> and said I gave her cancer.
> They carved her sweet hills out
> and still I couldn't answer.

The nakedness of the event is intensified by a nakedness of statement which the periphrasis of the next-to-last line only points up, and aptly so if "The Song of Songs" comes to mind, for affected is the entire possibility of love. The obtruding irrelevance of number (present in many poems) adds to the sharpness, evoking as in love-songs or magic rimes ("The first day of Christmas my true love gave to me . . .") the action of fate, its absurd yet demonically just jackpot. I would like to recall also that the journey Yeats' Platonists are forced to suffer against their will:

> Straddling each a dolphin's back
> And steadied by a fin,
> Those Innocents re-live their death,
> Their wounds open again . . .
> ("News for the Delphic Oracle")

Anne Sexton undertakes for a greater purpose even than to know herself and realize the Delphic (or Dolphin) imperative. It is to face a Mode of Being fatally estranged from her. She can revive it but not relive it; there can hardly be a deeper spiritual wound. And if she is so intent on turning wounds into words, is it not because many of them were originally inflicted by words, or their impossibility? This is the homeopathic magic of her verse, its true morality.

On *All My Pretty Ones*

(1962)

MAY SWENSON

With her first book, published only about two years ago, Anne Sexton threw a startling light over the poetic horizon; discerning poets and critics picked up their telescopes and reported something very like a new planet. Her material was startling and it had been lived through, in her own person or through persons closely around her: mental breakdown, accident, death in war, abortion, suicide, and "no special god to refer to." Her handling, in poetic form, of her own exposed and wounded psyche, seemed appalling, but courageous. With a technique apparently fully grown, she transposed her experiences out of their private realm and made them mesh with the instinctive knowledge we all carry of grief, guilt, compulsion, self-disintegration. But *To Bedlam and Part Way Back,* though shocking as a laparotomy, was an achievement not on the score of its subject matter, but because of its poetic mastery.

This is also true of Anne Sexton's second book, *All My Pretty Ones,* which continues to probe other parts of the same psychological terrain. Her method is as uninhibited as entries in a diary or letter writing (in fact several of the poems have "letters" as part of their titles or are addressed to specific persons); the diction seems effortless, yet when we examine for form we find it solidly there, and its expertness is a pleasurable thing in contrast to the often mercilous *débridement* taking place in the content:

> Concerning your letter in which you ask
> me to call a priest and in which you ask
> me to wear The Cross that you enclose;
> your own cross,
> your dog-bitten cross,
> no larger than a thumb,
> small and wooden, no thorns, this rose—
>
> I pray to its shadow,
> that gray place
> where it lies on your letter ... deep, deep.
> I detest my sins and I try to believe
> in The Cross. I touch its tender hips, its dark jawed face,
> its solid neck, its brown sleep.
>
> True. There is
> a beautiful Jesus.
> He is frozen to his bones like a chunk of beef.
> How desperately he wanted to pull his arms in!
> How desperately I touch his vertical and horizontal axes!
> But I can't. Need is not quite belief.

This poem, "With Mercy for the Greedy," states in the last stanza Mrs. Sexton's impelling impulse behind all her poetry so far: "My friend, my friend, I was born/doing reference work in sin, and born/ confessing it. This is what poems are. . . ."

The confessional element, as well as her kind of dexterity, reminds me a good deal of Robert Lowell; she is as savage with herself, as entangled with her New England background, as he. Her new book, however, seems less Lowell-like in its rhythms and pattern schemes than the first, while retaining her stance of the open soul. She says scathing things about her own sex in such poems as "Housewife" and "Woman With Girdle." And in "In the Deep Museum" she conducts us through several kinds of hell and hallucination, which is not to say that she deliberately deals in horror; these true and terrible poems are potential snapshots of any of our lives these days. In the midst of neurotic sadness are charming instances of humor and fantasy: "A Canada goose rides up,/ spread out like a gray suede shirt,/ honking his nose into the March wind." "Some ghosts are children./ Not angels, but ghosts;/ curling like pink tea cups/ on my pillow, or kicking,/ showing their innocent bottoms, wailing/ for Lucifer." "The fish are naked./ The fish are always awake./ They are the color of old spoons/ and caramels." "Over my right shoulder/ I see four nuns/ who sit like a bridge club,/ their faces poked out/ from under their habits,/ as good as good babies who/ have sunk into their carriages."

It seems to me that with the beginning in *All My Pretty Ones,* called "The Truth the Dead Know" (dedicated to her parents), Mrs. Sexton is perhaps laying away her past, to which she has written these re-markable epitaphs, and striding into a sunlight earned through grief. The form of this poem is bare and pure, musical and not tortured. It is a revelatory and healing poem, and quite different in tone from anything else in the book.

THOM GUNN

The split in Anne Sexton's book is between better and worse rather than between kinds or subjects. On the whole she is showing more control over her material than she did in her first book, where most of it was too close for her to speak about it very coherently. And the structure of her poems has become tighter and clearer. On the other hand, she has trouble in subduing the idiom of Lowell, which has evidently replaced Auden's as the most attractive of our time; her symbols are facile at times (one poem, for example, is entitled "Doors,

Doors, Doors"); and she can still relapse into bombast like the end of the following:

> My friend, my friend, I was born
> doing reference work in sin, and born
> confessing it. This is what poems are:
> with mercy
> for the greedy
> they are the tongue's wrangle,
> the world's pottage, the rat's star.

This is the last stanza of a poem addressed to a friend who has been trying to persuade her to take the sacrament of confession, so there is considerable point to the conceits of the first few lines quoted, though I doubt that any Catholic would be convinced by them. But the transition "this is what poems are" is too easy (she was not born writing poems, after all), the special relevance of "greedy" to the passage or the poem is not clear, and the last two lines appear to be there more for the suggestions of the words than for the meanings.

What is most encouraging about this collection is that she is getting rid of the faults of rhetoric and self-dramatization of her first book, in spite of all her admirers:

> A Canada goose rides up,
> spread out like a gray suede shirt,
> honking his nose into the March wind.
> In the entryway a cat breathes calmly
> into her watery blue fur.

These are only a couple of details, perhaps, but they are securely presented, solid in their own existence, and in no way distorted by the poet's intentions. And some of the other poems are impressive, not only in detail, but as wholes. "Old Dwarf Heart" is about the true seat of Adrienne Rich's "ignorant love," which turns out to be a bit like Chicken Little in Pohl and Kornbluth's *The Space Merchants*:

> Like an imbecile she was born old.
> Her eyes wobble as thirty-one thick folds
> of skin open to glare at me . . .

And in "In the Deep Museum," Jesus is transported from the tomb in the stomachs of rats. The poem is ingenious in conception and powerful in the writing. Jesus says, of the first rat:

> It is panting: it is an odor with a face
> like the skin of a donkey. It laps my sores.
> It is hurt, I think, as I touch its little head.

The last line, risking indifference by its understatement, is to me far more moving than anything in Miss Sexton's first book. It may well be that she is most credible when she fictionalizes her experience; certainly she is at her best when she presents it indirectly or from a distance.

LOUISE BOGAN

Anne Sexton, in her second book, *All My Pretty Ones,* as in her first, *To Bedlam and Part Way Back,* does take risks. She assumes the difficult and dangerous task of putting down the primary horrors of life, along with a good many of those secondary horrors which the imagination is able and willing to conjure up. Her realism deals with so many shocking secrets that her moderate use of Surrealistic language and method hardly counts; and these are almost always women's secrets that do not, in the ordinary way of things, get told. To outline personal relationships (and Mrs. Sexton's poems, unlike May Swenson's, are full of people) always at a high pitch of emotion requires courage; to describe fully the dark conflicts of the self without slipping over into the shrill voice of confession or the sobbing note of self-pity requires high control at every conscious and unconscious level. Mrs. Sexton sometimes crosses a boundary retrogressively— from large grief into small grievance, from natural fears to contrived ones. But she usually writes from the center of feminine experience, with the direct and open feeling that women, always vulnerable, have been shy of expressing in recent years.

IAN HAMILTON

Although Anne Sexton's *Selected Poems* show her to be by far the most promising new American poet to have appeared here for some time, there is a real danger, already evidenced by the salaaming *Critical Quarterly,* that she is to be translated into yet another cult-figure of neurotic breakdown, valued not for what she has written but for what her suffering seems to symptomatize. This sort of reading doesn't matter so much when the poet in question is dead—the poems, if they are any good, will outlive it; in the case of a young poet like Mrs. Sexton, however, it is likely to encourage exactly the kind of facile exhibitionism which is even now a constant worry in her work.

The present selection is from two American volumes, *To Bedlam and Part Way Back* (1960) and *All My Pretty Ones* (1962), and if there is any development between the two it is increasingly in the direction of mannerism and artifice, a thinning out and an often rather coy distancing of the intense antagonisms that beset the early poems, as well as a more meek capitulation to the influences of Lowell and Snodgrass and what has been called "the confessional orthodoxy" in current American verse. This is a pity because the first book is sometimes very strong indeed; richly detailed and assured in its excavations of the stable past, the breezy eccentricities, the wide-eyed, trusting tours of Mrs. Sexton's Victorian ancestors; nightmarishly adrift in its dramatising of the unhinged present, the asylum and her slow, uncertain escape from it back into the world, the old responsibilities and threats:

Wait Mister. Which way is home?
And the dark is moving in the corner.
There are no signposts in this room,
four ladies over eighty
in diapers every one of them.
La la la, Oh music swims back to me
And I can feel the tune they played
The night they left me
in this private institution on a hill.

This plaintive, passively victimised note is her most powerful; the voice really does seem to reach us from the wretched, sunken community into which it has awoken, but it is not mad. The four old ladies in diapers, this is the kind of unnerving detail that Mrs. Sexton is superbly good at catching; she notes, and then relinquishes, and although there is little figurative artifice in her best poems, there is a remorseless accuracy of observation that carries its own significance into what it seizes on. As in Williams and Lowell, there is the burden of minute personal detail, the family album, the local history, the pile of old letters, that swarms upon the poet as she digs back into her life; that so much complicated feeling could just have vanished, as mine is vanishing, is the constant exclamation—it is a moving one and has little room for what is not absurdly literal:

I am on the top deck now
holding my wallet, my cigarettes
and my car keys,
at 2 o'clock on a Tuesday
in August of 1960

At other times, though—in poems like "You, Doctor Martin" and "Ringing the Bell"—there is a somewhat slick offhandedness in Mrs. Sexton's approach to the horrors of asylum life, an ironic toning down that seems at some level to take rather too much pride in not having flinched or been more frantic, and this can often deteriorate into mere hardboiled whimsicality; in such poems one feels a restlessness with the sharp detail, the macabre figure and begins to look for some communication, not simply of what it feels like to be in a mental home but of what it feels like to be mentally ill. An impossible demand, probably, but Mrs. Sexton often seems to feel that she is answering it:

> You, Doctor Martin, walk
> from breakfast to madness. Late August,
> I speed through the antiseptic tunnel
> where the moving dead still talk
> of pushing their bones against the thrust
> of cure. And I am queen of this summer hotel
> or the laughing bee on a stalk
>
> of death.

There is a prosy cleverness here that undermines the effect of her horrific props; the distress seems flourished, with a wicked knowing air, and the incongruities are crudely engineered—"from breakfast to madness" could hardly be more full of its own vulgarity.

When Mrs. Sexton abandons her diarist's particularity and pushes towards a more metaphoric use of language this kind of falsity very often sets in; her similes, for instance—a device she is very fond of—invariably seem only to ornament the central factuality of her work. Of a woman, she can offer us her belly "soft as pudding," her nipples "as uninvolved as starfish," her thighs "thick as young pigs," her knees "like saucers"—this kind of freewheeling merely adds a decorative frill to the borders of her poem, making it impossible for us to take the subject very seriously. Again, in a single poem, a pine tree "waits like a fruit store," the wind is both "like a dying woman" and "like a wolf," birches are "like zebra fish," and "A pheasant moves/ by like a seal./ He's on show/ like a clown." The references glitter off into areas that are of no consistent usefulness to the poem, and they never return; what is on show is Mrs. Sexton's inventiveness and this is by no means her most remarkable quality. Clearly she will not rest content with her more documentary successes; to concentrate more colour and imaginative vigour into her language without succumbing to this kind of inert evocativeness is likely to be her most pressing task from now on. There is a good chance that she will succeed in it.

On *Live or Die*

(1966)

HAYDEN CARRUTH

The literary quality of Anne Sexton's new poems, in *Live or Die*, is impossible to judge, at least in the brief time given a reviewer; they raise the never-solved problem of what literature really is, where you draw the line between art and documentary. Certainly her book is one of the most moving I have read in a long time. It is the record of four years of emotional illness, the turns of fear and despair and suicidal depression, a heartbreaking account. The wonder is that she was able to write any poetry at all. What she has written is strong, clear, rather simple, never repressed and yet never out of hand. Some of the poems wander a little; they are unstructured, they start up, flag, then start again, or slip into references too private for us to understand. But I do not want to give the impression that they are jottings or notes, that they are merely documentary. They are poems. They are the work of a gifted, intelligent, woman almost in control of her material. Ultimately the question is, I suppose: how well can the imagination function in a condition of stress? I have the feeling that in the future— and the last poem in her book speaks confidently of the future—these

130

poems will serve as "starters" for further work, giving the poet ideas, images, snatches of language that may be strengthened and consolidated in more fully objectified, imagined poems.

CHARLES GULLANS

The materials of Anne Sexton's third book are already familiar to us. Wanting to die, resisting suicide, checking into the mental hospital, talking to one's psychiatrist, insanity and the threat of it, and one's desperate resistance to that insanity—any of these might well be the materials of a serious poem; but these are not poems, unless we conceive of a poem as the simple delineation of anguish, or literal confession. These are not poems at all and I feel that I have, without right or desire, been made a third party to her conversations with her psychiatrist. It is painful, embarrassing, and irritating. The immediacy and terror of her problem are painful; the personal character of the confessional detail is embarrassing; and the tone of hysterical melodrama which pervades most of the writing is finally irritating. Either this is the poetry of a monstrous self-indulgence, in which case it is despicable; or it is documentation of a neurosis, in which case to pretend to speak of it as literature at all is simply silly. It is raw material for the understanding, like any other confusing experience. For the author, one might feel pity, if she could not control herself. This would be the pity one feels for the victim of psychosis; but to mistake such feeling for literary response implies a confusion among readers and critics of cause and effect. The Romantic stereotype says that the poet is sensitive and suffers; the neo-Romantic stereotype says that anyone who is sensitive and suffers is a poet. In the former view, poetry was the product of anguish; in the latter, the anguish has become the poetry. To suffer is to be creative; I feel, therefore, I am: the more strongly I feel, the greater my Being. To invite the reader to participate in violent feeling for its own sake is the final cause of the poem. This is the sentimental view of literature and life, which argues that indulgence in feeling is a good in itself. The sentimental literature of the past invited us to participate in feeling of a rather idealized and genteel character; the sentimental literature of this century proposes violent feeling as a permanent mode of existence; one stumbles from disaster to disaster for the sake of the excitement which the disasters provoke. One might as reasonably propose Auschwitz as a model for communal living. But then, this is to take Miss Sexton's poems seriously; they are not poems, they are documents of modern psychiatry and their publication is a result of the confusion of critical standards in the general mind.

THOMAS P. McDONNELL

Anne Sexton's latest book of poems, *Live or Die,* presents a good opportunity to look at her achievement in three published volumes. It is by now a rather worn observation to say that her poetry is not only personal but clearly the autobiography of the psyche itself. (Poetry has come around again, since the excesses of nineteenth-century romanticism, to recognizing something like the existence of the soul.) It is the kind of poetry frequently written by Robert Lowell, W. D. Snodgrass, and Jon Silkin, and by Sylvia Plath in her last tragic years. And it is a kind of poetry that seems much in favor today, chiefly because it has been so long denied as legitimate matter for poetry by the art-as-dissociation critics.

Anne Sexton's poetry, however, is not a poetry of spasmodic revelation or of occasional incident transformed from similitude to artifact: in its continuing wholeness one perceives the suggestion of a journey. The journey is not a calculated one, marked with clear directions along the way (" . . . here are no signs to tell the way"), but a journey in and out of the various dark. The poems are fragments of light that illuminate not so much the general landscape as parts of the immediate terrain—and that only now and then.

In the first poem of her first book, *To Bedlam and Part Way Back,* Anne Sexton said: "Late August,/I speed through the antiseptic tunnel/where the moving dead still talk/ of pushing their bones against the thrust/of cure," in that immediate terrain where she is "queen of this summer hotel/or the laughing bee on a stalk/of death." Of course, "bones" has all but become a poetic cliché in modern verse and "thrust" a sociological one. Nevertheless, Anne Sexton very early wrote a kind of poetry in which you were not always sure whether the center was in motion and the periphery still, or the periphery in motion and the center still—with a stillness not of tranquillity but, ineffably, at the point of fear itself.

"Kind Sir," she says in a poem addressed to Thoreau, "lost and of your same kind,/I have turned around twice with my eyes sealed/and the woods were white and my night mind/saw such strange happenings, untold and unreal./And opening my eyes, I am afraid of course/to look—this inward look that society scorns—/Still, I search in these woods and find nothing worse/than myself, caught between the grapes and the thorns." But not all the early poems—remarkable poems, really—have "this inward look that society scorns," Anne Sexton looks outward, too, "up there" to the gulls "godding the whole blue world"; and she listens ("Oh, la la la") to the music that swims back to her:

> The night I came I danced a circle
> and was not afraid.
> Mister?

Not afraid, but still there is that implication—perhaps supplication—in "Mister?" at the end: thus in and out of the shadows of the still journey again.

What is at once perfectly clear about Anne Sexton's verse is that it so stunningly reveals the poetry of psychic disturbance in all its frightful fluctuations between terror and clarity—and the poetry is in both the terror and the clarity. A young Catholic girl, some years ago,

wrote a book of poems called *Songs of a Psychotic,* which was both
more naive and more innocent than the knowledgeable but dark world
of Anne Sexton. Where the younger poet was indeed all but otherworldly, Anne Sexton is a poet and woman intensely of this world.
It was evident, even in *To Bedlam and Part Way Back,* that we were
witness to a dimension of poetry unique in English literature, a poetry
uniquely ours in this post-Freudian era.

Such poetry exists, surely, in "Her Kind," "Ringing the Bells," "A
Story for Rose on the Midnight Flight to Boston," and "For John,
Who Begs Me Not to Enquire Further," which is a poetic statement
on the book's epigraph by Schopenhauer, and which also introduces
Part Two of the *Bedlam* poems. (Anne Sexton's epigraphs to the
several volumes, by the way, are extremely pertinent to the revelation
of the poems.) Too, in these poems of the first volume, we begin to
recognize certain tensions that later inform—though in larger free-
doms of organization—the stark yet delicate impact of Anne Sexton's
poetry.

In the last poem in *To Bedlam and Part Way Back,* "The Division
of Parts," autobiography becomes poetic catharsis on that Good Friday when "In Boston, the devout/work their cold knees/toward that
sweet martyrdom/that Christ planned." But "It does not please/my
yankee bones to watch/where the dying is done/in its ugly hours."
Still, "Such dangerous angels walk through Lent./Their walls creak
Anne! Convert! Convert!" At last, though, the poet herself resigns to
the non-miraculous grace of reality: "And Lent will keep its hurt/for
someone else. Christ knows enough/staunch guys have hitched on
him in trouble,/thinking his sticks were badges to wear."

In *All My Pretty Ones,* Anne Sexton reaches into the full power of
the autobiographical poem, at once, with "The Truth the Dead
Know," on the death by cancer of her mother, at fifty-seven, and of
her father by heart attack, at fifty-nine, only three months later. The
book's title poem begins: "Father, this year's jinx rides us apart"—
a line that comes much too close, perhaps, to the rub-off from Robert
Lowell's obvious influence on Anne Sexton. But the whole poem

manages to recover itself in the working out of her own authentic idiom. Disconcertingly, though, the poem ends: "Whether you are pretty or not, I outlive you,/bend down my strange face to yours and forgive you." Here, unfortunately, the reader cannot get close enough· to the personal anguish of the poet to disabuse himself of the notion that to forgive the dead is the ultimate condescension of the living.

The journey into autobiography continues in "The Operation"— surely one of the remarkable poems of its kind in English—and in "The Abortion" (*"Somebody who should have been born/is gone"*). This is followed by "With Mercy for the Greedy," with the epigraph, "For my friend, Ruth, who urges me to make an appointment for the Sacrament of Confession." The poem itself carries the journey farther: "Concerning your letter in which you ask/me to call a priest and in which you ask/me to wear The Cross that you enclose"; and the reader—at least this reader—says to himself: Oh, no, don't ask this of the poet, don't proselytize at this point of her genuine anguish, which is all confessional, anyway: and who are we to say whether it is sacramental in the formal sense or not, or even in the most understanding empathy of friendship, to press more upon the poet than is actually necessary? But the poet herself answers this best in the last stanza of the poem:

> My friend, my friend, I was born
> doing reference work in sin, and born
> confessing it. This is what poems are:
> with mercy
> for the greedy
> they are the tongue's wrangle,
> the world's pottage, the rat's star.

Poem follows remarkable poem: "For God While Sleeping," "In the Deep Museum," "Water," "Letter Written on a Ferry While Crossing Long Island Sound," each like a flash of light on the landscape of Anne Sexton's journey in and out of the dark. And not all dark at that, because in "From the Garden" Anne Sexton has written one of the loveliest poems of love that we have in contemporary

American poetry, and one of the most beautifully dark ones ("Though I was bony you found me fair") in "Love Song for K. Owyne."

Not so incidentally, by the way, Anne Sexton is a strikingly beautiful woman, as anyone can see from the photo on the back dust jacket of her latest volume, *Live or Die*. The fact is that press agents and movie makers do not know what authentic glamour is, chiefly because they don't know what a woman is; and Anne Sexton is one of the few women writing poetry in the United States today of whom it is possible to say that her womanness is totally at one with her poems—and never more so than when she partially and poetically, in "Consorting With Angels," denies it: "I was tired of being a woman. . . ./I'm no more a woman/than Christ was a man." But if a woman alone, in the physiological sense, could have written a poem like "Menstruation at Forty," then also a woman alone, in the fullest possible sense, could have written so exquisite a poem as "Little Girl, My String Bean, My Lovely Woman."

Now, in *Live or Die*, Anne Sexton is writing in a more powerful and a freer mode of poetic expression than that already, and almost at once, achieved in her two previous volumes. Her poems have a marvelously wrought discipline of free form in, say, "Flee on Your Donkey," as well as the discipline of strict form in "Cripples and Other Stories," notably so here, and in the elegy to a fellow New England poet in seven *a b a b* quatrains with the concluding couplet:

> John Holmes, cut from a single tree,
>   lie heavy in her hold
> and go down that river with the ivory,
>   the copra and the gold.

Sometimes, though rarely (as in "Those Times"), Anne Sexton's confessions become almost too much the poetry of the couch. Still, even here of course, it is a perfectly valid kind of poetry and surely in keeping with the journey backward as well as with the one that probes the present and the future tense: of the woman who "did not know the woman I would be/nor that blood would bloom in me/each month like an exotic flower." Too, the poem "To Lose the Earth" seems to me about as Freudian as a poem can get, even in these days when the couch has become a rack of pain rather than a bed of pleasure. In the poem on Sylvia Plath's suicide, "Sylvia's Death," one can almost read the terrible anguish of people who know not too little of themselves but perhaps too much.

Anne Sexton is a deeply religious poet in the existential sense of that depleted term. For her, the religious experience has nothing whatever to do with the ordinary comforts of piety; it daily involves one's struggle to survive, to somehow come to terms with the terrible mystery of existence and at last to find a measure of salvation in the life one has to live. For example, "For the Year of the Insane" is no idle prayer in poetry but the poetry of prayer itself. In following immediately upon "Protestant Easter," it perfectly reveals the modality from rote to authentic supplication.

The journey in and out of the dark continues in "Crossing the Atlantic," a passage in "steel staterooms where night goes on forever":

> Being inside them is, I think,
> the way one would dig into a planet
> and forget the word *light*.

But the journey always comes home again, from "Walking in Paris" to dialing a telephone number in Boston, and indeed walking again down Marlborough Street. The later poems in *Live or Die* — all dated 1965, and the last two, 1966—are powerful "meditations" of the kind the saints might reveal if they were poets (in the technical sense) as well as humanists caught in the terrors of the modern world; and I think it is folly to pretend that our world is no different, say, from the mystical age of the seventeenth century. These remarkable poems could have been written by no one not thoroughly a child of this century:

> . . . I am not what I expected.
>   Not an Eichmann.
> The poison just didn't take.

> So I won't hang around in my
>   hospital shift,
> repeating The Black Mass and all of it.
> I say *Live, Live* because of the sun,
> the dream, the excitable gift.

If the excitable gift is life itself, it is also life transformed by art as personal catharsis. In this age of dehumanization, Anne Sexton's is a necessary kind of poetry to have on the record. We need the poetry of a woman who couldn't drown the eight Dalmatians in the pails of water set aside for them. Anne Sexton is a woman and poet who "kept right on going on,/a sort of human statement," in that long and intricate journey where the dark is neither all nor forever.

On *Love Poems*

(1969)

MONA VAN DUYN

Miss Sexton must forgive me for my first reaction to *Love Poems,* which I read before being asked to review it. Having begun with the front inside jacket flap (which does no service to these solipsistic poems by asking one to relate them to great universals, "themes of departure, return, recurrence"), I proceeded to read straight through the story of illicit love, which includes "The Kiss" (the body is "shot full of these electric bolts. /Zing! A resurrection!"), the lover's exploration of the breasts, a poem "In Celebration of My Uterus," a poem "For My Lover, Returning to His Wife," "The Ballad of the Lonely Masturbator," a poem which celebrates being kissed on the back of the knee, and a final series of eighteen poems of mourning and memory called "Eighteen Days Without You" ("Then I think of you in bed/Your tongue half chocolate, half ocean.") and ended my reading on what seemed an unintentionally comic note, the first line of the inside back jacket flap, which informed me that Miss Sexton "lives now with her husband and two daughters" in Weston, Massachusetts.

But seriously: we are all by now aware that only the broken and invaded (by madness, surgery, doomed love, fractured bones, etc.) self, hers and hers alone, perilously put together again by will but permanently scarred, provokes her poems. In fact, as if the pain of a broken heart were not enough, this narrative includes a fall that results in a broken hip—one of the best poems in the book, with stanzas as effective as:

> for the soft, soft bones that were laid apart
> and were screwed together. They will knit.
> And the other corpse, the fractured heart,
> I feed it piecemeal, little chalice. I'm good to it.
>
> . . .
>
> This little town, this little country is real
> and thus it is so of the post and the cup
> and thus of the violent heart. The zeal
> of my house doth eat me up.

Love Poems is not sentimental, not trivial, it is simply not believable. The poems have little to do with believable love, having none of love's privacy and therefore too frequently repelling the reader; they have as little to do with believable sexuality as an act of intercourse performed onstage for an audience. Because neither revulsion nor amusement is a fair response to a poet with this much talent, one must, for the sake of the poet and the poems, totally suppress the word "confessional" and substitute the word "fictional." Only then, when the "I" is a character separate from the author, does the woman become as innocent of exhibitionism as Molly Bloom in her soliloquy. One would not, even then, return and return to these poems as one does to other love poems of past and present, because their self-absorption is too great to allow an empathic entrance. This degree of self-absorption I have seen equaled only by Norman Mailer, who took more than a hundred prose pages of strenuous effort to open his own shell widely enough to see that Robert Lowell is a decent human being. However, it is clear, I think, that it is from Miss Sexton's almost incredible feats of "indiscretion" in attitude and image, her grotesque, near-comic concentration on her every emotional and physical pore, and her delineation of femaleness, so fanatical that it makes one wonder, even after many years of being one, what a woman is, that her poems derive their originality and their power, as well as their limitations. To her admirers (among them, *if* I may pick and choose among all her poems I can include myself), I can say that the poetry is as good as ever.

DANIEL HUGHES

Anne Sexton's *Love Poems* might, one feared, show her at her worst, somewhere above *This Is My Beloved,* perhaps, but not far enough. Yet the direct intimacy of these poems actually strengthens the self to a curious inevitability, in a particularized reality that nearly becomes myth. In one poem, "For My Lover, Returning to His Wife," this dismissing, but dramatically appropriate gesture sets the tone for the collection:

> She is so naked and singular.
> She is the sum of yourself and your dream.
> Climb her like a monument, step after step.
>
> As for me, I am a watercolor.
> I wash off.

There are of course those poems of a typical Sextonish extravagance here, not watercolors, but blazing oils whose gaudiness makes one draw back from paint too heavily laid on; in "The Ballad of the Lonely Masturbator" or "In Celebration of My Uterus," the old strain and dazzle are present, but *Love Poems* depends less on shock tactics than any previous book by Anne Sexton. Her lyric gift, not her special subject matter, asserts itself in what we may take to be the tone sought for in the terrible, sometimes theatrical gestures of her previous books.

"It Is a Spring Afternoon," "Just Once," and "Moon Song, Woman Song" display a precise lyric gift finer than these Cummings-like titles may indicate. In her previous books, Mrs. Sexton had dared herself in one direction and now she seems to dare its opposite. At least, I can't think of a less likely *trouvaille* than a lover's eighteen-day absence on Air Force Reserve duty, but it is in "Eighteen Days Without You" that Mrs. Sexton's method finds its best means, in a dailiness sharply sensed and ringing its passionate changes. It is important, I think, that the woman writing these jottings lives in a natural setting, a country bungalow to which the lover will return; in his absence she defines herself within and outside the natural world. These are not poems of a fierce nostalgia, although there are a few selected recollections; rather, the sequence proceeds through a chart of feeling: loss, resentment, depression, excitement, and the glory of return. It is the tension between the diary and an art that would, for example, find carefully crafted but never asserted rhymes for its music that makes this unpromising narrative so attractive, so humanized.

Nature is the sign of the Other, not in an acceptation, but as a rhythm lonely as the poet's. On December 3rd she sees a dead rabbit in the road and muses: *"It's nature,* you would have said from habit-/and continued on to cocktails." On December 12, the poet visits the State School for the mentally retarded, but here the imagery Sexton has so often used to stun becomes no less terrible but part of a "natural" isolation too:

> Always I walk past the hydro-
> cephalic doorman on his stool,
> a five-year-old who sits
> all day and never speaks,
> his head like a twenty-five
> cent balloon, three times
> the regular size. It's nature
> but nature works such crimes.

Then even that doubtful consolation departs by December 15th:

> The day of the lonely drunk
> is here. No weather reports,
> no fox, no birds, no sweet chipmunks,
> no sofa game, no summer resorts.
>
> No whatever it was we had,
> no sky, no month—just booze.
> The half moon is acid, bitter, sad
> as I sing the Blended Whiskey Blues.

But the 18th brings the lover's return, and, if we pause to wonder what flashy new images for sex can be expected now as the runner breaks the tape, we find those images all right, but they are part of a restored sense of life, human *and* natural, passionately, wistfully true:

> Lock in! Be alert, my acrobat
> and I will be soft wood and you the nail
> and we will make fiery ovens for Jack Sprat
> and you will hurl yourself into my tiny jail
> and we will take a supper together and that
> will be that.

And that will be that. The lyric impulse has only pseudo-conclusions but they can be releasing-small, disengagingly-happy, *essential.*

JOYCE CAROL OATES

"My mouth blooms like a cut," Anne Sexton announces in a poem called "The Kiss." The unorthodox imagery is exactly right: her poems bloom, blossom like flowers, and yet they are small angry wounds, not to be forgotten easily. Her obsession is with the limitation of the body, its failure to be equal to the demands of the soul— specifically the failure of the female to be equal to her unbalanced ideal of herself, mother, daughter, beloved, "tiny jail," the poetess who cries out "my sex will be transfixed!"

Sexton has been criticized for the intensity of her preoccupations: always the self, the victimized, bullying, narcissistic self, half in love with sickness and madness and her own "violent heart." Yet *Love Poems,* which continues her earlier themes, is an extraordinary work —the language keen, musical, perfect, the haranguing voice exactly right, the ironic, deft touch never overdone, the sense of celebration (an element usually overlooked in her poetry) rigorous and convincing. "In celebration of the woman I am/and of the soul of the woman I am/and of the central creature and its delight/I sing for you. I dare to live."

There are certain poems in this collection that seem to me minor masterpieces, perfections of their kind. The voice does not vary much, but the intensity does; in such a poem as "For My Lover, Returning to his Wife," line after line is cast in elegant, hard, sardonic language, the achievement of an unanswerable argument. Sexton views the victorious wife in this way:

> . . . She is all harmony.
> She sees to oars and oarlocks for the dinghy,
> has placed the wild flowers at the window at breakfast,
> sat by the potter's wheel at midday,
> set forth three children under the moon,
> three cherubs drawn by Michelangelo. . . .

"As for me, I am a watercolor," Sexton says, "I wash off."

Many of these poems are bitterly reflective, a piling-on of bizarre images that remind me of Sylvia Plath's poems in *Ariel.* It is uncanny, as if Plath were somehow resurrected in Sexton (who admires her work)—the helpless acquiescence to a lover with a "Nazi hook," the blunt summing-up of a relationship ("we are a pair of scissors/who come together to cut"), the mechanical repetition of words at the end of lines, a desperate attempt to emphasize what has already been emphasized ("The trouble was not/in the kitchen or the tulips/but only in my head, my head"). But if Sylvia Plath has become a kind of minor legend, priestess of the Cult of Death and Madness who does not stint at sacrificing herself, Anne Sexton has already demonstrated a more durable talent and a willingness to explore in more detail the complexities of human relationships. For Plath, death is the most favored lover; for Sexton, life with its most agonizing contradictions is still preferable. Her self-preoccupation is tempered by a sense of humor. She is able to say to her lover, in the series of poems called "Eighteen Days Without You," "Catch me. I'm your disease." And she is able to bring to a conclusion this blunt and abrasive and exasperating group of love poems with an imperative that leaves us solidly on the side of life:

> Lock in! Be alert, my acrobat
> and I will be soft wood and you the nail
> and we will make fiery ovens for Jack Sprat
> and you will hurl yourself into my tiny jail
> and we will take a supper together and that
> will be that.

On *Transformations*

(1971)

CHRISTOPHER LEHMANN-HAUPT

The device of retelling *Grimms' Fairy Tales* is not an original one. After all, Donald Barthelme rewrote "Snow White" only a few years ago. Nevertheless, the device yields handsome returns for Anne Sexton in *Transformations,* her fifth and latest volume of poetry. For one thing, by retelling stories that are familiar to everyone, she has produced a delightfully accessible book. So *Tranformations* should win her an even wider audience than have her previous four books—*To Bedlam and Part Way Back, All My Pretty Ones, Live or Die,* and *Love Poems*—much praised and honored though these have been. For another, more important thing, by whispering her often terrifying visions into familiar and commonplace sounds, she has taken a long step toward solving a problem that has recurred in her earlier work.

The delights of *Transformations* are easily illustrated. No one has completely forgotten the complications that put Sleeping Beauty to sleep, or that brought the frog into the princess's bedchamber, or that indebted the miller's gold-spinning daughter to Rumpelstiltskin. But to have Miss Sexton remind us of the details with her seemingly casual sketches is as gratifying as the arrival of the repairman after a long day of bungling:

> There once was a miller
> with a daughter as lovely as a grape.
> He told the king that she could
> spin gold out of common straw.
> The king summoned the girl
> and locked her in a room full of straw
> and told her to spin it into gold
> or she would die like a criminal.
> Poor grape with no one to pick.
> Luscious and round and sleek.
> Poor thing.
> To die and never see Brooklyn.

Yes, I realize it's more than the ease of it that's charming. There's the surprise of odd juxtapositioning: similes that deflate romance, humor as black as ebony. There's Snow White "no more important/ than a dust mouse under the bed." There's "a king as wise as a dictionary." (So much for his wisdom and so much for dictionaries.) There's the doppelgänger inside all of us that Rumpelstiltskin represents—"a small old man . . . [who] speaks up as tiny as an earphone/ with Truman's asexual voice." It's cool. It's the narrator staking out huge territories in which to play, strike outrageous poses, draw previously undreamed-of parallels.

One of the more obvious purposes of which is to turn the fairy tales into comic strips and other pop-art artifacts, "As if an enlarged paper clip/could be a piece of sculpture./(And it could.)" Thus the philandering parson in "The Little Peasant" stood "rigid for a moment,/as real as a soup can." Rapunzel's song pierces the prince's heart "like a valentine." Hansel and Gretel "slept,/z's buzzing from their mouths like flies." And

> Cinderella and the prince,
> lived, they say, happily ever after,
> like two dolls in a museum case
> never bothered by diapers or dust,
> never arguing over the timing of an egg,
> never telling the same story twice,
> never getting a middle-aged spread,
> their darling smiles pasted on for eternity.
> Regular Bobbsey Twins. . . .

So much for "happily ever after."

Why this transformation to pop art? Well, that bitter note at the end of "Cinderella" obviously stresses the difference between fairy tales and real domestic life. But it also throws us back to Miss Sexton's prologue to "Cinderella": "You always read about it:/the plumber with twelve children who wins the Irish Sweepstakes./From toilets to riches./That story." It never happens to me—just as all the tales are caricatures that thrust us back to the prologues that Miss Sexton has composed for them. Which brings me to her more important accomplishment.

If her poetry has betrayed any weakness in the past, it has been her tendency to allow its content to do the work—a tendency to record raw disasters without curing them with her art. Her tortured confessions seemed to be personal yelps rather than universal cries. Perhaps this reflected the fact that she was working too impulsively from first-hand experience, as some critics have accused her of doing. Perhaps not. In any case, by using the artificial as the raw material of *Transformations* and working her way backwards to the immediacy of her personal vision, she draws her readers in more willingly, and thereby makes them more vulnerable to her sudden plunges into personal nightmare.

The technique works effectively in the concluding poem, "Briar Rose (Sleeping Beauty)." We are asked in the prologue to

> Consider
> a girl who keeps slipping off,
> arms limp as old carrots,
> into the hypnotist's trance,
> into a spirit world
> speaking with the gift of tongues.
> . . . Little doll child,
> come here to Papa.
> Sit on my knee.
> I have kisses for the back of your neck.

Next, the fable of the princess who sleeps off a hundred-year curse unfolds more or less conventionally until the prince

kissed Briar Rose
and she woke crying:
Daddy! Daddy!
Presto! She's out of prison! She married the prince
and all went well
except for the fear—
the fear of sleep.

And in concluding stanzas that thrust us back into the tortured
world of Miss Sexton's earlier poetry, she writes:

Each night I am nailed into place
and I forget who I am.
Daddy?
That's another kind of prison.
It's not the prince at all, but my father
drunkenly bent over my bed,
circling the abyss like a shark,
my father thick upon me
like some sleeping jellyfish.
What voyage this, little girl?
This coming out of prison?
God help—
this life after death?

But the technique works elsewhere, too. And the result is a funny,
mad, witty, frightening, charming, haunting book.

VERNON YOUNG

I'm relieved not to have to cope with Anne Sexton's customary war
on her own gender. In *Transformations,* while her impatience with
biology and destiny remains, she pursues another beast. She undermines the fairy tale with deadly address and a merciless employment
of city-American idioms: occasionally vulgar, often brilliant, nearly
always hilarious, to *my* cruel mind! She is no Thurber; the elegant

master-spook of the graphic and English arts was a True Believer. His versions of Grimm or Andersen, however salty, set out to rival the originals; his ear was in thrall to Lewis Carroll and his wit, in this area, was less clinical than linguistic. Anne Sexton is out to *get* the brothers Grimm, armed with illuminations supplied by Freud but as much by the wised-up modern's experience of having been victimized by grandmother and recaptured by the pragmatic test. In such endeavors, tone is everything. Here's how she launches "Cinderella":

> You always read about it:
> the plumber with twelve children
> who wins the Irish Sweepstakes.
> From toilets to riches.
> That story.
>
> Or the nursemaid,
> some luscious sweet from Denmark
> who captures the oldest son's heart.
> From diapers to Dior.
> That story.

And here's how she ends the tale:

> Cinderella and the prince
> lived, they say, happily ever after,
> like two dolls in a museum case
> never bothered by diapers or dust,
> never arguing over the timing of an egg,
> never telling the same story twice,
> never getting a middle-aged spread,
> their darling smiles pasted on for eternity.
> That story.

Corner-of-the-mouth stuff? Ideal for reading aloud to friends or to guests who won't thaw? But there are other passages where, sustained by her fine art of inflection and an uncanny choice of impertinent simile, she achieves a truly diabolical lyricism: in "Hansel and Gretel," in "One-Eye, Two Eyes, Three Eyes," in "The Sleeping Beauty"

(where Briar Rose audibly becomes Electra) and in "Rapunzel," from
which this romping stanza:

> Rapunzel, Rapunzel, let down your hair,
> and thus they met and he declared his love.
> What is this beast, she thought,
> with muscles on his arms
> like a bag of snakes?
> What is this moss on his legs?
> What prickly plant grows on his cheeks?
> What is this voice as deep as a dog?
> Yet he dazzled her with his answers.
> Yet he dazzled her with his dancing stick.
> They lay together upon the yellowy threads,
> swimming through them
> like minnows through kelp
> and they sang out benedictions like the Pope.

The drawings of Barbara Swan incisively complement the poems.
Their designs are what they should be: importunate and macabre;
Gothic and placental.

On *The Book of Folly*

(1972)

ARTHUR OBERG

Anne Sexton in *The Book of Folly* shares Galway Kinnell's wish to move through and beyond the way, or ways, of the world, to a visionary humor that can reject the world's foolish fools for the unworldly wise fools to whose rank the poet has always made some claim. Although Anne Sexton has been intensely aware of herself as a woman and a woman poet, there is a new militancy here that I have never detected in her previous work. At best, it is part of a larger impulse in the book which would challenge not just what are male and female worlds, but what constitutes sane and insane, prosaic and poetic, sacred and secular domain.

A concern with breakthrough, as much as breakdown, continues to distinguish Anne Sexton's work in this book; and, since literary influences are quirky, tricky matters, I kept having to remind myself that if I found some bad, unfortunate debts to Robert Lowell and Sylvia Plath in these pieces, that it was Anne Sexton who was also important in influencing Plath and possibly even Lowell. What I am more worried over, however, is how this new book raises the same problems that have marked her books—an unevenness that often derives from the inclusion of unmistakably bad poems and even entire, unsuccessful sequences: an overuse of apostrophe and appositives to conceal some terrible failures of language and imagination, feeling, and thought; recurrent metaphor and simile that are either too banal or not outrageous enough to work. These may seem like harsh criticisms, but I say them because I also find here important poems by an important poet, and a poet whose best poems ought not to run the risk of being dwarfed by lesser things. At its best, *The Book of Folly* has poems and prose poems—"The Ambition Bird," "The Doctor of the Heart," "Oh," "The Wifebeater," "The One-Legged Man," "The Red Shoes," "The Death of the Fathers," "Three Stories"—that can stand up to the stronger pieces in what for me are her best books, *To Bedlam and Part Way Back, All My Pretty Ones,* and *Love Poems,* this last book a book that never received the kind of attention it deserved.

Earlier I talked about a new militancy in *The Book of Folly.* It is part of the letting down of the hair, which just happens also to be the title of one of the poetic prose fables in one section of the book. Her earlier books gave off some sense of this exposure and dispersal. Yet this sense, now in *The Book of Folly,* is meaningfully, painfully complicated by her situation of aging, middle-aged woman and mother with daughters who are growing up and becoming women themselves, by fame and by older and new loves, by new losses she must confront and sustain, and by war that continues rather than ends.

What moves me most in this book is the relentless vision and weird abundance which marked the best of Anne Sexton's earlier work, a hard-earned knowing that need is not quite belief. I conclude with the ending of the opening poem of the book, "The Ambition Bird"; in it, there are anger and energy which want to create a love song that still must acknowledge the dangerous possibility of art as sarcophagus:

> He wants to light a kitchen match
> and immolate himself.
>
> He wants to fly into the hand of Michelangelo
> and come out painted on a ceiling.

He wants to pierce the hornet's nest
and come out with a long godhead.

He wants to take bread and wine
and bring forth a man happily floating in the Caribbean.

He wants to be pressed out like a key
so he can unlock the Magi.

He wants to take leave among strangers
passing out bits of his heart like hors d'oeuvres.

He wants to die changing his clothes
and bolt for the sun like a diamond.

He wants, I want.
Dear God, wouldn't it be
good enough to just drink cocoa?

I must get a new bird
and a new immortality box.
There is folly enough inside this one.

If these lines recall the art and life of Sylvia Plath, they also go on to establish an authentic voice and to reject what that less fortunate poet was unable to put aside. Here, there is irony as loving, saving grace. In poems like "The Ambition Bird," Anne Sexton shows how triumphant, achieved a poetry she has always been capable of setting down.

MURIEL RUKEYSER

At a reading at the Guggenheim Museum, Anne Sexton—after three books of poems—finished one of her poems and said, "But it is not true." That hall feels cold and artificial. It was a beautiful woman standing there, in a beautiful dress. The expectation and the gossip around one was of confessional poetry. Now this is a curious genre, one taken to promise a new order of secret, and one finds secrets that everyone knows; taken to promise emergent men, emergent women, who may bring to speech the lives of these generations; too, one is often given disposable poems, made without the structural reinforcements, those lattices on which the crystal grows.

However, when Anne Sexton said, "But it is not true," a waver went through the audience. No, I cannot say that, I can speak only for myself. I thought, "It may very well be true." She had cut through the entire nonsense about confessional writing, and returned me to the poem.

The issue in most of Anne Sexton's poems has been survival, piece by piece of the body, step by step of poetic experience, and even more the life entire, sprung from our matrix of parental madness. It is these people, who have come this way, who have most usefulness for us, they are among our veterans, and we need them to look at their lives and at us. It is the receivers of these "confessions" who are the welcomers and the further damagers of the poets among whom Anne Sexton stands, with her father, her mother, the trains of relatives, doctors, nurses, lovers who populate this landscape, and the children in whom we find the same traits, with a difference: they may be dealing with them differently, their poems may be otherwise.

The two books of poems before *The Book of Folly* (published in 1972 and now before us) gave us a gathering-together of forces. I remember the signs. There had been books even earlier: *Live or Die* was shown to me in manuscript with the page on whose back Saul Bellow had written a letter. It was on the front of that page—a draft of his novel—that Anne Sexton had found her title, and it was in the work that was before a group of us at that moment that the instigation for her next work, running along with the poems in *Love Poems,* came.

For Herbert Kohl, speaking to us as we worked the Writers–Teachers group, said as he said to the high-school students he knew, ("Why not write fables? Or make something based on fables and childhood stories?) Anne Sexton's *Transformations* followed that reminder. I do not know whether her play, *Mercy Street,* was written after that period, or whether the production I saw was based on earlier writing, but the density of those works—the play of the early flailing life in which our father's fantasies overcome our own, and the poems of the next phase of our other childhood fantasies, inherited from Grimm and the rest—this reality, has fed the last two books.

Love Poems opens with a statement of theme in "The Touch."

> For months my hand had been sealed off
> in a tin box. Nothing was there but subway railings.
> Perhaps it is bruised, I thought,
> and that is why they have locked it up.

The hand lies there like an unconscious woman. It has collapsed:

> Nothing but vulnerable.
>
> And all this is metaphor.

And then we are given all the people and reasons for the trouble:

> Then all this became history.
> Your hand found mine.
> Life rushed to my fingers like a blood clot.
> Oh, my carpenter, the fingers are rebuilt.
> They dance with yours.
> They dance in the attic and in Vienna.
> My hand is alive all over America.
> Not even death will stop it,
> death shedding her blood.
> Nothing will stop it, for this is the kingdom
> and the kingdom come.

In the next poem, "The Kiss,"

> Before today my body was useless.
> .... Where there was silence
> the drums, the strings are incurably playing. You did this.
> Pure genius at work. Darling, the composer has stepped
> into fire.

These excerpted lines have some of the breadth of her speech and her assumption of relation, but it is in the sequence of the book itself that the declaration here is made. It goes on with the architectural statement of Herbert's *The Temple:* "The Breast," "That Day," and one of the few poems in which a woman has come to the fact as symbol, the center after many years of silence and taboo: "In Celebration of My Uterus." We have allowed the language of sex when it was accompanied—really superseded—by wit; or, in this year, accompanied by strobe lights and lack of words on the stage; or, in film, when it is ripped away from the rest of life, ripped away from the exchange of fantasies that is deep in relation; or, as in *Portnoy's Complaint,* when it is really prison literature, so that one's genitals become the image of the world, the only beautiful thing, the only loved thing. In Anne Sexton's poems, the world is here—Capri, Vietnam, Boston, Africa, Washington, the house, the bedroom—and the other person is here, or absent so strongly that he is

> a weird stone man
> who sleepwalked in, whose features did not change.

Although Anne Sexton wrote poems in high school, she soon stopped. What happened to let her come through to this Afterlife of the American Girl, to take the reality and dance it, physical it, allow it always its whiskey and its gold skin, its psalms and the Papa and Mama dance?

There are traps here. There is always the chance to fall over into total sanity, a kind of fashionable grotto, the death of Elinor Wylie, in which the world is "gorgeous" and "crystal." But here is a woman who *was* a model, who *was* a librarian. Sometimes you think it is going to be the marriage of E. E. Cummings and Marion Morehouse that is doing the writing. But these poems always ride steady again, furious and seductive; the woman is swimming, lying on the water,

> The walls of that grotto
> were everycolor blue and
> you said, "Look! Your eyes

are seacolor. Look! Your eyes
are skycolor." And my eyes
shut down as if they were
suddenly ashamed.

It is that movement that brings the poems through the narcissism, the
breakage, the wounds. Into what? Song and connection and delight,
brought through by a poet who has transformed acrid experience into
her own words and her own touch reaching another person.* Reaching the reader superbly, as in this poem of one of the days of absence
in the group "Eighteen Days Without You":

Then I think of you in bed.
your tongue half chocolate, half ocean,
of the houses that you swing into,
of the steel wool hair on your head,
of your persistent hands and then
how we gnaw at the barrier because we are two.

How you come and take my blood cup
and link me together and take my brine.
We are bare. We are stripped to the bone.
and we swim in tandem and go up and up

the river, the identical river called Mine
and we enter together. No one's alone.

The Book of Folly draws on all Anne Sexton's earlier work, and a
fertile transformation can be seen.

Once there was blood
as in a murder
but now there is nothing

*Reaching past her earlier poems in mastery, echoing the earlier knowledge of "The
Truth the Dead Know,"

My darling, the wind falls in like stones
from the whitehearted water and when we touch
we enter touch entirely. No one's alone.
Men kill for this, or for as much. . . .

gives us a theme. The parts are here, one's mother's breasts, Mary's breasts for Jesus, his "penis sang like a dog," and the angels, the rather Spanish angels, "Angel of blizzards and blackouts, do you know raspberries ... ?" and the larger statement, which when it comes, sounds too much like Sandburg,

> We are America.
> We are the coffin fillers.
> We are the grocers of death.
> We pack them in crates like cauliflowers.

But it goes on, a little further,

> And the woman?
> The woman is bathing her heart.
> It has been torn out of her
> and because it is burnt
> and as a last act
> she is rinsing it off in the river.
> This is the death market.

The "confessional poem" is beginning to turn into something, and I think we have waited for this for a long time.

I heard a woman-poet say, "It's really the distinction between those woman poets who are attractive and those who really aren't, like poor —— ——, isn't it?" Well, of course it isn't, but that adheres to the name in its own time, and beyond. When the live woman is attractive, is part of her own and Sylvia Plath's fable, works with a music group, trails clouds of Robert Lowell, has a Pulitzer and various epaulets, you have also an actress-persona, and actress before you.

But when the live poet is a woman writing sonnets of angels:

> Angel of fire and genitals, do you know slime,
> that green mama who first forced me to sing,
> who put me first in the latrine, that pantomime
> of brown where I was beggar and she was king?
> I said, "The devil is down that festering hole."
> Then he bit me in the buttocks and took over my soul.

and, in "Going Gone,"

Although you are in a hurry
you stop to open a small basket
and under layers of petticoats
you show her the tiger-striped eyes
that you have lately plucked,
you show her your specialty, the lips,
those two small bundles,
you show her the two hands
that grip each other fiercely,
one being mine, one being yours.
Torn right off at the wrist bone
when you started in your
impossible going, gone.

—then one sees that the long walk out the other side of the struggle, madness, into the other struggle, to use madness, has made a poet who no longer looks at the audience to see how the confession is going. For those confessions had to have their "other"—and the other, the audience, battened on confessions, not even eating, they were not nourished by them, not using them in any way at all.

It has remained for the poet to use the early confessions and make a second poetry out of them. We see the gossip produced by that period all around us, and we also see the result of several battles, in their slightest, lightest terms, as well as the ones we all know. Still men talk about Emily Dickinson—last week, on a remote island in Canada, I heard a doctor and a student ask each other whether she really slept with him, she certainly wanted to, all her life. And I had a book-length manuscript from a woman poet—the stamps the package carried were twelve Emily Dickinsons and one Planned Parenthood.

The contortions here, the deaths, the fathers, the silences, all turning into

Father,
we are two birds on fire

give us the versions of any one experience—even in the stories that begin to enter these books, here in "Dancing the Jig" and the others. The variousness reminds me of the great example out of Coleridge,

who wrote to his wife, "a stye, or something of that kind, has come
upon me and enourmously swelled my eyelids, so that it is painful or
improper for me to read or write," and wrote to Wordsworth,

> O! what a life is the eye! what a strange and inscrutable essence!
> Him that is utterly blind, nor glimpses the fire that warns him; . . . .
> Even for him it exists, it moves and stirs in its prison;
> Lives with a separate life, and "Is it a Spirit?" he murmurs;
> "Sure it has thoughts of its own, and to see is only a language."

I think of his "confessionals" and the nonsense the critics have issued
about him, speaking of his incompleteness when he is the one who
knows of the search for completeness.

What, then, is the place reached now by the women who have gone
through the steps, as Anne Sexton has? What processes are brought
together? Can these poems bring the moment through? "Folly," the
word in its title, speaks for the book. Sanity and madness as daily life
—the folly that offers

> . . . . air to have. . . .
> There are gulls kissing the boat.
> There is the sun as big as a nose.
> And here are the three of us
> dividing our deaths,
> bailing the boat
> and closing out
> the cold wing that has clasped us
> this bright August day.

On *The Death Notebooks*
(1974)

SANDRA M. GILBERT

No matter what else you think about Anne Sexton's poetry, you have to concede its extraordinary and persistent vitality. Like that awful child with the curl, when she's good Anne Sexton is very, very good, and when she's bad she sometimes really is rather horrid—but, nonetheless, vital. Always energetic, always brimful of her own pains and passions, as if *she,* whoever and whatever she is (and that's an issue which continually concerns her) is about to leap out of her own skin in her ironic/demonic quest for Love, Life, Art, Intensity.

All of which may seem, at first, particularly odd in view of the brooding, apparently "neurotic" preoccupation with death which her poetry has displayed from *To Bedlam and Part Way Back* onwards, and which now surfaces fully in *The Death Notebooks,* her latest collection. Yet even in her earliest books, Sexton's thoughts of death were expressed with a breathless and often comic vitality that lightened what might otherwise have been unmitigated gloom. Death—the deaths of friends and relatives, her own death, domesticated as suicide —rose yeastily in the oven of her mind, like a loaf of exotic bread. But

if she confessed a perverse taste for such fare, she was herself ironically (and healthily) aware of her own perversity. "I am queen of this
summer hotel,/or the laughing bee on a stalk/of death . . ." she wrote
of her own institutionalization in *To Bedlam*. And later, in an obviously compassionate elegy for Sylvia Plath, she nevertheless depicted
her own (and her dead friend's) suicidal longings with sardonic good
humor:

> Thief!—
> how did you crawl into,
>
> crawl down alone
> into the death I wanted so badly and for so long,
>
> the death we said we both outgrew,
> the one we wore on our skinny breasts,
>
> the one we talked of so often each time
> we downed three extra dry martinis in Boston. . . .

Even in "Somewhere in Africa," that marvelous and wholly serious
elegy for John Holmes, her imaginative vitality redeemed her death-
vision from both terror and perversity:

> Let there be this God who is a woman who will place you
> upon her shallow boat, who is a woman naked to the waist,
> moist with palm oil and sweat, a woman of some virtue
> and wild breasts, her limbs excellent, unbruised and chaste.
>
> Let her take you. She will put twelve strong men at the oars
> for you are stronger than mahogany and your bones fill
> the boat high as with fruit and bark from the interior.
> She will have you now, you whom the funeral cannot kill.

Vital as these early volumes were, however, *The Death Notebooks*
goes far beyond them in making luminous art out of the night-
thoughts that have haunted this poet for so long. The book's epigraph
is a line from Hemingway's *A Moveable Feast*—"Look, you con man,
make a living out of your death"—which succinctly summarizes the

poet's goal, a goal both shrewdly ironic (at least she can write, and thus make a living out of her obsession) and ambitiously metaphysical (what is there to make a *living* from except death?). But if irony and shrewdness have always characterized Anne Sexton's work, the largeness of her metaphysical ambition is what is newly notable about *The Death Notebooks.* The seductions of suicide no longer concern her; the deaths of friends and relatives are secondary. Now, like John Donne, she is lying down in the inescapable coffin that is her own, "trying on," as she tells us, her "black necessary trousseau." In doing this, she has inevitably to define the death that is neither a handful of pills nor somebody else's funeral but, in a sense, a precondition of life itself. And so she joins the company of writers who have asserted with Gertrude Stein that "being dead is not ending it is being dead and being dead is something," or with Wallace Stevens that "Death is the mother of beauty, mystical/Within whose burning bosom we devise /Our earthly mothers, waiting, sleeplessly."

I think the book, like all of Sexton's work, has many flaws, but I'd prefer not to dwell too lengthily on them. It is probably true that (as someone once said of Stevens) Sexton publishes too many "practice poems"—hence her volumes are marred by occasional prolixity, flatness, cuteness, sentimentality: "Even crazy, I'm as nice/As a chocolate bar," she wrote in *Live or Die,* and in *The Death Notebooks* we encounter Rod McKuen-ish passages like "The soul presses a button. /Is the cry saying something?/Does it mean *help*?/Or hello?" Yet even Sexton's bad qualities seem, curiously, to be aspects of her vitality. The Romantic self-absorption we admire trembles on the edge of self-indulgence. Ought we, we wonder, to forgive the Wordsworthian "egotistical sublime" when it manifests itself in the work of a modern poet? Does Sexton's continuing, "confessional" search for Anne signify, to those of us who are searching for ourselves, anything beyond *Anne's* quest? Would this poet's voice be muffled or stifled if she enclosed herself more, set herself a few more formal limits? The answer to all these questions appears, in Sexton's case, to be yes. Yes, she probably had to cultivate self-absorption, speak in a deliberately naive or flat tone, risk sentimentality and cuteness, in order to achieve

the triumphs of this new collection which, by narrowly skirting melodrama, wins through to a kind of grandeur.

Less flawed than her earlier volumes, *The Death Notebooks* moves
from a witty opening statement that describes her search in almost
vaudevillean terms ("Mrs. Sexton went out looking for the gods./She
began looking in the sky—/expecting a large angel with a blue
crotch. . . . She made a pilgrimage to the great poet/and he belched
in her face . . . ") through several carefully elaborated poem-sequences
("The Death Baby," "The Furies," "Hurry Up Please") to an extraordinary concluding series of psalms ("O Ye Tongues"). All of these
works have merit, but "The Death Baby" and "Hurry Up Please" still
have all those weaknesses familiar to Sexton's readers. Some of "The
Death Baby," for instance, seems in cadence, style, theme, like watered-down Plath:

> I rock. I rock.
> You are my stone child
> with still eyes like marbles.
> There is a death baby
> for each of us.
> We own him.
> His smell is our smell.
> Beware. Beware.
> There is a tenderness.
> There is a love
> for this dumb traveler
> waiting in his pink covers.

And "Hurry Up Please," as the title suggests, is tiresomely Eliotian,
without the impersonal terseness and bite of Eliot.

We forgive, however, we forgive, by the time we've arrived at "O
Ye Tongues." For this final psalm-sequence, the ornament of the
collection, is poetry that anyone would flirt with almost any disasters
to write. Organized by Biblical parallelisms into a series of deceptively
simple statements ("Let there be a God as large as a sunlamp to laugh
his heat at you./Let there be an earth with a form like a jigsaw and
let it fit for all of ye./Let there be the darkness of a darkroom out of

the deep. A worm room"), the first psalm gives us Sexton's personal re-vision of Genesis. Then the second gives us her *own* genesis and —significantly—the genesis of her imaginary twin, Christopher ("Let Anne and Christopher appear with two robins whose worms are sweet and pink as lipstick"). Soon it is clear that Christopher, though Sexton never tells us this, is—*must* be—the great, mad eighteenth-century poet Christopher Smart, of whom Sexton, with her trips to the mad-house, her fits and starts of inspiration, her poetry written against all odds, is a modern echo. Now speaking from the Bedlam of death, he tells her where she is and what to do:

> For I was in a boundary of wool and painted boards. Where are we Christopher? Jail, he said.

> For the room itself was a box. Four thick walls of roses. A ceiling Christopher found low and menacing.

> For I smiled and there was no one to notice. Christopher was asleep. He was making a sea sound . . .

> For birth was a disease and Christopher and I invented the cure.

> For we swallow magic and we deliver Anne.

Together, using the technique of parallel stanzas beginning with "Let" and "For" that Christopher Smart devised for *Jubilate Agno* (Rejoice in the Lamb) his own series of affirmative psalms, they work their way from womb to tomb, from birth to death to God. And there is, though I don't mean this pejoratively, an inspired awkwardness about "their" poetry, as though Sexton were reinventing language just for the two of them and just for this occasion. In the end, perhaps because of this totally new-minted quality, the poems carry rare con-viction. I believe Sexton when she tells me that "God did not forsake [Anne and Christopher] but put the blood angel to look after them until such time as they would enter their star./For the sky dogs jumped out and shoveled snow upon us and we lay in our quiet blood./For God was as large as a sunlamp and laughed his heat at us and therefore we did not cringe at the death hole." I believe her because she confronts death with such complete vitality that there is no longer any room in her lines for egotism, evasion, or dishonesty. Her "God as large as a sunlamp" is a plausible avatar of Christopher Smart's divinity, whose "Sun's at work to make me a garment and the Moon is at work for my wife." "For," said Christopher Smart (and Anne Sexton was listening) "the approaches of Death are by illumination."

On *The Awful Rowing Toward God*

(1975)

JOYCE CAROL OATES

In an intensely personal, frank memoir of her friend Sylvia Plath ("The Barfly Ought to Sing," *TriQuarterly* 7, 1970), Anne Sexton claimed that suicides are a special people. "We talked death," she said, "and this was life for us." These two young, gifted and very attractive women spent hours exchanging details of their suicide attempts; and after Sylvia Plath's successful attempt some years later, Anne Sexton wrote a poem that belongs with the most terrible and yet the most intelligent and convincing work of what is loosely called the "confessional mode." The poem is "Wanting to Die," and it is included in *Live or Die,* Anne Sexton's third volume. Too long to be quoted here, it is probably the poet's central poem, the calm, dispassionate and sparely-crafted statement that makes the familiar charges of "hysteria" quite irrelevant:

Since you ask,
  most days I cannot remember.
I walk in my clothing,
  unmarked by that voyage.
Then the almost unnameable
  lust returns.

Even then I have nothing
  against life.
I know well the grass
  blades you mention,
the furniture you have
  placed under the sun.

But suicides have a special language.
Like carpenters they want to know
  which tools.
They never ask *why build.*

Ironically, the thirty-nine poems of Sexton's posthumous volume, *The Awful Rowing Toward God,* do set out reasons, explanations and occasionally rueful apologies for her emotional predicament; like some of the finest poems of *The Book of Folly* of 1972, these poems attempt not simply the poetic expression of emotion—that "unstoppered fullness" Robert Lowell praised—but intelligent and sometimes highly critical analysis of the suicidal impulse. In fact, we are mercifully not told which tools so much as instructed in the much more valuable why build. *The Awful Rowing Toward God* contains poems of superb, unforgettable power, but it would be disingenuous of any reviewer to suppose that the book will be bought and eagerly read for the excellence of its craft. (Many contemporary poets are fine craftsmen, in fact; never have so many people been capable of writing so well, and with so little possibility of being justly recognized.) The book will probably be bought because it is the posthumous volume Anne Sexton had planned and because it describes with more candor and wit and warmth than Sylvia Plath allowed herself, the stages of the "rowing" toward what Sexton calls "God."

The volume begins with a poem called "Rowing" and ends with "The Rowing Endeth" and the "untamable, eternal, gut-driven *ha-ha*" that is the triumph of the union of God and man. Between are poems of sorrow, poems of anger, poems of befuddlement and terror and love, and while some are almost too painful to read ("The Sickness Unto Death," "The Big Heart"), many are as slangy and direct as those "Eighteen Days Without You" that conclude the volume *Love Poems,* my personal favorite among her eight books. In "The Play," for instance, the poet describes herself as the only actor in the play that is her life; she knows her concerns are dismayingly solipsistic, she knows the speeches she gives are "all soliloquies" and that the audience will boo her:

> Despite that I go on to the last lines:
> To be without God is to be a snake
> who wants to swallow an elephant.
> The curtain falls.
> The audience rushes out.
> It was a bad performance.
> That's because I'm the only actor
> and there are few humans whose lives
> will make an interesting play.
> Don't you agree?

There are poets who seem to choose their surreal images with fastidious care, as if seeking physical images to describe what are primarily intellectual or even ideological beliefs; Anne Sexton, however, gives the impression of selecting from a great flood of dreamlike or nightmarish images precisely those which communicate most directly to the reader (and to the poet herself). Her painful honesty is well known. What her unsympathetic critics have charged her with —an overvaluing of her private sorrows to the exclusion of the rest of the world—seems to have been felt by Sexton herself. This sort of knowledge, however, rarely brings with it the ability to change. The hearty optimism of a certain kind of American temperament—these days, most obviously illustrated by the plethora of "easy" psychotherapies—is absolutely balked by the fact that some people are unchangeable despite their own deepest wishes; optimists either turn aside from the problem of "evil" (or unhealth), or deny strenuously that it is really a problem. The death-driven personality, whether fated to murder others or itself, is only "neurotic" and can be made more "healthy" by being subjected to the right treatment. Anne Sexton, then, can be dismissed as "sick" and her poetry dismissed as the outpouring of a pathologically egocentric imagination—unless one is willing to make the risky claim, which will not be a popular one, that poets like Sexton, Plath, and John Berryman have dealt in excruciating detail with collective (and not merely individual) pathologies of our time.

It is probable that a serious artist exercises relatively little control over the choice of subjects of his or her art. The more fortunate artist is simply one who, for reasons not known, identifies powerfully with a unit larger than the self: Faulkner with his "postage stamp" of earth, Shakespeare with the glorious, astounding variety of human personality, Dostoevsky with all of Russia. Such artists surely dramatize their own emotions, but they give life to the world outside the self by means of these emotions and in so doing often draw up into consciousness aspects of the collective human self that would otherwise not be tapped. If this sounds like a mysterious process, it must be admitted that it is mysterious: but most artists understand it intuitively. Anne Sexton yearned for that larger experience, that rush of near-divine certainty that the self *is* immortal; she knew it existed but she could not reach it. "The place I live in/is a kind of maze/and I keep seeking/the exit or the home" ("The Children"). Trapped within her specific, private self, she seems to have despaired of any remedy short of death—

> . . . I have a body
> and I cannot escape from it.
> I would like to fly out of my head,
> but that is out of the question.
> It is written on the tablet of destiny
> that I am stuck here in this human form.

That being the case
I would like to call attention to
   my problem.
            ("The Poet of Ignorance")

Only my books anoint me,
and a few friends,
those who reach into my veins.
Maybe I am becoming a hermit,
opening the door for only
a few special animals?
Maybe my skull is too crowded
and it has no opening through which
to feed it soup?
Maybe I have plugged up my sockets
to keep the gods in?
                  ("The Witch's Life")

Sexton's God is masculine; being masculine, he is necessarily outside her—far away, inaccessible in this life. When she rows to The
Island of God, He and she play cards and He wins "because He holds
five aces"; she does not regret His victory, however, but joins Him in
His laughter: "Then I laugh, the fishy dock laughs/the sea laughs. The
Island laughs./The Absurd laughs" ("The Rowing Endeth"). For
Sexton there must have been little comfort in the near-universal religious assurance that the Kingdom of God (or the potentiality for
divine experience) is within human beings. Despite her yearning,
despite her obvious intelligence and her sense of humor (usually one
measure of health), she simply did not find her "God" near at hand.
And it is surely not for others to judge her as harshly as she judged
herself.

ROBERT MAZZOCCO

One of Schopenhauer's stranger ideas is that the will to live is so
universal, so strong, that no man can ever really say "I'll kill myself."

He can of course do away with his body but his "will" goes marching on. This (I suspect) is the old notion of the immortality of the soul in another (and absurd) guise, and beyond that, morally, perhaps vengefully, the conviction that no matter what we can never escape judgment. But it seems to me it's precisely escaping judgment that the suicide wants and, for all we know, finally achieves. For a suicide is the ultimate bankrupt, he cancels all debts, wipes the slate clean, plays the last trump, what the analysts call the "superlative bid"—he not only dies but sacrifices *himself.* So what more can one ask?

This fascination with "death and what death invents" or what death erases, with *tabula rasa,* with "never having been," is the melody we hear most often, I think, in the poetry of the late Anne Sexton. Sometimes it is barely audible, sometimes it is strident, sometimes it is a sort of fugue contrasting the will to live with the will to die. Sometimes the "music swims back" to the poet and she is less afraid, sometimes soaring on "black wings" it enters a major key, brings forth *"good news good news."* But the latter occurrence of course is rare.

Many of the early poems depict intensely introverted states in a highly extroverted style, are desperate in spirit but have a breezy air. Colloquial in statement, clever in juxtapositions, they are sleek too in a certain recurring employment of nuances, rhymes, couplets. The later poems, though, seem to me less commanding, strike dissonant strains, chromatize the keyboard, or become programmatic, a little like Gray's "moody madness laughing wild amidst severest woe." And the language suffers. Often in *The Book of Folly* and *The Death Notebooks,* and now in her posthumous collection, *The Awful Rowing Toward God,* the churning of a symbol, the intrusion of a raw memory betray Anne Sexton almost as ludicrously as the ass in the lion's skin betrayed himself when he began to bray:

> I am filling the room
> with words from my pen.
> Words leak out of it like a miscarriage.
> I am zinging words out into the air
> and they come back like squash balls. . . .

Anne Sexton often wrote of the cruelty of life and the cruelty of people, particularly the ungiving nature of her parents, yet unlike Sylvia Plath she seems always to have been asking to be forgiven. Plath had a colder heart, perhaps, but wrote fiercer, purer poetry—was indeed a genius. Sylvia Plath refused to forgive the world and there's always something triumphant about that refusal. Plath is always, as she says, "ready for enormity," crossing the frontier, with no carols to be sung, no Whitmanian salutations to accompany the hearse —and one has to honor her. Faithful to her demons, she seems, in the end, a conqueror, victorious.

Anne Sexton dealt with the theme of vulnerability directly, bluntly. Also the theme of melancholia, often picturing herself as a "possessed witch," or speaking of "mensturation at forty," or laughing at herself as a housewife mixing the martinis. But these highly womanly images were never any match for the presence that really haunted the poems, the specter of herself as a dependent, arrested in the past, the child with the "night mind" or night wound.

When she retreats to the "scene of the disordered senses," the sanatorium, she has to lecture herself as if she were elsewhere, back with the family: "for this is a mental hospital / not a child's game"; to her bachelor analyst she's his "third grader / with a blue star on my forehead"; her fellow patients chew in rows above their plates, these "permanent guests" beset with faces that are "still small / like babies with jaundice"; while the guignol of therapy, "the skull that waits for its dose / of electric power," assumes the shape of a classroom horror. And even when she becomes a mother herself, Sexton sees it as a means of remaining a daughter, clarifying her childhood or redeeming it:

> I, who was never quite sure
> about being a girl, needed another
> life, another image to remind me.
> And this was my worst guilt; you could not cure
> nor soothe it. I made you to find me.

Full of doubts over the essential conventional truths of maturity, she was nonetheless never an iconoclast; always looking for answers she knew she would "die full of questions." Often she dramatized herself as the unwilling beneficiary of what others would give her ("they gave me your ash and bony shells") or awarded with what she felt she could not use or didn't deserve, "the division of money," her mother's legacy. In one of the poems she creates a persona for herself, a woman with a bastard child, who represents "sin and nothing more." Guilty, she gathered "guilt like a young intern / his symptoms, his certain evidence."

The clinical detail of many of the poems has often been remarked, but the guilt is really of the old nether world, invented long before Freud, and it is in that world that her repeated suicide attempts occur which are always unforgivable (" 'I cannot forgive your suicide,' my mother said. / And she never could"). The guilt is there, most condemnatory, in the remembered deaths of her parents, which are always the real deaths of her life: watching over her mother as she lay dying of cancer, "blown up, at last, / like a pregnant pig," her daughter seeming to be her mother's "dreamy evil eye," or recalling her father, "a cured old alcoholic" who went out "on crooked feet and useless hands."

Later the sense of guilt attempts to move away from the embodiment of her parents as earthly judges, agonizes a bit over the possibility that her father was not her "real father" (a concern also strikingly illustrated in two of the short stories she wrote during her last years, which are far better than the later poems), and finally fastens on some sort of heavenly intercession. Not the earlier panoply of Christ and Lent and Crucifix, but instead a cyclopic or totemic god, a god who appears to be grotesquely as "large as a sunlamp," whose universe includes a manic America, a moon that has a "naggy voice," and a sky out of which dogs jump.

These poems, irreverently called "psalms," are, no doubt, deliberately horrific, meant to zap the Almighty, paradoxically to assuage the terrors or mock them. But Anne Sexton's sense of violence was always faltering. Violence seems never to have enhanced her work as it did that of Mishima and Plath. With these figures there's an objectification or theatricalization of the body—Plath and her "Greek ritual," Mishima's head severed with the single stroke of a sword—that's not apparent in Sexton. The murderous impulses that lie buried in her work always verge on the lurid or the awkward; the cry of "my hungers! my hungers!" is a cry of absence, of feelings that can neither be named nor stanched. The flute player in *Live or Die,* whose eerie music intoxicates the poet, is a dwarf with an "enormous misshapen mouth," who sits in a cave, "a great hole in the earth," with its "tons of suffocating dirt," the distance in which his listener must enter in order to be fed.

Nietzsche says, speaking of the creativity of the artist, that "one does not get over a passion by representing it, rather it is over *when* one is able to represent it." But that *when* Sexton, I believe, never fully reached. Beneath the recklessness of so much of her language there's always a strange passivity, a great unknowingness or fear. In the brittle, excitable music of the last poems, including those of *The Awful Rowing Toward God,* the theme of stability often sounds, the poet admonishing herself to put a pot of soup on the stove and "light up the cave." But Anne Sexton's sensibility always went the other way. For her poems are never about how to gain things or how to consolidate things, but about how to get rid of what she already has, how to lose friends, home, children, lovers, how indeed to move *backward,* to hold death in her arms "like a child," the "death baby," with the " glass eye, ice eye," to be "wedded to my teddy," to bed down against the "stony head of death," to inherit, in other words, her parents' graves, and there finally to be forgiven—that is to say, forgotten, unreflective and unreflecting.

Her best poems—poems like "Flee on Your Donkey," "To Lose the Earth," "Letter Written on a Ferry While Crossing Long Island Sound"—are delicate, visceral, poignant. The throes of a dire need run through them. Others, less successful, are a diary of scars where the reader can discern his own. But good or bad, because the protagonist is so often so dreadfully unhappy they are poems one can never take lightly.

Yet reading her one has to ask: is it really unhappiness that kills? I would doubt it. Unhappiness steadies one usually, if it does anything, adds gravity to what's inevitable or implacable. What kills, I

REVIEWS 177

think, is something simpler and deeper, the horror, as Anne Sexton
knew again and again, of being unable to see or feel clearly, to be
always, as she says, only part way back from Bedlam; that inability
to "for once make a deliberate decision," to arrive at no conclusions
whatever except the most desperate of all. It's the sense of the frag-
mentary that buries us, because things don't connect, so we don't add
up, we become useless to ourselves and to others.

With Sexton life seems a sort of "trick," even sickness becomes
something one no longer has "the knack of." "Bells," "lighthouse,"
"Clorox and Duz," "sixteen-in-the-pants," "bedside radio," "cash"
and "car keys"—these emblems of the everyday became for her signs
of the disfavored or disfigured, the unrealized. Nor did having a
"career," being an "ambition bird," honored in a way other poets
have never been, seem to ease her plight. It's as she says in one of her
earliest poems, which points to all the later ones, where the people at
Atlantic City are sitting around praying for "impossible loves," for "a
new skin," for "another child," or are playing at the gaming tables
of Reno where they never win, waiting for the lost ingredient, like
waiting for Godot, whose absence must keep them incomplete:

> Today is made of yesterday, each time I steal
> toward rites I do not know, waiting for the lost
> ingredient, as if salt or money or even lust
> would keep us calm and prove us whole at last.

BEN HOWARD

Two of the most conspicuous features of postwar American verse
have been its drift toward simplicity of style and its preoccupation
with self-disclosure. Of the dozens of influential poets who have exemplified one or both of these tendencies—Lowell, Berryman, Plath,
James Wright, to name only a few—no one has done so more dramatically than the late Anne Sexton. And nowhere in Mrs. Sexton's work
are these tendencies carried to greater extremes than in the three

present volumes. In these final statements the poet lays her most private moments—and her nastiest fantasies—at the reader's feet, and she reduces a once-graceful style to its barest, crudest essentials. Whatever one might think of these poems, it would seem unwise to underestimate their importance. To begin with, they are the last testament of a gifted and widely recognized American poet. Beyond that, they are a form of evidence: a field of glass around a shattered windshield. In their extremity they prompt the question of where American poetry has been during the past decade, and where it might be heading.

Anne Sexton began her career fifteen years ago as a formalist poet. Her early poems were anguished in tone and autobiographical in content, but they were well-made, polished pieces, formally inventive and often ironic. In view of their subjects, they were remarkably reticent:

> The town does not exist
> except where one black-haired tree slips
> up like a drowned woman into the hot sky.
> The town is silent. The night boils with eleven stars.
> O starry starry night! This is how
> I want to die.
>
> ("The Starry Night")

Over the years Mrs. Sexton abandoned the formalist manner. Her imagery grew bold, her syntax elemental. She seemed determined to share with her growing audience the most intimate details of her private life, and she seemed increasingly indifferent toward subtlety and polish. The solidity of her early work survives in her *Love Poems* (1967), but in *Transformations* (1971), her colloquial renditions of Grimms' fairy tales, it is almost nowhere to be found. And what becomes of style in these final poems? "Gods" will suffice as an example:

> Mrs. Sexton went out looking for the gods.
> She began looking in the sky—
> expecting a large white angel with a blue crotch.

No one.

She looked next in all the learned books
and the print spat back at her.

No one.

She made a pilgrimage to the great poet
and he belched in her face.

No one.

She prayed in all the churches of the world
and learned a great deal about culture.

No one.

She went to the Atlantic, the Pacific, for surely God . . .

No one.

She went to the Buddha, the Brahma, the Pyramids
and found immense postcards.

No one.

Then she journeyed back to her own house
and the gods of the world were shut in the lavatory.

At last!
she cried out,
and locked the door.

Naming herself, the poet mocks herself. Reducing diction, imagery, and syntax to their simplest terms, she reduces her religious anxiety and religious quest to a kind of verbal cartoon. The episodic structure and pattern of comic humiliations call to mind nothing so much as the daily comic strip, or even more, the animated cartoon, whose miniature antihero suffers a string of defeats. Here the sought object is not a mouse or roadrunner but an elusive company of gods, and the chase is mysteriously successful. But the two structures are otherwise much the same. The pathetic figure of "Mrs. Sexton" reminds one less of St. Teresa than of Charlie Brown.

Episodic structure is prominent in these three volumes [*The Book of Folly, The Death Notebooks, The Awful Rowing Toward God*], both in the syntax of individual poems and in the structural relationships of poems grouped as sequences. *The Death Notebooks* contains three such sequences—"The Death Baby," "The Furies," and "O Ye Tongues"—and *The Book of Folly* three more: "Angels of the Love Affair," "The Death of the Fathers," and "The Jesus Papers." Poetic sequences have become common in postwar American poetry, but to my knowledge there have not been any sequences quite like these. On the whole, they create little or no sense of progression, whether dramatic or thematic, nor do they present multiple perspectives on a single subject or situation. More than anything, they evoke a sense of succession and repetition, of events following one another in predictable and usually empty patterns. The poems themselves generate a similar mood, with their frequent catalogs ("the hating eyes of martyrs, / presidents, bus collectors, / bank managers, soldiers"), their parallelisms ("Sing me a thrush, bone. / Sing me a nest of cup and pestle. / Sing me a sweetbread for an old grandfather. / Sing me a foot and a doorknob . . ."), and their elemental narratives:

> Oysters we ate,
> sweet blue babies,
> twelve eyes looked up at me,
> running with lemon and Tabasco.
> I was afraid to eat this father-food
> and Father laughed
> and drank down his martini,
> clear as tears.
> It was a soft medicine
> that came from the sea into my mouth,
> moist and plump.
> I swallowed.
> It went down like a large pudding.
> Then I ate one o'clock and two o'clock.
> Then I laughed and then we laughed
> and let me take note—
> there was a death,
> the death of childhood

> there at the Union Oyster House
> for I was fifteen
> and eating oysters
> and the child was defeated.
> The woman won.
>
> ("Oysters")

Mrs. Sexton's reduction of syntax and structure to an episodic, childlike simplicity has its counterpart in the diction of these poems, which is often that of the nursery. Diverse voices can be heard, among them Sylvia Plath's ("Beware. Beware." "my own little Jew"), Theodore Roethke's ("Sing me a thrush, bone," "Someone lives in a cave / eating his toes, / I know that much"), the mature voice of Mrs. Sexton's *Love Poems* ("I talk to God and ask Him / to speak of my failures, my successes, / ask Him to morally make an assessment"), and the offhand colloquial voice of *Transformations* ("If someone had brought [daisies] / to Van Gogh's room daily / his ear would have stayed on"). But the dominant voice is that of the cute, defiant, and often naughty little girl. "Why shouldn't I pull down my pants," the poet asks, "and show my little cunny to Tom / and Albert? / They wee-wee funny." "I am wedded to my teddy," she declares, in a poem addressed to her mother. And speaking of the Biblical Jonah, whose predicament she likens to her own: "Give praise with the whale who will make a big warm home for Jonah and let him hang his very own pictures up." It remains puzzling, at least to this reader, why an artist capable of eloquence should have chosen so limiting an idiom. In the sequence entitled "The Death of the Fathers," Mrs. Sexton employs the childlike voice as part of an effort to re-create scenes from her childhood and to confront, among other things, the question of whether her alcoholic father, who appears variously as Santa Claus, the skipper of a Chris-Craft, a dancing partner, and a storyteller, is her "real" father. Elsewhere, the childlike voice serves an ironic purpose, dramatizing the disparity between childlike innocence and adult experience: "She is the house. / He is the steeple. / When they fuck they are God. / When they break away they are God." Most of the time, however, Mrs. Sexton's reduction of speech to the level of

Run-Spot-Run is merely distracting. It may represent an effort to satirize childish elements in herself and in the social role she felt compelled to play. But it has neither the variety nor the acute focus of effective satire, and it very soon wears thin.

If one of Mrs. Sexton's purposes is, in fact, to satirize her predicament as an American woman, she is well-assisted by her imagery, which in these last poems becomes a bizarre blend of Gothic and domestic. Here, as in her previous work, her metaphoric range is unusually wide. By turns her imagery is sentimental, sexual, violent, freakish, surreal, maternal, religious, and scatological. She puts bees in her mouth and hatpins through the pupils of her enemies. She presents us with a one-legged man, a man with a knife in his armpit, and a "Hitler-mouth psychiatrist." Words become squash-balls in one context, and in another, dung. The sea turns into the pond of urine; the poet dreams that she can "piss in God's eye"; and the penis of Jesus is made to sing "like a dog." For all its sensationalism, Mrs. Sexton's imagery does carry conviction, and it is sometimes striking in ways that are not sensational, as when she supplicates her doctor to let her "dilate like a bad debt," or when she speaks of "someone drowning into his own mouth." Her most characteristic kind of metaphor fuses imagery of violence and death with imagery of the kitchen, suggesting a close, even inevitable relationship between them. Rarely have poems been so well-stocked with household products and brand-names—Kleenex, Lysol, Clorox, Bab-O—and with domestic objects generally. The immediate effect of such imagery is to evoke the Mad Housewife, driven to distraction by suburban confinement. More seriously, Mrs. Sexton's images evoke the horror of suburban sterility, the suppressed violence and irrational fear of a woman enmeshed in domestic routine. "Blood fingers" tie the poet's shoe; she discovers blood in her gravy; and blood flows from the kitchen pump. Mrs. Sexton has traveled leagues from Dr. Johnson, who objected to the use of the domestic "knife" in tragic drama. To a large extent, however, Mrs. Sexton's personal tragedy seems to have been bound up in domestic objects, both as literal impediments and as symbols of her role; and through those objects she seems to have been developing, at the end of her life, a vision of her predicament. That vision is far from integrated or fully realized in these poems, but its discrete elements, set in close proximity, speak with force and insight.

Mrs. Sexton's household is also the theater for her religious struggle. These poems often call to mind T. S. Eliot's description of the poet's capacity to amalgamate Spinoza and the smell of cooking, forming new wholes of disparate experiences. In these poems Mrs. Sexton amalgmates the smell of cooking—and cleaning, and laundry —with a wide spectrum of religious sentiments and attitudes, which range from sarcastic irreverence to a desperate, if self-ironic, religious striving. In some poems the domestic order appears as an impediment to spiritual fulfillment. "Hail mary coffee toast," the poet prays; and speaking of her death she asks, "God, you don't mind if I bring all my kitchens." At other times the poet's quarrel is with the perverse indifference of a God who "has turned his backside to us," who is "too busy / to be here on earth," and who is compared to "that washerwoman / who walks out / when you're clean / but not ironed." In the absence of a sympathetic personal God the poet invents substitutes, declaring that "All the cocks of the world are God" and even "I am God, la de dah." Or she strikes a pose of nonchalance:

> Interrogator:
> Why talk to God?
>
> Anne:
> It's better than playing bridge.
> ("Hurry Up Please It's Time")

But indifference is a thin disguise for a poet who knows that "To pray . . . is to be a man carrying a man" and who speaks often of being "swallowed" by a God who is even now "opening His teeth." Mrs. Sexton's "rowing toward God" is indeed awful, in the oldest sense of that word. Beneath the domestic clutter and confused self-mockery of these last poems there runs a current of religious terror, as though the poet were writing, willy-nilly, her personal *Dies Irae*.

What she was not writing, it seems clear, were suicide notes. Nor, for the most part, are these poems cries for help. On the whole, their character is that of a preparatory ritual, in advance of a death which could come at any time. At one point, Mrs. Sexton explicitly rejects the role of the "suicide bitch," declaring (to an imagined "Herr Doktor"), "I am no longer the suicide / with her raft and paddle. . . . I'll no longer die / to spite you. . . ." Obsessed as she is with her death, the poet's imagination plays not upon forms of suicide or its effect upon her survivors but upon the necessary preparations for the final event. At the center of those preparations lies the imagining of that event. She portrays herself dying "like a nice girl / smelling of Clorox and Duz." She presents herself as a spectacle, attracting voyeurs:

> But when it comes to my death let it be slow,
> let it be pantomine, this last peep show,
> so that I may squat at the edge trying on
> my black necessary trousseau.
>   ("For Mr. Death Who Stands With His Door Open")

And in the last of her nine "psalms," the final poem of *The Death Notebooks,* she seems to speak with confidence, as though she had recovered her faith and had faced her deepest fear:

> For God was as large as a sunlamp and laughed his heat at us
> and therefore we did not cringe at the death hole.

It has been little more than a year since Mrs. Sexton's death, and it is surely too soon to attempt an overview of her life and work. How much help these last books will provide remains to be seen. Mrs. Sexton's last poems provide many glimpses of her private life, and they express her sense of spirtual deprivation. But nowhere do they provide a statement of belief, or a rejection of belief, or a fully-developed vision of the poet's life and the forces threatening it. Perhaps that is too much to ask of so troubled a poet. The task might best be left to those who will pick up these sharp-edged and sometimes radiant pieces.

What these last poems do provide, however, is an extreme instance of a common predicament, namely that of American poets in the aftermath of formalism. For all her uniqueness, Mrs. Sexton was one of a large number of American poets who have rejected the conventions of formalism and its doctrine of impersonality and have had to shape a style and a coherent aesthetic to replace them. In this sense Mrs. Sexton's shattered art speaks not only for a troubled American psyche but for the poets of her generation and the one presently succeeding it.

On *45 Mercy Street*

(1976)

PATRICIA MEYER SPACKS

Harder to detect than banalities about young love and springtime, the various sentimentalities of madness and suicide have peculiar appeal in our era. Anne Sexton's biography authenticates her poetry, her self-inflicted death attesting to the reality of her pain: how unfeeling, then, for a reader to complain about the facility with which she renders human suffering. Yet *45 Mercy Street*, a poet's record of the miseries of divorce, sexuality, daughterhood, shows the devices of self-revelation hardened into mannerism. However genuine the anguish, its rendition here raises large questions about the esthetic possibilities of raw confession in poetry. How, for instance, can one properly respond to lines as grotesquely uncontrolled as these?

> . . . having ripped the cross off Jesus
> and left only the nails,
> Husband,
> Husband,
> I hold up my hand and see
> only nails.

Or, in a different vein,

The moth, grinning like a pear,
or is it teeth
clamping the iron maiden shut?

Sentimentalism, by a common handbook definition, means "an overindulgence in emotion, especially the conscious effort to induce emotion in order to analyze or enjoy it; also the failure to restrain or evaluate emotion through the exercise of the judgment." In Anne Sexton's earlier books, imagery and poetic action often served to restrain and evaluate.

We chew in rows, our plates
scratch and whine like chalk

in school.

This evocation of a meal in a mental hospital (from *To Bedlam and Part Way Back,* 1960) suggests the personal diminutions of institutional existence with a precision of observation and association that transcends simple self-pity. Some of the lyrics in that first book remain undiminished in vigor and freshness, their material a kind of experience conventionally kept private, their technique demonstrating the author's awareness not only of such immediate and obvious precursors as Robert Lowell but of older poetic and religious traditions and of a world outside the self. When Sexton writes,

Still, I search in these woods and
find nothing worse
than myself, caught between
the grapes and the thorns.

she implicitly judges her self-absorption, understanding it as cause and symptom of mental distress. The second book too (*All My Pretty Ones,* 1962) has its telling moments, particularly when the poet functions as observer ("Woman with Girdle," "Housewife") rather than self-devouring subject of the work. The title poem, accepting the discipline of rhyme and of closely observed detail, keeps emotional extravagance in check; other pieces occasionally manage moments of epigrammatic economy.

But even these first volumes lapse frequently into bathos, betraying an apparent incapacity for self-criticism either moral or esthetic, and such lapses multiply as the career continues. In a sense, Anne Sexton can be seen as a victim of an era in which it has become easy to dramatize self-indulgence, stylish to invent unexpected imagery regardless of its relevance, fashionable to be a woman and as a woman to display one's misery. Her poetry became increasingly popular as it manifested increasing slovenliness. In *Live or Die* (1966), which won the Pulitzer Prize, the speaker describes herself in one poem as daughter, sweet-meat, priest, mouth, and bird of the sun: images of altogether uncritical self-adoration. A poem on the death of Sylvia Plath quickly becomes yet another means for talking about the self, that self endlessly jealous of attention. The shrill narcissism of such lyrics appears to have attracted more readers than it repelled. Perhaps the mounting stress on self-loathing and self-punishment—also fashionable modes of grandiosity—helped to obscure the limitation of range, perception, accuracy, the effect of being trapped in a not-very-interesting mind with no capacity to see beyond its own insistent mirroring. Sentimentalism in both its definitions mars most of the lyrics in *Live or Die;* the conscious effort to induce emotion for its own sake, the failure to evaluate it by any rational standard.

This sentimentalism has increased, becoming painfully marked in the first posthumous volume, *The Awful Rowing Toward God* (1975), with its embarrassments of religious pretension. A poem beginning, "I am torn in two/ but I will conquer myself," continues by evoking "God dressed up like a whore/ in a slime of green algae," and concludes by asserting the speaker's determination to "build a new soul" and sing "a song of myself." The problem of internal division, the perception of divinity, the will to rebuild the soul: all alike register unconvincingly. The poetry through which these vast themes are rendered is simply not good enough.

Which brings us to *45 Mercy Street*: definitively now, the poetry is not good enough. Inaccurate metaphors—the planets cutting "holes in their nets" to "let our childhood out." Arbitrary associations—"a seal/ with wide wings,/ made of vinegar and little boys." Vulgar imagery—"we became a home,/up into the elbows of each other's soul"; "I sweat into the bathtub of his being." Lines so devoid of melody as to be virtually unsayable: "from the public voyeury eyes/of my typewriter keys." A disturbing repetitiousness of tone and technique pervades the book. Words like "little" and "tiny" recur again and again, part of the falsely deprecatory litany of self-pity. Whether poems begin with apostrophe—"God, Jack of all trades"; "You with your wings like spatulas"—or with the first-person pronoun, their true and monotonous concern remains that self explicitly declared inadequate but nonetheless the speaker's only real interest. These poems may claim to talk about moles or seagulls or Orphan Annie (in " 'Daddy' Warbucks," one of the better efforts here); the poet can sound cute (as when she imagines sending children back to God by "real air mail") or angry or despairing; but always there is only obsessive misery to declare. Occasionally an image ("The brains as/ helpless as oysters in a pint container") or a sequence of lines (in "The Break Away," for example) returns to the imaginative force of the best early poems. More often, the verse implicitly argues that anguish is self-justifying, neither permitting nor demanding the further pain of balanced self-knowledge or the illuminations of controlled imagination and poetic technique. In life we forgive sufferers the necessities of their obsessions. In literature we must ask more: acknowledging the pain that produces such work as Anne Sexton's later poems, yet remembering that art requires more than emotional indulgence, requires a saving respect for disciplines and realities beyond the crying needs, the unrelenting appetites, of the self.

PART V

Overviews

RICHARD HOWARD

Anne Sexton: "Some Tribal Female Who Is Known But Forbidden"

There are some areas of experience in modern life, Theodore Roethke has said, that simply cannot be rendered by either the formal
lyric or straight prose. We must realize—and who could have en-
forced the realization upon us better than Roethke—that the writer
in "freer forms" must have an even greater fidelity to his subject
matter or his substance than the poet who has the support of form—
of received form. He must be imaginatively "right," his rhythm must
move as the mind moves, or he is lost. "On the simplest level, something must happen in this kind of poem." By which Roethke meant,
I am certain, that it is not enough to report something happening in
your life merely—it must be made to happen in your poem. You must
begin somewhere, though, generally with your life, above all with
your life when it seems to you to welter in a particular exemplary
status. Such is Anne Sexton's case, and she has begun indeed with the
report of her case:

> Oh! Honor and relish the facts!
> Do not think of the intense sensation
> I have as I tell you this
> but thing only. . . .

In fact, she has reported more than anyone else—anyone else who has set out to write poems—has ever cared or dared, and thereby she has gained, perhaps at the expense of her poetry, a kind of sacerdotal stature, the elevation of a priestess celebrating mysteries which are no less mysterious for having been conducted in all the hard glare of the marketplace and with all the explicitness mere print can afford.

Anne Sexton is the true Massachusetts heiress of little Pearl, who as the procession of Worthies passes by asks Hester Prynne if one man in it is the same minister who kissed her by the brook. "Hold thy peace, dear little Pearl," whispers her mother. "We must not always talk in the marketplace of what happens to us in the forest." Like the sibylline, often insufferable Pearl, Anne Sexton *does* speak of such things, and in such places, and it makes her, again like Pearl, both more and less than a mere "person," something beyond a "character"; it makes her, rather, what we call a *figure,* the form of a tragic function. If you are wearing not only your heart on your sleeve, your liver on your lapel and the other organs affixed to various articles of your attire, but also a whole alphabet in scarlet on your breast, then your poetry must bear with losing the notion of *private parts* altogether and with gaining a certain publicity that has nothing to do with the personal. Further, if you regard, as Anne Sexton does, the poem as "a lie that tells the truth" (it was Cocteau who first spoke of himself this way), then you face the corresponding peril that the truth you tell will become a lie: "there is no translating that ocean," as Miss Sexton says. And it will become a lie because you have not taken enough care to "make something happen"—in short, to lie in the way poems must lie, by devising that imaginative rightness which Roethke located primarily in rhythm, but which has everything to do as well with the consecration of images, the shape language makes as it is deposited in the reader's mind, the transactions between beginnings and endings, the *devices*—no less—of art.

"Even one alone verse sometimes makes a perfect poem," Ben Jonson declared, and so much praise (it is the kind of praise that leaves out of the reckoning a great deal of waste, a great deal of botched work) it will be easy, and what is more it will be necessary, to give Anne Sexton; like the preposterous sprite whose "demon-offspring" impulses she resumes, this poet is likely, *at any moment,* to say those oracular, outrageous things we least can bear but most require:

> Fee-fi-fo-fum
> Now I'm borrowed
> Now I'm numb.

It is when she speaks beyond the moment, speaks as it were consecutively that Anne Sexton finds herself in difficulties; if we are concerned with the poem as it grows from one verse to the next, enlarging itself by means of itself, like a growing pearl, the real one (Hawthorne's, for all he tells us, never grew up), then we must discover an Anne Sexton dead set, by her third book of poems, against any such process. Hers is the truth that cancels poetry, and her career as an artist an excruciating trajectory of self-destruction, so that it is by her failures in her own enterprise that she succeeds, and by her successes as an artist that she fails herself.

In 1960 Miss Sexton's first collection of poems, *To Bedlam and Part Way Back* was published with an epigraph from a letter of Schopenhauer to Goethe echoing Hester Prynne's reproof: "Most of us carry in our heart the Jocasta who begs Oedipus for God's sake not to inquire further. . . ." The poems begin right there in Bedlam, unacclimated, unexplained, and take shape, apparently, as a therapeutic project—the very ingenuity of their shape, indeed, has something of the basket-weaver's patience about it, it is the work of a *patient.* The very first, addressed to the doctor "who walks from breakfast to madness," refers to the speaker and the other inmates as "magic talking to itself,/noisy and alone." Only gradually are we given a hint of the circumstances that brought her there, circumstances it will be Sexton's life work to adumbrate until the shadows fall indeed over her entire existence as a poet—here we simply start out in the asylum, where "my night mind/saw such strange happenings." The poet is in her own dark forest:

> ... I am afraid of course
> to look—this inward look that society scorns—
> Still, I search these woods and find nothing worse
> than myself, caught between the grapes and the thorns.

She is even, like Daphne, her own tree:

> I live in my wooden legs and O
> my green green hands ...
> I am a fist of my unease
> as I spill toward the stars in the empty years.
> I build the air with the crown of honor; it keys
> my out of time and luckless appetite.
> You gave me honor too soon, Apollo.
> There is no one left who understands
> how I wait
> here in my wooden legs and O
> my green green hands.

That strikes the proper note of the priestess: it is the voice of a woman defiled by the very life she would expose, and whose knowledge has been granted by her defilement and is thereby partial, momentary and changing: "caught between a shape and a shape and then returned to me."

In these first poems, Anne Sexton has already mastered not only an idiosyncratic stanza, but a verse paragraph whose characteristic diction has, in Robert Lowell's choppy wake, restored to our poetry not only the lyric of self-dramatization which had hidden out in the novel for so long, but an unmistakable notation of events—not witty but always *grinçant,* and without more music than mere accuracy affords:

> It is a summer evening.
> The yellow moths sag
> against the locked screens
> and the faded curtains
> suck over the window sills

and from another building
a goat calls in his dreams.
This is the TV parlor
in the best ward at Bedlam.
The night nurse is passing
out the evening pills.
She walks on two erasers,
padding by us one by one.

The line break at "passing," the intermittent rhyme and the rhythmic
subtlety, particularly in the last two lines, suggest the gifts employed
here (Flaubert himself would have been pleased with that second
sentence), even or especially when the matter is "given" so unbearably
that no further gifts can, in short, matter:

> . . . because we mind by instinct,
> like bees caught in the wrong hive,
> we are the circle of the crazy ladies
> who sit in the lounge of the mental house
> and smile . . . .

There is, demonstrably, a care in these first poems for the poem's
making; invariably it is Sexton's practice to use rhyme to bind the
poem, irregularly invoked, abandoned when inconvenient, psychologically convincing. It is the rhyme introduced into English verse by
Arnold, refined by Eliot, and roughed up here by Miss Sexton, who
seeks to recover for poetry the expressive resources of chaos and is not
to be coerced, "in that narrow diary of her mind," to any spurious
regularity:

> Today is made of yesterday, each time I steal
> toward rites I do not know, waiting for the lost
> ingredient, as if salt or money or even lust
> would keep us calm and prove us whole at last.

She conducts her funneling and furious tour of the wards, in this
collection, so that the final third of the book is focused on the purely
private horrors: on the separation from individual impulse that leaves
us

> ... too alien to know
> our sameness and how our sameness survives;

and on the terrible demands, nonetheless, of the ego imprisoned in the woman's wanting body:

> My dear, it was a time,
> butchered from time,
> that we must tell of quickly
> before we lost the sound of our own
> mouths calling mine, mine, mine.

The last three poems, "For John, Who Begs Me Not to Enquire Further," "The Double Image" and "The Division of Parts" are specifically concerned with a disengagement from the sacred world of madness and a weary return to sanity, or at least to a version of secular (bourgeois) life which must seem sane for being so bleak. The painful poems to the estranged daughter, to the mother dying of cancer, and about the two suicide attempts (Sexton is more than half in love with easeful death; as her envying poem to Sylvia Plath insists, she is altogether enamored of a difficult one) are an exorcism, a caveat and a mustering of forces; to the daughter is assigned the disabused confession:

> I, who was never quite sure
> about being a girl, needed another
> life, another image to remind me.
> And this was my worst guilt; you could not cure
> nor soothe it. I made you to find me.

And to the mother, an outraged voice with whom Sexton is to wrestle in almost every poem, a deferred reconciliation:

> You come, a brave ghost, to fix
> in my mind without praise
> or paradise
> to make me your inheritor.

While to herself the entire book stands as a valorization of the present, a way of facing up to a perishable existence, all transgressions acknowledged and even embraced—were they not the source of ecstasy? —and of recognizing the daily extinctions that make suicide not undesirable but unnecessary:

> Today the yellow leaves
> go queer. You ask me where they go. I say today believed
> in itself, or else it fell.

"Her first book, especially the best poems, spills into the second and somehow adds to it," Robert Lowell said when *All My Pretty Ones* was published in 1962: the title comes, of course, from the "one fell swoop" passage in *Macbeth,* in which the operative phrase, for Miss Sexton's retrospective purposes, quite defines the volume's enterprise:

> I cannot but remember such things were,
> That were most precious to me.

There is also an inner epigraph, parallel to the remark from Schopenhauer in the first collection, this time from a letter of Kafka's, to the effect that "a book should serve as the ax for the frozen sea within us." Thus the therapeutic requirement is still served, along with the memorial function, by these poems which, as Lowell remarked, pursue what Anne Sexton has always had in view, "the tongue's wrangle, the world's pottage, the rat's star," the minimal furniture, too, of a life confined but also privileged by madness, disease, death and violence to "spells and fetishes":

> I cannot promise very much.
> I give you the images I know.

Such knowledge has afforded the poet a certain abundance, and if the harshness of her concern makes us wonder with her "how anything fragile survives," there is in *All My Pretty Ones* an intimation of survival that is the more powerful, not the less, for its obsessive mortality. "Nothing is sure. No one. I wait in doubt," Anne Sexton confesses after surgery, "my stomach laced up like a football/for the game." Attending to herself between the periods when those other attendants must take over, she continues to catalog the ills not only the flesh is heir to, but the mind and the body politic as well, always convulsively yet with a vividness generally associated with a more sanguine view:

> Outside the bittersweet turns orange.
> Before she died my mother and I picked these fat
> branches, finding orange nipples
> on the gray wire strands.
> We weeded the forest, curing trees like cripples.

It is strong stuff and invariably brought to a devastating close—by postponed rhymes, or by pruning down the stanza to the simplest terminal phrase, standing alone as a line: "my son," or "I wish I were dead"—the cadences of agony, loss and division. What a relief when the design works against the poet's distemper, as in "The Abortion" and "The Operation," instead of surrendering—condescending, really —to the awfulness of it all. Such titles suggest Sexton's preoccupations, but not the lucid obstruction to sentimentality which her firm control, at her best, of the stanza and her fine colloquial diction set up. I cannot guess what another generation—before or after our own —might make of such incisions as this, from "Housewife":

> Men enter by force, drawn back like Jonah
> into their fleshy mothers.
> A woman *is* her mother.
> That's the main thing.

But abjuring incantation of any obvious kind for statement, choosing truth and taking the always discreditable consequences does not, for all that, mean that Anne Sexton has given over the oracular role, the Pythian occasion. Once she is on the tripod, it does not matter that images are extinguished, metaphors dissipated, words harrowed. What is left is a poem which utter necessity seems to have reduced

to absence and which, nonetheless, is acknowledged in such absence
as the image—the final image—of an absolute plenitude. Though
nothing is smooth or caressing here—it is a rough magic indeed that
Sexton, unlike Prospero, refuses to abjure—it is still "The Black Art"
she practices, as in the poem of that name:

> A woman who writes feels too much,
> those trances and portents!
> As if cycles and children and islands
> weren't enough; as if mourners and gossips
> and vegetables were never enough.
> She thinks she can warn the stars. . . .

By 1966, Miss Sexton had completed another book of poems, with
the almost expected, certainly self-parodying title *Live or Die*—from
Bellow's *Herzog,* and the quote goes on, in what I take to be an
exacerbated self-adjuration: "But don't poison everything"—and also
written a full-length, theater-of-the-mind play called *Tell Me Your
Answer True.* It is not surprising, after the tremendous series of
intimacies to which she has made us a party, to find now in any one
poem not only a case-history versified into its most painful crises, the
analects of continuing dissolution ("life enlarges, life takes aim"), but
also accounts of drug addiction, the bloody accidents of children, the
death by cancer of at least one parent, and certainly the disappearance
of God ("need is not belief").* A lessening of attention to what
happens in the poem, as Roethke prophesied, has obliged Sexton to
move into it every kind of event that can compel *our* shocked atten-

---

*Typical titles: "Menstruation at Forty," "Wanting to Die," "Pain for a Daughter,"
"Suicide Note." The accommodation of violence, always a matter of diminishing
returns, becomes, with its characteristic dependence on cruel verbs, the *raison d'être*
of whatever consecutive discourse is to be found in these poems:

> The thoroughbred has stood on her foot . . .
> The marks of the horseshoe printed
> into her flesh, the tips of her toes
> ripped off like pieces of leather,
> three toenails swirled like shells
> and left to float in blood in her riding boot.

tion, if not our assent, to that other world, the world where "I am the target." The poet's attitude toward her art is defined, I think, by the fact that many of the speeches in her garishly articulated psychodrama are the word-for-word texts of poems from the third collection, written out as prose and simply *uttered,* always by Daisy, the self-exploring heroine who is "tired of the gender of things":

> Dreams came into the ring
> like third-string fighters ...
> each one a bad bet
> who might win
> because there was no other.
>
> I stared at them
> concentrating on the abyss,
> the way one looks down into a rock quarry ...
>
> You taught me
> to believe in dreams,
> thus I was the dredger.
>
> I have come back
> but disorder is not what it was.
> I have lost the trick of it!
>
> I stand at this old window
> complaining ...
> allowing myself the wasted life.
>
> This is madness
> but a kind of hunger ....

However effective, and ultimately reductive, such utterance may sound within the play, the mere fact that it is set down there as merely spoken prose suggests what Sexton's entire career—"submerged in my own past/and my own madness"—has imposed upon her talent: the priestess' commitment to survival at the expense of artifice or appearance:

> To be occupied or conquered is nothing—
> to remain is all! ...

and again, from the final "affirmative" poem, "Live":

> Even so,
> I kept right on going on,
> a sort of human statement,
> lugging myself as if
> I were a sawed-off body
> in the trunk . . .

a hostage to the perpetuation of the self, even if it is in "the domain of silence,/the kingdom of the crazy and the sleeper." So assured, in these poems which won her a Pulitzer Prize, and in the ones to come after, is Anne Sexton of her hieratic position ("Everyone has left me/except my muse *that good nurse*") that she can afford, literally, to say anything and know that for all the dross it will be, in some way, a poem. "I am an identical being," she proclaims, and it might indeed be the sibyl talking, confident that what is said has its virulent, its vatic status because *she says it,* out of the welter of love, "that red disease," and of death, "an old belonging"—

> I am your daughter, your sweetmeat,
> your priest, your mouth and your bird
> and I will tell you all stories
> until I am laid away forever,
> a thin gray banner.

ROBERT BOYERS

Live or Die:
The Achievement
of Anne Sexton

Anne Sexton's *Live or Die* is the culmination, indeed the crowning achievement, of the confessional mode which has largely dominated American poetry in the last decade. No doubt, the very term "confessional poetry" may dismay many people, but it is a convenient catchall for the kind of work we have come to associate with the names of such poets as Robert Lowell, the late Sylvia Plath, W. D. Snodgrass, and Frederick Seidel, not to mention numerous other, if less distinguished, practitioners. Mr. Lowell's *Life Studies* is generally acknowledged as the driving force, perhaps even the inspiration for much of this poetry, and its influence on Miss Sexton's work has always been obvious. In her latest volume, though, Miss Sexton has brilliantly transcended, without wholly discarding, her allegiance to Lowell's verse, with its resolute dredging of a complex domestic past, its morbid self-disparagement, and its remorseless pursuit of an identity which is at once genuine and acceptable.

Miss Sexton's confessional, like Mr. Lowell's, is by no means wholly therapeutic in either purpose or effect. As Allen Alvarez recently remarked of Sylvia Plath's later poetry, the Freudian notion that the artist is relieved of his fantasies simply by expressing them does not hold water: "the act of formal expression merely makes the dredged-up material more readily available." In the case of Miss Plath, the full destructive potential of the material was released by her violently excessive straining for authenticity, by her unquenchable desire to examine what was most unthinkable in herself and in history. Miss Sexton's propensities are similarly violent and suicidal, but she convinces herself, and her reader, that she has something to live for. We are grateful to Miss Sexton as we can be to few poets, for she has distinctly enlarged and enhanced the possibilities of endurance in that air of lost connections which so many of us inhabit.

Miss Sexton's is a poetry of the nerves and heart. She is never abstract, never permits herself to be distracted from her one true subject—herself and her emotions. It is remarkable that she never flinches from the task at hand, never attempts to use her art as a device for warding off final perception. Unlike a poet like Frederick Seidel, she is willing to make her connections explicit. Her poems lack that hurtling momentum which keeps diverse elements in a sort of perpetual disrelation in the work of Seidel. Miss Sexton is painfully direct, and she refuses to keep her meaning at a tolerable distance. *Live or Die* projects an anguish which is profoundly disturbing precisely because its sources are effable, because the pressure of fantasy has not been permitted to distort or mediate Miss Sexton's vision.

One must admit that several poems in this volume are less than total successes. There are occasional crudities which should not be overlooked. Frequently, the debt to poets as far apart as Lowell, Roethke, and Emily Dickinson strikes one as almost obscenely unconcealed, nakedly thrusting itself before a gaping awareness. In the poem "Flee on Your Donkey," describing one of Miss Sexton's sojourns in a mental hospital, one is continually reminded of Mr. Lowell's poems on the same subject. One does not so much resent the echoing of details from Mr. Lowell as one resents the appropriation of his characteristic tone. And it is striking that whenever Miss Sexton mimics the man who was at one time her teacher, she comes off a very poor second. In the following passage, Miss Sexton sounds like a colorist, a collector of faintly absurd minutiae: "in another room someone tries to eat a shoe;/ meanwhile an adolescent pads up and down/ the hall in his white tennis socks." And later: "The permanent guests have done nothing new./ Their faces are still small/ like babies with jaundice." One shudders to compare this with lines from Mr. Lowell's "Waking In the Blue": "and see the shaky future grow familiar/ in the pinched, indigenous faces/ of these thoroughbred mental cases,/ twice my age and half my weight." At another point in her poem, Miss Sexton tries to establish a more detached vantage point. She vaguely wonders why she has returned to the institution that confines her, but concludes "what good are my questions/ in this hierarchy of death," precisely as Mr. Lowell concluded after mentally making the rounds: "What use is my sense of humor?" Even the names of places and people echo from *Life Studies,* including such familiars as Marlborough Street and L. L. Bean, but they lack resonance in Miss Sexton's poem.

In a few of these poems, Miss Sexton demonstrates a grasp of poetic nuance which is hardly satisfactory. Her similes are often imprecise, or simply gratuitous. In "Flee on Your Donkey," she writes: "recommitted,/ fastened to the wall like a bathroom plunger,/ held like a prisoner/ who was so poor/ he fell in love with jail." One must be excessively charitable to grant validity to Miss Sexton's "bathroom plunger." It does not in any way make more distinctively manifest Miss Sexton's anxiety over recommitment to the asylum. The effect of the second simile is even less justifiable, for it strikes one as wholly unnecessary and irrelevant, as a sort of very feeble joke having no relation to the dominating seriousness of the poem. Even in a beautiful little piece like "Three Green Windows," one has questions to ask about some of Miss Sexton's similes.

On occasion, the poet grows rather too self-conscious about her role as a writer. She wants us to be sure and listen very carefully, now. In one poem, "The Legend of the One-Eyed Man," she dictates "Do not think of the intense sensation/ I have as I tell you this/ but think only. . . ." In "Flee on Your Donkey," she takes measures to ensure we are solemn enough for what she has to convey: " . . . for this is a mental hospital,/ Not a child's game." Neither is the poet's taste always security against excessive self-dramatization, even spilling into undertones of self-pity. In "Two Sons" she announces "I grow old on my bitterness," and proceeds to establish the disparity between the bustling past and her present loneliness, only Miss Sexton never quite succeeds in evoking the gilded past which comes alive in the work of Mr. Lowell. Her writing is strangely flat and unaffecting where one would expect her to invest a great deal of nostalgic enthusiasm, as though she did not quite believe the memories of a more baroque and securely enclosed heritage: "I sit in an old lady's room/ where families used to feast/ where the wind blows in like soot/ from north-northeast." One would care more about the soot if one had more of the sense of decline which Miss Sexton obviously wished to convey.

Notwithstanding such defects as these, Miss Sexton is an extraordinarily accomplished artist. It is a mark of her distinction that one never hesitates to grant her the privilege of being wholly self-centered in her poems. There is no real inclination to insist that she get beyond the relatively narrow range of problems that haunt her, for her evocation of these problems gives them a resonance which is unmistakably general, universally relevant. Miss Sexton's is a poetry of victimization, in which she is at once victim and tormentor. She has an inalienable sense of guilt and responsibility which is rendered pathetic by her recognition of contingency and ultimate chaos in the world. In "The Legend of the One-Eyed Man," she identifies with Judas Iscariot, and one has no doubt that she is convinced of her own guilt: "look into my face/ and you will know that crimes dropped upon me/ as from a high building." She wants desperately to be judged, for if her sins can be legitimately punished, so too might she be the recipient of a grace which is nowhere forthcoming. But she lacks proper faith. Her imagination is too bizarre to relax with singular explanations. It is always playing with alternatives, wryly amusing possibilities. In "Protestant Easter," she recaptures the naive meanderings of an eight-year-old, skeptical about conventional legends, who wonders whether the resurrected Jesus was able to accomplish his "miracle" by mere sleight of hand. She thinks of a tunnel she used to hide in as a child: "Maybe Jesus knew my tunnel/ and crawled right through to the river/ so he could wash all the blood off."

The naive archness, even cuteness of this poem is far from characteristic of Miss Sexton, whose tone is generally severe and intense. Her abasement is frequently so extreme that it threatens to become either mawkish or simply unbearable, but she succeeds nonetheless. An instance of her daring and skill is "For the Year of the Insane," in which she struggles valiantly to escape what she is, to transcend her condition, the arrogance of a mind which demands explanations where there are none. Her obsession with words is seen as ugly and corrupt, a sign of insufficient spirituality. She forces herself into a posture of utter abasement, but the exacerbation of will is everywhere apparent. Indeed, the frightful tension and pain implicit in the acquiescence indicates that Miss Sexton's salvational ordeal can be only temporarily relieved. She cannot truly be innocent again, as she wants to be. She is too aware of guilt and pain, too self-conscious ever to be open and free and humbly grateful. During communion, reverently silent and deliberately pious, "I am handed wine as a child is handed milk." But the mood is quickly broken. Miss Sexton's awareness of herself, imperfect and sinful, intrudes: "I have this fear of coughing." She sips the wine clumsily: "I see two thin streaks burn down my chin./ I see myself as one would see another./ I have been cut in two."

Miss Sexton's continuing, and largely unsuccessful struggle is to escape the image of herself which dominates and in a sense pollutes her projections of future possibility. Part of her self-disgust is not uncommon. She is dissatisfied with her performance as mother and wife, though the demands she customarily lays on herself are hardly conventional. The intimacy of married life seems absurdly ludicrous, with strangers inhabiting a common situation, powerless to affect the essential loneliness of the individual psyche. In "Man and Wife," Miss Sexton's image beautifully evokes the futility of the marital arrangement, and the peculiarly insufficient intimacy it often involves: "Now they are together/ like strangers in a two-seater outhouse,/ eating and squatting together."

Miss Sexton is terribly annoyed with herself. She hates to be a spectacle, a nuisance. Though her past is a nightmare of grisly proportions, she cannot evade its urgent appeals to her consciousness. In "Those Times," probably the best single poem in this volume, Miss Sexton recounts the humiliations of a childhood marked by early sexual distress, and dominated by the sense that she was an unwanted expediency used by her mother "to keep Father/ from his divorce." She cannot really fight back, but withdraws instead. She delights in stillness, but fears everything. The young child is projected as "the me who stepped on the noses of dolls/ she couldn't break . . ./ They came from a mysterious country/ without the pang of birth,/ born quietly and well." What envy seethes in those lines, at once so fragile and violent! And what terrible transformations the poetic imagination at its best is capable of achieving. In "Those Times," the most conventionally beneficent phenomena are imbued with a quality of awesomeness that is both strange and disturbing. There is a sense of violent dislocation, as objects are ripped out of their familiar emotional contexts and charged with an electricity we had thought them incapable of transmitting. The rose in this poem becomes wholly different from what we expect, for its natural growth has been arrested. It is fixed in the endlessly repetitive, undeveloping pattern of wallpaper. The child thinks once, and then again, of "the same terrible rose repeating on the walls." What had been lovely and free to bloom and die in its own way is trapped, denied its autonomy.

The feeling is developed, made somewhat more explicit, in a further image, as the child hides from life in a closet, only to find that the inexorable voracity of her imagination inclines it to devour and transform everything, to invest the most mundane objects with an aura of menacing potency. An ordinary array of dresses is described as follows: "and then the dresses swinging above me,/ always above me, empty and sensible/ with sashes and puffs,/ with collars and two-inch hems/ and evil fortunes in their belts." The effect of these lines is to render everything intimidating, and to dwarf the huddling, frightened child by contrast. The experience which we have learned to live with, to tolerate as relatively benign and uncomplicated, appears suddenly to have acquired appalling dimensions. It is a revelation which brings us back to the root of things, to the nature of the freedom upon which we predicate our smugness, individually and collectively. The momentum of the poem marvelously prepares us to acquiesce in the development of Miss Sexton's vision, which grows more terrifying as it becomes more explicitly violent. The terrible rose becomes " . . . the wallpaper of the room/ where tongues bloomed over and over,/ bursting from lips like sea flowers—" and the window is described as " . . . an ugly eye/ through which birds coughed,/ chained to the heaving trees."

Everywhere in this volume the sense of entrapment is acute, and the spectre of violation is equally pervasive. The poetry is not correspondingly claustrophobic. The succession of images does not hammer one into painful submission before the spectacle of humanity furiously plundered and abandoned. Miss Sexton's ambience is severe, as suggested, but not torrential. At her best, the rhetoric is subdued. She employs irony as a counterpoint to intensity. In several poems, Miss Sexton expresses her sense of violation in terms of the sophisticated preoccupations "responsible" people are supposed to have, including a wide spectrum of items, from social problems and family affairs to literary fashions. She is always on the run from one thing or another, expressing in this the contours of an instinct for escape and purification which must obsess a great many of us. In "Walking in Paris," she announces "I have deserted my husband and my children,/ the Negro issue, the late news and the hot baths," but her construction of a new possibility, a new reality, is flawed. The patchwork cannot hide its seams, for the tone of longing and faint regret, and the consciousness of what must be left behind, cling in the mind like foul odors which cannot be washed away. Miss Sexton is brave, and resolute, but her essential honesty prevents her from any easy accessions of peace and renewal. She identifies herself with Zola's Nana, and with Nana's Paris, "as if I might clear off/ the made woman you became,/ withered and constipated." What pain and desire ring in her assertion that "to be occupied or conquered is nothing—to remain is all." One might almost be willing to tolerate such a sentiment, if only one could believe Miss Sexton capable of accepting it. Her longing is ultimately pathetic, however, and strangely beautiful in the very fact that it cannot be satisfied or assuaged. Miss Sexton must know, conjure as she will, that glorious invocations like "Come, my sister/ we are two virgins,/ our lives once more perfected/ and unused" cannot mitigate the pain she knows too well. There is a knowledge beyond words, which words must be forever powerless to affect.

The anonymity of Miss Sexton's oppressors makes her struggle all the more representative and relevant, for today we have all learned what it is like to perpetually stifle our complaints, not knowing to whom we can rightfully attribute a primary responsibility. Surrounded by middle-men, faceless bureaucrats and managers, we turn our anger inwards, growing bitter in the face of liberal platitudes about meaning well, respect for due process, and basic human frailty. Rarely, Miss Sexton erupts with a sputter of furious accusation, but she soon lapses into the tone of dogged, agonized reminiscence which we recognize. There is release, a kind of pyrrhic gratification, in a poem like "Cripples and Other Stories," with its "God damn it, father-doctor./ I'm really thirty-six./ I see dead rats in the toilet./ I'm one of the lunatics." But Miss Sexton knows that her father is only part of the story, a dubious source of her misery. She is confused about him, as about so many other things, earnestly groping for an image of consistency where there is always essential contradiction. She is mystified by tenderness, by apparently genuine displays of affection and whispers of love.

In search of an oppressor, of an object for the venomous resentment she carries in her like a knife, she seizes upon her mother in "Christmas Eve." The setting is evoked in words of bitter directness, memory stirred roughly as with a stick. Fiercely she stares at a portrait of her late mother, lighted by the multicolored bulbs of the Christmas tree: "Then they were a beehive,/ blue, yellow, green, red;/ each with its own juice, each hot and alive/ stinging your face. But you did not move." And later: "Then I thought of your body/ as one thinks of murder. . . ." One would suppose that passages of such ferocity would tend to alienate their witness, that the myopic eye of anguish, as one

critic said of Sylvia Plath's work, would so obliterate the contours of
the known and acceptable, that true participation on the part of
readers would be rendered highly unlikely. It is not so. In this poetry,
the passion to punish, to point an unswervingly accusatory finger, is
everywhere balanced by a conviction of personal failure, by an altogether remarkable complexity in single lines, where one cannot be
too hastily disposed to make absolute judgments. Even as the poet's
mother is mercilessly dissected, with a simultaneously obsessive and
self-conscious objectivity, there is a strange admixture of pervasive
sorrow, a regret for an intimacy that might have flourished. The object
of so much hatred and derision is a frail creature, pathetically human:
"Then I watched how the sun hit/ your red sweater, your withered
neck,/ your badly painted flesh-pink skin."

Where do such projections take us, and Miss Sexton? Presumably
to guilt, impatience with our collective inability to fix blame and at
least quell a bitterness that we more and more allow to turn inwards,
and ultimately to the final despair of suicidal negation. Miss Sexton
feels not only thwarted and impotent, but actively put upon, not only
violated, but regularly manipulated. While her writing resists overt
political commentary, she is very much aware of the unique character
of our century, of the levelling of standards and the rampant destruction of individual identity at the roots of mass society. This awareness
is reflected in "Self in 1958," where Miss Sexton sees herself as a
plaster doll, "with eyes that cut open without landfall or nightfall/
upon some shellacked and grinning person." The standard faces and
counterfeit courtesy of our civilization, with its regular diet of homi-
letic banalities shoveled out with impeccable execution by statesmen
and Presidents, is remarkably conveyed in that image of "some shellacked and grinning person." How Miss Sexton loathes the way in
which we have agreed to be dominated by the synthetic comforts we
crave. Her house is a doll's house, with neat little, carefully measured
cubicles thinly separated from one another, with "the all-electric
kitchen," "a cardboard floor," "a counterfeit table," and, in a description suggesting total alienation from the world modern technology
has wrought, "windows that flash open on someone's city,/ and little

more." The poet sees herself as a sort of free-floating element in a
world at once confining and inhospitable, a world she can in no way
embrace as belonging to her. She inhabits a universe which Robert
Lowell has described as "our monotonous sublime," in which we must
often wonder whom to properly acknowledge as the agents of our
actions. "Someone plays with me," complains Miss Sexton. "Someone
pretends with me—I am walled in solid by their noise." She knows
what is expected of her, that she also must pretend to satisfy others,
that she must show "no evidence of ruin or fears," no sign of the chaos
within her and the senseless terror and destruction outside of her. She
wants to flee from contingency, from her habits of acquiescence and
patient self-hatred. She wants to be transcendently beautiful, unclas-
sified, not a woman but something rare and detached, like the angelic
creatures in "Consorting with Angels," "each one like a poem obeying
itself,/ performing God's function,/ a people apart."

Miss Sexton concludes her sequence with a poem called "Live," an
affirmation of such "mundane" qualities as simple fortitude, self-
reliance, and love of dogs and children. The poem is a triumph of
determination and insight, a final resolution of irreconcilabilities that
had threatened to remain perpetually suspended and apart. Miss Sexton's affirmation represents a rebirth of astounding proportions, a
veritable reconstruction of her self-image in the face of a corrupt and
corrupting universe. The poet strengthens herself by struggling to
identify with her children, with the spontaneity of their responses to
life. Miss Sexton's indomitable need to engage the reality of her own
peculiar obsessions, jealousies, and cruelties does not spoil the poems
in which she draws ever closer to her children, but instead imbues
them with an air of desperation to which we cannot help responding.
In the midst of "A Little Uncomplicated Hymn" for the daughter she
names Joy, she fears that she is being dishonest, that she does not
deserve to sing songs of pure peace and harmony. She yearns to
participate in the innocent games and delightful fantasies of childhood, but she wonders, in another poem, watching her daughter's eyes
open after retreating under closed lids: "Perhaps they will say nothing,/ perhaps they will be dark and leaden,/ having played their own

game/ somewhere else,/ somewhere far off." As always, the poet is beset by uncertainties. She is still dependent, even with relation to her young daughter. She cannot take the initiative.

What Miss Sexton comes to see in the course of her book, covering three stormy years, is that to maintain innocence, an openness to life and a regular communion with diverse phenomena, the child must be oblivious to certain fundamental considerations. The innocence of the child is really nothing less than an ability to live blithely in the face of contingency, to live as though we held the key to our own fate. In "Your Face on the Dog's Neck," Miss Sexton recoils at her daughter's pastoral intimacy with "this spayed and flatulent bitch," "that infectious dog," but she sees that to truly enter the child's world, to partake of her simple vision, she must banish her inveterate hesitancy, and embrace life joyously in all its soiled and spotted variety. She must not be too mindful of the neighbor's symbolic lawnmower, as it " . . . bites and spits out/ some new little rows of innocent grass."

Miss Sexton's salvation lies in her twin capacities for irony and love. At moments of intense depression, she retains an attitude of sardonic anger towards herself and towards a world which will not help her. This sardonic streak, obviously also a component of Miss Plath's later work, intermittently erupts as a peculiarly laughable and bitter form of self-mockery, as in "The Addict," where she describes herself as "the queen of this condition," "something of a chemical/mixture./ That's it!" and "a little buttercup in my yellow nightie." This poem is wonderfully effective in the way it undercuts the terrible worry and concern that originally occasioned the poem. Miss Sexton seems genuinely amused that her condition should have progressed as far as it has, that she is indeed a grotesque spectacle, as unbearable to herself as she must be to others. The irony, the mockery, has as its object, of course, a distancing, making tolerable that which is too painful to contemplate. The literary antecedents for such an aesthetic device are legion, though rarely has an artist been so deft and inventive as Miss Sexton in carrying it to great extremes. Aside from the aesthetic accomplishment, though, a poem like "The Addict" permits Miss Sexton to step back from herself, from the image of herself with which she is so constantly at odds. It permits her, that is, to accomplish, even if only for a moment, what she so desperately wanted—to escape the self-absorption which has kept her a prisoner of her own fantasies and delusions. The control implicit in the poet's manipulation of her self-image for aesthetic purposes becomes demonstration of a capacity which had for too long lain unused and forgotten.

Miss Sexton's poems, then, come as close as we can expect anyone to come to that creation of a poetic universe which is at the same time a re-creation of the self, a restructuring of a general orientation to reality. As such, it is invigorating and significant in a way we had not thought great poetry could any longer be: it renews our capacity for delight and joy in the created world of the poem, and in the world of men which we inhabit. There is something awesome, even sublime in a woman who is not afraid to sound crude or shrill so long as she is honest, who in her best work sounds neither shrill nor crude precisely because she is honest. At the end of this long journey, this dark night of the soul, Miss Sexton emerges triumphant, deciding not to kill the eight inconvenient Dalmatian puppies everyone advises her to drown: "I promise to love more if they come,/ because in spite of cruelty/ and the stuffed railroad cars for the ovens,/ I am not what I expected. Not an Eichmann./ The poison just didn't take./ So I won't hang around in my hospital shift,/ repeating the Black Mass and all of it." Miss Sexton's decision to live, with her eyes open, and the responsibility for human values planted firmly on her competent shoulders, is a major statement of our poetry.

JANE McCABE

"A Woman Who Writes": A Feminist Approach to the Early Poetry of Anne Sexton

Not that it was beautiful,
but that, in the end, there was
a certain sense of order there;
something worth learning
in that narrow diary of my mind,
in the commonplaces of the asylum

At first it was private.
Then it was more than myself;
it was you, or your house
or your kitchen.

(*BPWB* 51)[1]

Anne Sexton was not and never claimed to be a feminist. Although many feminist critics have tried to claim her, they have had to turn a deaf ear to some of her best poetry to do so. So much of Sexton's flirtatious parading, her glamorous posing, her sexual exhibitionism —understandable and forgivable—is clearly unacceptable to a feminist's sense of the sources of her own value. But, like so much poetry by contemporary women, Sexton's poems about personal experience often point to larger issues; although she does not necessarily offer any solutions, many of her poems isolate and describe the difficulties of being a woman in our society. And this is of course a subject of primary interest to any feminist.

The sources of Anne Sexton's poetry are her own life, what happens in "that narrow diary of my mind." Her poems are about personal relationships and about the intensities of her own emotions. She actually began writing poetry as a kind of therapy following a nervous breakdown, and it is clear that by an ordering of experience through language, she is trying to discover and accept herself. Conversely, she, like any committed artist, is after that "sense of order," that way of giving form to experience which transforms "commonplaces" into art. And unless we are content to remain voyeurs rather than critics, or to consider Sexton as a personality rather than as a poet, we must ask that her poetry be about more than the private life of Anne Sexton. And I believe that much of it is.

Sexton is intent on finding ways to think and feel about the female body—in heterosexual, homosexual, even onanistic contexts. She is especially concerned with sexual, extramarital relations with men, and much of her poetry is charged with the energy and tensions that come from those relations. But the special, nonsexual relations with women—her mother, her sister, her daughters, her friends—are also central to her poetry.

Anne Sexton was brought up to be an affluent, middle-class, suburban housewife. In a 1968 interview, she said,

> All I wanted was a little piece of life, to be married, to have children. . . . I was trying my damnedest to lead a conventional life, for that was how I was brought up, and it was what my husband wanted of me. But one can't build little white picket fences to keep the nightmares out.[2]

And I think that Sexton differed from most of her successful female peers in that when she wasn't in the hospital, she lived in comfort behind the white picket fences. She was not urban; she was not an academic (her formal education ended at Garland Junior College); and she was not really an intellectual. She lived very comfortably— a sunken living room, a swimming pool—in suburban Weston, Massachusetts: the look of the country, the convenience of town. But this life worried her; she felt personally at odds with its rather dismal comforts. And although she played her part—"I ... answered the phone,/ served cocktails as a wife/ should, made love among my petticoats,/ and August tan ... "—she was also concerned with the pressure of isolation and uneasy with the particular kind of social expectation that faces a suburban housewife, especially one who is also a poet. She defined her alienation as witchery, and as a "middle-aged witch" she had the magic of words with which to transform even the calmest and most orderly of suburban lawns into a landscape of both nightmare and vision. And this often led her to explore the dangerous borderland between imagination and insanity:

> I have gone out, a possessed witch,
> haunting the black air, braver at night;
> dreaming evil, I have done my hitch
> over the plain houses, light by light:
> lonely thing, twelve-fingered, out of mind.
> A woman like that is not a woman, quite.
> I have been her kind.
>
> (*BPWB*, 21)

And that kind is "a woman who writes." So, although I would not suggest that Anne Sexton is a feminist poet, I think that her poetry catches the feminist's eye and ear in special ways. Many of her experiences and feelings are the product of a society that oppresses women. The anger and excess that run through so much of her poetry are uniquely hers, but there are echoes of the same kind of rage in the poetry of many of her more explicitly feminist contemporaries.

Feminist critic Suzanne Juhasz says: "Until the twentieth century, there was no body of poetry by women in English. Now one exists." This seems fair enough. But she goes on to suggest not only that we suddenly have a great deal of writing by women, but that it is signifi-

cantly different from the writing by contemporary men; that it constitutes, in fact, a "new tradition." She calls the old tradition
"masculine: an expression and reflection of the male norms and values
of a patriarchal cultures."[3] I instinctively agree with such assessments
and find myself thinking in terms of "domination," "colonialism,"
"capitalism," law rather than love, greed instead of generosity, publicity instead of intimacy. And I know that these "male norms and
values" affect men too and make them suffer as well as women. But
they suffer differently.

It is certainly not difficult to argue that sexual difference is significant; what is terribly difficult is to define the terms of that significance
and at the same time to avoid the kind of qualitative statements that
determined the sexual stereotypes in the first place. From the very
beginning of the "second wave" of feminism, female literary critics
with strong sympathies for the movement have been making easy or
uneasy attempts to talk about women writers in new ways and to
establish, like Juhasz, that women writers are not simply writing
more, but that they are writing differently from their male peers, using
language in a way unavailable to male poets. In a recent anthology,
Psyche: The Feminine Poetic Consciousness, which gives considerable
space to Anne Sexton's work, the editors insist that "a private personal voice and almost solipsistic vision, an overly modest opinion of
her own worth, a conflict between passivity and rebellion against the
male-oriented universe" are "typical of the women poet."[4] The anthology is valuable and full of diversity; it is a genuine celebration of
the "Feminine Poetic Consciousness," but in its introduction it comes
dangerously near to suggesting that that consciousness is *by its nature,*
rather than as a result of cultural pressure, passive, vain, private, and
low in public self-esteem.

This has a familiar, unpleasant ring; these are not states of mind
that anyone should especially celebrate. An analogous argument is
that the experience of living in a patriarchal society alters the sensibility in such a way that when a woman writes poetry, the aesthetic
result is significantly different from the comparable result in poetry
written by men. I am willing to agree that an altered sensibility might

well result in an altered poetry, that a life of privacy will offer different kinds of insights from a life lived mostly under public scrutiny; but I am quite unable to discuss—in aesthetic terms—the difference between the poetry of men in general and the poetry of women. And in fact, when they actually discuss the work of individual poets, the editors of *Psyche* pay most attention to *what* those women are writing about rather than the way they write it. For example, they claim, in a rather sweeping fashion, that Anne Sexton's poetry "catalogues most of the significant events that can happen in a woman's life."[5] But they don't describe how her manner of cataloguing is in any way particularly female. Suzanne Juhasz tries a different method. She makes a distinction between "feminine" and feminist poetry (the quotation marks are hers). The first kind includes writing in which the poet's female identity is clear, poetry in which the "feminine experience contributes more directly to the themes and the forms"[6] of the poems. In feminist poetry, however, the poet realizes and analyzes the political implications of being both female and a poet. According to Juhasz, Sexton, along with Sylvia Plath and Denise Levertov, falls into the first category. This, like her book's opening statement, seems fair enough. But she pushes it too far when she goes on to say that Sexton's "therapy was occasioned by her womanhood itself, by the very real strains and conflicts that Sexton experienced while attempting to exist in her world as a woman."[7] How could Juhasz possibly know this?

The politics of the present women's movement is unique in that it is based on small, private groups of women talking to each other, realizing the wealth and potential of their commonality, and recognizing perhaps the sources, certainly the results, of their separation from each other. I have found no better description of this process than in these lines from a poem by Adrienne Rich:

> Two women sit at a table by a window. Light breaks
> unevenly on both of them.
>
> Loneliness has been part of their story for twenty years,
>
> While they speak the lightning flashes purple.

It is strange to be so many women,
eating and drinking at the same table,
those who bathed their children in the same basin
who kept secrets from each other
walked the floors of their lives in separate rooms
and flow into history now as the woman of their time
living in the prime of life
as in a city where nothing is forbidden
and nothing is permanent.[8]

Clearly, women poets are now writing about certain subjects from perspectives unavailable to men. Sexton, for example, writes about masturbation, abortion, female sexuality, being a mother, having daughters. But you could also say that if and when they write, poor people, black people, city people, or for that matter Norwegians have different perspectives from rich people, farmers, Parsees, and Turks. The questions for literary critics are: Are women using the language differently? Are the availability of various "new" subjects—the experience of childbirth or menopause, the oppression of housework, the female experience of sex—and an insistence on a revised attitude toward these subjects strong enough criteria to be the basis of a new *tradition* of poetry? Has there been a break as significant as that from Pope to Wordsworth, or from Tennyson to Eliot?

Much of the poetry by contemporary women is written in anger; the voice often rages after it recognizes its oppression, suppression. Diane Wakoski, Alta, Robin Morgan spring to mind here. But in this context Anne Sexton does not. Her biggest enemy seems to be herself; her mind leads her into dangerous, sometimes thrilling places, away from love of herself, away from life. She rarely accuses. In "Wanting To Die" (*LD*, 58), she explains:

Since you ask, most days I cannot remember.
I walk in my clothing, unmarked by that voyage.
Then the almost unnameable lust returns.

To thrust all that life under your tongue!—
that, all by itself, becomes a passion.
Death's a sad bone; bruised, you'd say,

and yet she waits for me, year after year,
to so delicately undo an old wound,
to empty my breath from its bad prison.

Balanced there suicides sometimes meet,
raging at the fruit, a pumped-up moon,
leaving the bread they mistook for a kiss,

leaving the page of the book carelessly open,
something unsaid, the phone off the hook
and the love, whatever it was, an infection.

Surely the anger of poets like Wakoski, Alta, and Morgan is aestheti-
cally more limiting than Sexton's self-destructiveness. Wakoski, for
example, begins one poem,

God damn it,
at last I am going to dance on your grave,
old man;
          you've stepped on my shadow once too often,
you've been unfaithful to me with other women,
women so cheap and insipid it psychs me out to think I might
ever
be put
in the same category with them;

*†. I'm going to dance on your grave
because you are
          dead
          dead
          dead
under the earth with the rest of the shit,[9]

The world perceived through anger is, in many ways, a world that can
be plotted in straight lines. As with all flat worlds, the danger lies in
falling off. As Wallace Stevens wrote in "Esthétique du Mal," the
dilemma is that of

          . . . the lunatic of one idea
          In a world of ideas, who would have all the people
          Live, work, suffer and die in that idea
          In a world of ideas.

Through anger, the truth looks simple. And it may even be necessary to reduce the world and even truth to radical simplicity in order to find ways of leading anger back to its source; but simple anger never was the proper mode for art. We want poetry to be rich in ambiguity, subtlety, and passion. When necessary, we always want to insist on having it both or even several ways. Anne Sexton is inconsistent and contradictory and cannot be stuffed into a single category of writers, and she is consequently a far more interesting poet than Wakoski or Alta or Morgan.

I am not suggesting that feminist poetry loses *anything* by its insistence on making political as well as aesthetic statements; Adrienne Rich, for example, is able to do both brilliantly. Robin Morgan, on the other hand, often throws aesthetic considerations out the window. Good feminist poetry is rare, and what defines it as feminist are its lines of inquiry rather than its aesthetic mode. And feminist criticism, as one critic put it, is "criticism whose first loyalties are political. Its major lines of inquiry tend to be into the distortions and limitations that a male culture has imposed on women";[10] it should not insist on a new consideration of style.

Nevertheless, in discussing the poetry of Anne Sexton, a poet who in all her writing insisted on an explicitly female persona, it is impossible to avoid making something of how she experienced herself as a woman. Women experience the world through different bodies than men. This is nowhere more clear than in Sexton's poetry. It simply feels different to be a woman and will continue to feel different even in the most "liberated" society. It feels different to move, to have sex, to stand up, to sleep.

But although women and men do not and will never share the same kind of body, they do share the same language. Of course, we all use language according to the occasion; we talk differently to the motor vehicle clerk than we do to our lovers. Public talk has a different cadence than private talk. But women cannot claim to have introduced a personal, colloquial language into poetry. Perhaps they use it more naturally now because they are more thoroughly used to it, but it cannot be said to have been invented by women as a new approach to poetry. Wordsworth, after all, wanted in 1800 "to choose incidents and situations from common life, and to relate or describe them, throughout, as far as was possible in a selection of language really used by men. . . . My purpose was to imitate, and, as far as possible to adopt the very language of men. . . . " And we think of Whitman or Williams or Ginsberg or Lowell or a dozen other male poets.

What is unfortunately significant about the literature of women, as of other oppressed groups—the working class, ethnic minorities—is its scarcity. And this startling absence of literary record makes Juhasz's opening statement ("there was no body of poetry by women. . . . Now one exists") really very important. But finally this kind of observation leads mainly to social and political rather than aesthetic judgments. Of course, if you listen to the language of black preachers, the talk of black kids on street corners, the way men talk to each other in working-class bars, or the way working-class women talk to each other over back fences, you are likely to hear different rhythms of speech, a different vocabulary than you might hear in academic middle-class discussions. But good poets—black, white, rich, poor, male, female—tend to have waggling ears and pick up what's alive in contemporary speech even if it is not the way that they talk to their mothers or students. Eliot, Lowell, Berryman. . . .

Still, I *am* a feminist critic and am very interested in the writing of contemporary women, work which often exhibits an exciting sense of power, of political solidarity, and a sense that there is an audience sympathetic to what they have to say—willing to identify the poet's experience as either imaginatively or actually their own, and who are grateful for the talent that can articulate those experiences. Like many contemporary black poets, women poets have to some extent created a new audience—people who did not read poetry as a habit but who began to understand that they were being addressed.

Now I want to write more directly about Anne Sexton, about her as a woman and as a poet, and about how those two identities were connected. It is probably true that Sexton's work would not have its present stature if Robert Lowell's pioneering "confessional" writing had not preceded it, or if she had not written in a time when there were shelves in bookstores marked "Women's Studies," or, more likely, if she had not led such a dramatic and tragic life. But she once remarked to one of her students, "No, I do not want to be known as the mad suicide poet, the live Sylvia Plath." And, taking her at her word, I do not want to write about her this way. What I am interested in here are the poems that would have survived without Robert Lowell, without the vogue of Women's Studies, and without the current morbid and destructive fascination with the connection between creativity and suicide.

I want, for the most part, to talk about the early poems, quite simply because they are Sexton's best poems. In her last four books, turned out at an increasingly rapid rate, she became more and more obsessed with death in a strangely religious way. Unfortunately, this obsession seemed to make her lose control of her language at the same time that she lost control of her life. *Nothing* remained private; the dynamic relation between private and public faded into a simple publicizing of the private—quite a different thing. Although she could clearly still turn a good line, they became random; the poet no longer seemed to be self-critical and she handed her public whatever occurred to her, in whatever form it occurred. It seems to me that Anne Sexton is a good poet in her early books, less so in the last ones, and that there is little value in laboring over poetry which she herself knew was diminishing in quality even as it increased in quantity.

Until *Transformations,* Sexton was concerned with herself mainly as a regular woman. The early poems about witchery, like "Her Kind" and "Black Art," are really about the life of the imagination for a woman who has the magic of language in her thrall. In the later, God-obsessed poems, she became truly a frightening figure, but it is the power of the obsession, not the language, that inspires fear:

> I am not lazy
> I am on the amphetamine of the soul.
> I am, each day,

> typing out the God
> my typewriter believes in.
> Very quick. Very intense,
> like a wolf at a live heart.
> Not lazy.
> When a lazy man, they say,
> looks toward heaven,
> the angels close their windows.
>   (*ARTG,* 76)

In her best poems, Anne Sexton is writing about herself as a woman
not a witch, about her relationships with men, and more successfully
about her relationships with women, as the daughter of a mother, the
mother of daughters. Successful, too, are the poems in which she
explores herself as a woman poet, poems in which the pressures of
"feminine" expectation on the middle-class suburban housewife are
countered by the forces of creativity. Juhasz says, "A woman is not
defined by a profession, such as poet, but by her personal relationships
as daughter, sister, wife, mother."[11] True as this may often be, in
Sexton's case her profession *was* poet, a profession which for her often
meant giving aesthetic meaning to personal relationships, to what it
means to be "daughter, sister, wife, mother."

Sexton is often caught in what is a uniquely feminine trap of simultaneously celebrating herself, exploiting herself, letting herself be exploited, and apologizing for herself. This seems especially true in her
poems about men. Her uncertainty about her body as she displays
it, exploits it, and denies it is certainly a feminist issue. In her best
poems, she is trying to clear away what is irrelevant and to find affirmation in a self that so often hides behind both a sense of glamor
and a sense of ugliness. In "You, Doctor Martin" (*BPWB,* 3), she
states with measured triumph, "I am queen of all my sins/ forgotten.
Am I still lost?/ Once I was beautiful. Now I am myself. . . . " But
despite the affirmation, the question still nags. The poem that follows
begins with an epigraph from Thoreau, "Not til we are lost . . . do we
begin to find ourselves," and ends with Sexton saying, brave but
frightened:

And opening my eyes, I am afriad of course
to look—this inward look that society scorns—
Still, I search in these woods and find nothing worse
than myself, caught between the grapes and the thorns.

One of the most interesting aspects of Sexton's poetry is her attempt
first to identify which are the grapes, which the thorns, and then to
decide which to choose. The thorns, for her, were very tempting, not
only for their obviously suicidal attraction, but as one version of
sexual identity that was masochistic:

You have seen my father whip me.
You have seen me stroke my father's whip.
(*DN*, 16)

But more interesting is the attempt to identify "myself" once it has
sprung free of what catches it. Sexton is very uneasy with her femaleness; she writes to her daughter:

I, who was never quite sure
about being a girl, needed another
life, another image to remind me.
And this was my worst guilt; you could not cure
nor soothe it. I made you to find me.
(*BPWB*, 61)

After looking at all those glamorous pictures on the backs of her
books, and listening to lines like,

So tell me anything but track me like a climber
for here is the eye, here is the jewel,
here is the excitement the nipple learns,
(*LP*, 5)

or

Loving me with my shoes off
means loving my long brown legs,
sweet dears, as good as spoons;
(*LP*, 35)

I am at first surprised that she "was never quite sure about being a girl," but taking a closer look, I see that in most of the poems about her body, she is offering it rather than claiming it; men often create it for her:

> Once it was a boat, quite wooden
> ... It was no more
> than a group of boards. But you hoisted her, rigged her.
> She's been elected
>
> ... Where there was silence
> The drums, the strings are incurably playing. You did this
> Pure genius at work. . . .
>
> (*LP*, 3)

And there are many more examples in poems like "Mr. Mine," "Us," and "Barefoot," where she says

> And I'm your barefoot wench for a
> whole week. Do you care for salami?
> No. You'd rather not have a scotch?
> No. You don't really drink. You do
> drink me.
>
> (*LP*, 35)

Alone with her body in "The Ballad of the Lonely Masturbator," she is angered, abandoned, betrayed:

> I break out of my body this way,
> an annoying miracle. Could I
> put the dream market on display?
> I am spread out. I crucify.
>
> (*LP*, 33)

So, for all the ostensible glamor and sexual confidence in Sexton's poetry, there is an increasingly clear sense that her body is only hers and admirable when it is given to men. In so many of her poems about extramarital affairs, she is hopelessly sentimental:

> We were in our bodies
> (that room will bury us)
> and you were in my body
> (that room will outlive us)
> and at first I rubbed your
> feet dry with a towel
> because I was your slave
> and then you called me princess.
> Princess!
>
> (*LP,* 41)

But the travestied Magdalen turns angry, bitter, or despondent when she describes her marriage—she sees it mainly as a trap. In "Man and Wife," for example, she says:

> We are not lovers.
> We do not know each other.
> We look alike
> but we have nothing to say.
>
> A soldier is forced to stay with a soldier
> because they share the same dirt
> and the same blows.
>
> (*LD,* 27)

This is, by the way, amazingly close to Adrienne Rich's description of *her* "Marriage in the Sixties":

> Today we stalk
> in the raging desert of our thought
> whose single drop of mercy is
> each knows the other there.
> Two strangers, thrust for life upon a rock,
> may have at last the perfect hour of talk
> that language aches for; still—
> two minds, two messages.[12]

But Sexton becomes more vindictive. In "Again and Again and Again," she writes,

> Oh the blackness is murderous
> and the milk tip brimming
> and I will kiss you when
> I cut up one dozen new men
> and you will die somewhat,
> again and again.
>
> (*LP,* 29)

The problem—clearly unresolved in these poems—is that identity cannot be had vicariously, either by giving yourself away to emerge through someone else or by revenge. It is, I suppose, a common enough problem, but I think women more often than men tend to seek identity through sexual relationships. The social pressure simply to find a mate is clearly heavier on women, and this is partly because women have been taught that theirs is the domain of love, affection, and intimacy; that is their share of the marriage pact. Men too are burdened in marriage, but it is with more public duties—to support, provide, protect, to stand between the family and the outside world. Schematic and simplistic as this may sound, I really think that to suffer the whip and also to stroke it, to want to be both slave and princess, to dance while the man builds a museum ("Mr. Mine," *LP,* 43) suggests a kind of self-denial that is a particularly feminine trait. The point, easily said, difficult to live out, is to love yourself—and this includes, of course, loving your own body—so that love from others, when it comes, is an even exchange, one which does not demand a blending, which does not provide identity but simply illuminates it. Anne Sexton *knows* this when she says to one daughter:

> What I want to say, Linda,
> is that there is nothing in your body that lies.
> All that is new is telling the truth.
> I'm here, that somebody else,
> an old tree in the background.
>
> Darling,
> stand still at your door,
> sure of yourself, a white stone, a good stone—
> as exceptional as laughter

> you will strike fire,
> that new thing!
> *(LD,* 64–65)

and even more complexly to the other,

> Today, my small child, Joyce,
> love your self's self where it lives.
> There is no special God to refer to; or if there is,
> why did I let you grow
> in another place. . . .
>
> *(BPWB, 54)*

She is telling her female children to do what she could never do, and even in the telling strangles herself with guilt. What at first seems ostentatious self-love in Sexton's poems, the startling glamor, finally hides the frightened child who thrives on the love of others and is afraid that she is unloveable. I am not saying that men do not, or even should not, thrive on love; I am saying that women are *expected* to, and, so very often, they offer themselves in ways that leave little of that self for *them* to love. Sexton's need is made quite clear in "The Touch," a poem which opens with her looking abstractly at her hand as if it were foreign to her: "For months my hand had been sealed off/ in a tin box." But after some elaboration, she admits that after all it is really "An ordinary hand—just lonely/ for something to touch/ that touches back." She is unsatisfied with the animal affection of her dogs, who like her indiscriminately—"I'm no better than a case of dogfood." Her sisters "live in school" and her parents seem to reserve their affection for each other; her father "lives in a machine made by my mother/ and well oiled by his job, his job." The answer finally comes from the inevitably male "you."

> Your hand found mine,
> Life rushed to my fingers like a blood clot.
> Oh, my carpenter,
> the fingers are rebuilt.
>
> *(LP,* 2)

In "The Farmer's Wife," one of the few poems in *To Bedlam and Part Way Back* written in the third person, Sexton discusses the dreary life of a farm couple in Illinois, where for ten years "she has been his habit." At night, habitually, "he'll say/ honey bunch let's go" and she does not really mind; she even wants "the raucous bed . . ./ the slow braille touch of him/ like a heavy god grown light," but although she says nothing, she wonders if there shouldn't be "more to living/ than this brief bright bridge" of sex; and when the sex is over,

> it leaves her still alone,
> built back again at last,
> mind's apart from him, living
> her own self in her own words
> and hating the sweat of the house.
>
> (*BPWB*, 27)

Depressing as this is, she finds something strong in her aloneness; she is "built back again at last" as herself; her separateness from him is part of her strength. The quality of this strength is not unlike that longed for in Sylvia Plath's "Lesbos," when from the stench of the smoky kitchen she imagines herself, like the moon, "normal,/ Hard and apart and white." But this is not how Sexton's housewife imagines her liberation from the "sweat of the house." She reimagines her husband not herself. And the result is a maimed, and therefore weakly romantic, figure.

> She wishes him cripple, or poet,
> or even lonely; or sometimes
> better, my lover, dead.
>
> (*BPWB*, 27)

The last line, of course, is slightly ambiguous. Does she wish him dead so she can indulge herself in dramatic mourning, or so that she can find another life? Had he been cripple, poet (an interesting twist), lonely, or dead, her sensibility, stifled by "their local life in Illinois," might find an airhole, but it would not be her own. It remains a pathetic situation, understandable enough but of no good to anyone.

So the search for "myself, caught between the grapes and the thorns" cannot be conducted in bed. The search in Sexton's poetry seems more imaginatively right when she turns to the women in her family: her great-aunt, her mother, and her daughters. Here the need for love, the giving of it, and its acceptance and rejection are much more real:

> I will speak of the little childhood cruelties,
> being a third child,
> the last given
> and the last taken—
>
> being the unwanted, the mistake
> that Mother used to keep Father
> from his divorce.
> Divorce!
>
> (*LD*, 29)

Feeling unloved and unwanted, Sexton (it seems clear that we are to make no or very little distinction between poet and speaker) describes how she would hide in the closet all day waiting, yet afraid to grow up, silently enduring the humiliations of childhood. She refers to her mother as "the large one" and seems to fear that growing up might mean becoming her mother. In an earlier poem, "Housewife," she insists, "A woman *is* her mother./ That's the main thing" (*AMPO*, 48). And it is a trap. But this later poem, "Those Times," ends in a celebrated liberation from "the large one"—the sense that she is not doomed to become her mother, that she can be both a woman and a mother on her own terms:

> I did not know the woman I would be
> nor that blood would bloom in me
> each month like an exotic flower,
> nor that children,
> two monuments,
> would break from between my legs
> two cramped girls breathing carelessly,
> each asleep in her tiny beauty.
> I did not know that my life, in the end,
> would run over my mother's like a truck

> and all that would remain
> from the year I was six
> was a small hole in my heart, a deaf spot,
> so that I might hear
> the unsaid more clearly.
>
> (*LD*, 32)

In what is surely one of Sexton's best poems, "The Double Image," this celebrated liberation is much more complex. The poem begins in impressive, even elegant simplicity, and in subject even in its elegaic tone echoes Hopkins' "Spring and Fall":

> I am thirty this November.
> You are still small, in your fourth year.
> We stand watching the yellow leaves go queer,
> flapping in the winter rain,
> falling flat and washed. And I remember
> mostly the three autumns you did not live here.
> They said I'd never get you back again.
> I tell you what you'll never really know:
> all the medical hypothesis
> that explained my brain will never be as true as these
> struck leaves letting go.
>
> (*BPWB*, 53)

It is a melancholy meditation on time; watching the year die, the poet is reminded that she chose to die soon after the birth of her second child, the child addressed in this poem. Throughout the poem, the forces of life and the forces of death intermingle. When the child becomes ill, just months after her birth, the mother feels that she is somehow to blame. Then in almost Faustian exchange,

> The day life made you well and whole
> I let the witches take away my guilty soul.
> I pretended I was dead.

In keeping with the title, "The Double Image," there is a similar exchange later in the poem. As the mother becomes increasingly "well and whole," *her* mother begins to die:

> They hung my portrait in the chill
> north light, matching
> me to keep me well.
> Only my mother grew ill.
> She turned from me as if death were catching,
> as if death transferred. . . .
>
> (*BPWB*, 56)

The seven sections are connected by recurring double images that are skillfully bound together in a strong rhyme scheme. The poet's control here in itself suggests one of the poem's subjects, the need to grasp the past in order to take control of the future. Sexton's tone varies from meditative elegy to jaunty balladry and this also signals the return of the poet to life, health, and motherhood. It is a complex and very moving poem in which Sexton tries to deal with the guilt she feels for abandoning her child, and the guilt she feels about her mother abandoning her.

> That August you were two, but I timed my days with doubt.
> On the first of September she looked at me
> and said I gave her cancer.
> They carved her sweet hills out
> and still I couldn't answer.

The ferocity and unfairness of the accusation underlined by the strict memory of the exact date—"On the first of September"—emphasize the intensity of guilt; a sudden lyricism in the line, "They carved your sweet hills out," coupled with the horror of its meaning suggest a terrible confusion: "and still I couldn't answer." Precision disappears and neither the answer nor its question is clear.

Portraits of mother and daughter face each other; daughter sees in her mother

> . . . my mocking mirror, my overthrown
> love, my first image. . . .

> And this was the cave of the mirror,
> that double woman who stares
> at herself as if she were petrified
> in time—. . . .

And then, looking at her child, she also sees herself:

> And you resembled me; unaquainted
> with my face, you wore it. But you were mine
> after all.

How can she escape the inevitability of generation? How can time become unpetrified; how can it be stopped from repeating itself? If her mother is unable to forgive her attempt at suicide, will her child be able to?

The poem, then, is about the struggle against the notion that life can only be purchased with death. It also explores Sexton's uncertainty about herself as a woman. It is an uncertainty that is never really resolved for her. In a very late poem, she is still writing:

> The trouble with being a woman, Skeezix,
> is being a little girl in the first place.
> Not all the books in the world will change that.
> I have swallowed an orange, being a woman.
> You have swallowed a ruler, being a man.
> Yet waiting to die we are the same thing.
>
> (DN, 63)

But in "The Double Image," an earlier, more optimistic, more interesting poem, Sexton is trying to figure out a way to be a different kind of woman, one who does not swallow oranges. And so finally this poem is about learning to love oneself so that love for others is possible.

> . . . And I had to learn
> why I would rather
> die than love. . . .
>
> (BPWB, 58)

The advice that Sexton gives her daughter in the first part—"love yourself's self where it lives"—is the advice that she is ultimately trying to give herself. It involves cutting through debilitating, petrifying guilt—what she believed was "an old debt I must assume." She must face herself when she faces her mother and her daughter, and this means trusting what it means to be a woman. She acknowledges her connections, the reflections of herself that she sees in her mother and her child, but refuses to be entirely bound by them. She needs to find herself in her own present as well as in the past and future versions of herself that she sees in her mother and her daughter; the reflection, after all, is bound to distort.

"The Double Image" is artful therapy; in explaining her absence to her child, she is also explaining it to herself, working her way slowly part way back from Bedlam. In the poem's final section, the child identifies her mother, names her *mother,* and claims her in simple need:

> ... You scrape your knee. You learn my name,
> wobbling up the sidewalk, calling and crying.
> You call me *mother* and I remember my mother again,
> somewhere in greater Boston, dying.
>
> (*BPWB,* 61)

The witches that enforce the false guilt in Part One and who announce the guilty truth in Part Two ("Too late,/ too late, to live with your mother, the witches said") have, for the time being at least, been exorcised. The daughter–poet accepts and reclaims her living child in the face of the death of her mother and, in doing so, affirms her own life. Her worst guilt, that she made this child to find herself, cannot be cured by the child. Finally the double image must be focused into a single one and only then are the connections and resemblances valuable.

Many of the other especially successful poems in Sexton's early work are explorations of what it means to be a woman in terms of other women: "The Fortress" (*AMPO*), "Woman with Girdle" (*AMPO*), and "Rapunzel" (*Trans*), where she says, "A woman/ who loves a woman/ is forever young." In one of the poems about her

daughters, "Pain for a Daughter," the injured child, suddenly no
longer a child in her pain, cries

> *Oh my God, help me!*
> Where a child would have cried *Mama!*
> Where a child would have believed *Mama!*
> she bit the towel and called on God
> and I saw her life stretch out . . .
> I saw her torn in childbirth,
> and I saw her, at that moment,
> in her own death and I knew that she
> knew.
>
> (*LD,* 84)

This, like "The Double Image," confronts the vital connections between women—mothers and daughters—when they are alone in
themselves.

In her last three books, there is almost no mention at all of human
relationships (the one notable exception is "The Death of the Fathers"
in *The Book of Folly*), but especially absent is discussion of relationships with men. The fifth book, *Transformations*—one which marks
a definite shift in style and subject—is a series of jazzily retold fairy
tales. Here gardener meets princess, charwoman meets prince, but
Sexton insists on her own angle. Young girls are exploited by lecher-
ous old men and the most interesting, loving relationships are between
women. In "Rapunzel," for example, the old witch, Mother Gothel,
hides her young, long-haired beauty in a tower and together they play
the intriguing and quite clearly Lesbian "mother-me-do." Describing
the homosexual relationship, Sexton writes,

> We are two birds
> washing in the same mirror.
> We were fair game
> but we have kept out of the cesspool.
> We are strong.
> We are the good ones.

> They play mother-me-do
> all day.
> A woman
> who loves a woman
> is forever young.
> *(Trans,* 39)

The inevitable prince arrives; Rapunzel is fascinated and falls into the cesspool—described with fierce irony:

> They lived happily ever after as you might expect
> proving that mother-me-do
> can be outgrown,
> just as fish on Friday,
> just as a tricycle.
> The world, some say,
> is made up of couples.
> A rose must have a stem.
> *(Trans,* 42)

And all sympathy is reserved for the suffering, languishing Mother Gothel.

> and only as she dreamt of the yellow hair
> did moonlight sift into her mouth.

In Sexton's version of Cinderella, the most dynamic relation is between the badly treated step-daughter and the spirit of her dead mother, a white dove/fairy godmother. When the deal is finally clinched with the prince, they live "happily ever after" even more hideously than Rapunzel and her spouse:

> Cinderella and the prince
> lived, they say, happily ever after,
> like two dolls in a museum case
> never bothered by diapers or dust,
> never arguing over the timing of an egg,
> never telling the same story twice,
> never getting a middle-aged spread,

their darling smiles pasted on for eternity.
Regular Bobbsey Twins.
That story.

(*Trans,* 56–57)

It is illuminating—if not liberating—that in this book, at least, Sexton finds sexual, emotional, even spiritual relationships with women much more interesting than the inevitable "happy" endings with men.

"Song for a Lady," which appears in *Love Poems* along with all those other love poems in which the woman is created by the adoring man, stands out. Clearly, the voice is androgynous if not explicitly homosexual. It is an earlier and better version of "two birds/ washing in the same mirror." And even if Sexton is imagining herself as a male speaker, which I doubt, the force of the poem comes from the sense of physical love and tenderness for her own body worn by another. I quote it in full:

> On the day of breasts and small hips
> the window pocked with bad rain,
> rain coming on like a minister,
> we coupled, so sane and insane.
> We lay like spoons while the sinister
> rain dropped like flies on our lips
> and our glad eyes and our small hips.
>
> "The room is too cold with rain," you said
> and you, feminine you, with your flower
> said novenas to my ankles and elbows.
> You are a national product and power.
> Oh my swan, my drudge, my dear wooly rose,
> even a notary would notarize our bed
> as you knead me and I rise like bread.

(*LP,* 44)

As a lover, Sexton offers an uncertain identity; as a mother, she is clearer about herself and clearer about her own self-doubt. As the poet who is also a woman—"a woman who writes"—her situation is difficult. She feels uneasy in middle-class suburbia's sad approaches to human comfort. Suburban matrons are not expected to write poetry, much less publish such intimate details of their not so regular lives.

The social context in which she lived much of her life must have put heavy pressures on her, must have made her feel acutely the presence of those ghosts, ugly angels, and witches that plagued and also fed her imagination. In "The Funnel" (*BPWB,* 28–29), she envies the rich, excessive life of her great-grandfather, who not only "Begat eight/ genius children," but who also "bought twelve almost new/ grand pianos" and "built seven arking houses and they still stand." In one of these houses, which "still dominates its costal edge of land,"

> . . . those eight children danced
> their starfish summers, the thirty-six pines sighing,
> that bearded men walked giant steps and chanced
> his gifts as numbers.

Meanwhile, Anne Sexton returns from that great-grandfather's grave, to her quite different house, "to question this diminishing and feed a minimum/ of children their careful slice of suburban cake." It is not so much that she envies the wealth or even the material extravagance of her great-grandfather; rather, she seems to admire the style of his excess. It is a kind of style, of genius, of bravado conspicuously absent in the careful suburbs.

Looking through old letters of her great-aunt, until then known only to her niece as a deaf, prim spinster, Sexton discovers a different life: an affair with a married count—skating to Strauss in Berlin, climbing Mount San Salvatore, where "The count sweated/ with his coat off as you waded through top snow./ He held your hand and kissed you. You rattled/ down on the train to catch a steamboat for home;/ or other postmarks: Paris, Verona, Rome." And then the niece who lives in Weston warns the spirit of her dead aunt of her future:

> . . . You will accept
> your America back to live like a prim thing
> on the farm in Maine. I tell you, you will come
> here, to the suburbs of Boston, to see the blue-nose
> world go drunk each night, to see the handsome
> children jitterbug. . . .
>
> (*BPWB,* 15)

242   ANNE SEXTON

And this is where Anne Sexton lives part of her life. But there is quite
another life being led in that not so "narrow diary of [her] mind." She
senses, she really knows that there is something in her life that is not
"diminishing," something that is foreign to her physical environment
but nonetheless persists:

> . . . It is as real
> as splinters stuck in your ear. The noise we steal
> is half a bell. And outside cars whisk on the suburban street
>
> and are there are true.
> What else is this, this intricate shape of air?
> calling me, calling you.
>
> (*BPWB,* 36)

It is this life that makes her poet, not housewife. And it must come
to women poets from a different route, because they live in different
places than men do; the suburbs—as well as the city and the farm—
trap them in different ways. But however it gets there, it transforms
that diminished suburban world of Weston, Massachusetts, into one
which is both frightening and magical, a world of demons and angels
who both lie and tell the truth—sometimes at the same time. Although Anne Sexton admits in "Housewife" that "some women
marry houses" (*AMPO,* 48), she also insists on another kind of house-
keeping:

> I have found the warm caves in the woods,
> filled them with skillets, carvings, shelves,
> closets, silks, innumerable goods;
> fixed the suppers for the worms and the elves:
> whining, rearranging the disaligned.
> A woman like that is misunderstood.
> I have been her kind.
>
> I have ridden in your cart, driver,
> waved my nude arms at villages going by,
> learning the last bright routes, survivor
> where your flames still bite my thigh
> and my ribs crack where your wheels wind.
> A woman like that is not ashamed to die.
> I have been her kind.
>
> (*BPWB,* 21)

The thrill, even the strange contradictions—the witch who keeps house for worms and elves, the survivor who is not ashamed to die —come from a kind of declaration of separation from that careful, diminishing suburban world; it is an insistence on being "a woman who writes."

> A woman who writes feels too much,
> those trances and portents!
> As if cycles and children and islands
> weren't enough; as if mourners and gossips
> and vegetables were never enough.
> She thinks she can warn the stars.
> A writer is essentially a spy.
> Dear love, I am that girl.
>
> *(AMPO,* 65)

The claims and apologies in this stanza from "Black Art" are telling in both the discussion of Sexton's work and that of many of her female contemporary poets. It slips us a rather facile explanation of why women write poetry: "As if cycles and children and islands/ weren't enough." But it also points out a particular kind of complexity in the writing of women: "A writer is essentially a spy." In the next stanza, which begins, "A man who/ writes knows too much," the comparable line is "A writer is a crook." Both are thieves, but the booty is significantly different.

J. D. McCLATCHY

Anne Sexton:
Somehow To Endure

Even the covers of an Anne Sexton book are contradictory. The
poet posed demurely on their jackets: a sun-streaked porch, white
wicker, the beads and pleated skirt, the casual cigarette. Their tame
titles—literary or allusive: *To Bedlam and Part Way Back, All My
Pretty Ones, Love Poems, Transformations, The Book of Folly.* And
yet beyond, inside, are extraordinary revelations of pain and loss, an
intensely private record of a life hungering for madness and stalked
by great loves, the getting and spending of privileged moments and
suffered years. The terrible urgency of the poems, in fact, seems to
invite another sort of contradiction, the kind we feel only with strong
poets: disappointments. Occasionally there are poems which frankly
misfire for being awkward or repetitious, stilted or prosaic. One critic
has caught it:

> So her work veers between good and terrible almost indiscriminately.
> It is not a question of her writing bad poems from time to time, like
> everybody else; she also prints them cheek by jowl with her purest
> work. The reason, I suppose, is that the bad poems are bad in much
> the same way as her good ones are good: in their head-on intimacy and
> their persistence in exploring whatever is most painful to the author.[1]

244

The influences on her poetry—ranging from Rilke, Lawrence, Rimbaud and Smart, to Jarrell, Roethke, Lowell, Plath, and C. K. Williams—were easily acquired, obviously displayed, and often quickly discarded, while a few deeper influences—like that of Neruda—were absorbed and recast. She described herself as "a primitive," yet was master of intricate formal techniques. Her voice steadily evolved and varied and, at times, sought to escape speaking of the self, but her strongest poems consistently return to her narrow thematic range and the open voice of familiar feelings. *Do I contradict myself? Very well then I contradict myself.* For the source of her first fame continued as the focus of her work: she was the most persistent and daring of the confessionalists. Her peers have their covers: Lowell's allusiveness, Snodgrass's lyricism, Berryman's dazzle, Plath's expressionism. More than the others, Sexton resisted the temptations to dodge or distort, and the continuity and strength of her achievement remain the primary witness to the ability of confessional art to render a life into poems with all the intimacy and complexity of feeling and response with which that life has been endured.

Endurance was always her concern: why must we? how can we? why we must, how we do: "to endure,/somehow to endure." It is a theme which reenacts not only the sustained source of her poetry but its original impulse as well. At the age of twenty-eight, while recovering from a psychotic breakdown and suicide attempt, she began writing poems on the advice of her psychiatrist: "In the beginning, the doctor said, 'Write down your feelings because someday they might mean something to somebody. No matter how despairing you are, there are other people going through this who can't express it, and if they should read it they would feel less alone.' And so he gave me my little reason to go on; it shifted around, but that was always a driving, driving force."[2] The essentially practical motive here, and the fact of her coming to write so late and unlearned, accounts for her ironic fortune in pursuing a poetry not only then unfashionable but also difficult to achieve without a kind of clumsy innocence: "I couldn't do anything else," she said.

The spur to more serious concentration—the conscious conversion of a means for survival into a necessary art—was her reading of five poems by W. D. Snodgrass from his "Heart's Needle" sequence, published by Hall, Pack and Simpson in their important 1957 anthology, *New Poets of England and America.* The impact of Snodgrass's poems came as an affirmation of Sexton's own effort to write personally. Not the influence of his achievement, but the encouragement of his example mattered, and she left to study with him at the 1958 Antioch Writers Conference, where she showed him her poem "Unknown Girl in the Maternity Ward," written in direct response to "Heart's Needle" and dealing too with the loss of a child. Snodgrass sensed that her poem was a disguise and advised her simply, "Tell the real story." The result, written over many months and in obvious imitation of the strategies of "Heart's Needle," became one of her best-known poems, "The Double Image." Snodgrass also told her to study with Robert Lowell, which she returned to Boston to do in the fall of 1958. She later evaluated Lowell's influence: "He helped me to distrust the easy musical phrase and to look for the frankness of ordinary speech. If you have enough natural energy he can show you how to chain it in. He didn't teach me what to put in a poem, but what to leave out."[3] At the same time, she was studying at the Boston Adult Center with John Holmes, who discouraged her confessional impulse and tried to impose a more traditional subject matter on her. "I couldn't do anything else. I tried, but I couldn't do it. I mean, I did a couple. There's a stupid poem called 'Venus and the Ark,' which should never have been in that first book, that is the sort of thing that was approved of. That's one of the attempts; I do it, and then think, 'No!' "[4] There are a few other false starts among the poems she had gathered by 1959, but *To Bedlam and Part Way Back* (1960) has fewer hollows and sags than betray most beginners because it is the product not only of several years of determined effort but of the longer years which, to paraphrase Shelley, had learned in suffering what they teach in song.

It may be appropriate first to consider the general problem of the confessional aesthetic which Sexton's poetry helped establish. Even if it were possible, any description of the psychogenesis and psychopathology of confessionalism could only be reductive. More general psychoanalytical theories of poetry are either so broad as to be impractical for this special use of poetry, or so vague and unmanageable as to be of no use at all. Freud's sense of poetry as compensatory gratification is not really applicable for confessional poetry, and more recent theories—for instance, art as "restitution" or symbolic recreation of what the artist's aggressive fantasies have already destroyed—still cannot account for a poetry which largely avoids the symbolic approach and instead seeks naked revelation. In fact, surprisingly little has been written with any authority on the subject of confessionalism, which has become, under the rubric of "sincerity," an impulse behind many of the significant social movements and styles since 1960.

One of the few studies available is Theodor Reik's *The Compulsion to Confess,* a work which, while hardly exhaustive, at least opens up a few theoretical approaches toward an understanding of the "compulsion" and its results. Broadly, Reik defines a confession as "a statement about impulses or drives which are felt or recognized as forbidden," and their expression involves both the repressed tendency and the repressing forces. If this secular interpretation seems to exclude the usual religious (and even legal) sense of the term as narrowed to facts and intentions, they can easily be added to Reik's definition without any loss to the force of his point. The confessional situation—most obvious in analytical sessions—resides in "the transformation of a primitive urge for expression into the compulsion to confess," occasioned by social and psychic restraints and "the reactive reinforcement which the intensity of the drive experiences through repression," so that "confession is a repetition of action or of certain behavior substituted by displacement and with different emotional material, as words must substitute for action." This weakened repetition allows its own gratifications, indulging as it does both guilt and the need for punishment, even while the "reproduction through narration" achieves "the retroactive annulment of repression." That is to say, confession is at once the process of exorcism and the plea for absolution. And the result, in Reik's view, is that "the disintegrating of the personality is at least temporarily halted by the confession. The communication between the ego and that part of the ego from which it was estranged is restored."[5]

Although Freud recognized the "flexibility of repression" in artists, allowing them greater access to the unconscious and what Ernst Kris calls "functional regression" in service to the ego and its art, Reik's discussion is more directly apt for the poetry by Sexton under discussion in this essay. At the same time, it must be admitted that however much such sequences as "The Death of the Fathers" (in *The Book of Folly*) or "The Divorce Papers" (in *45 Mercy Street*) may have served Sexton as punishments for sins confessed, such an explanation, if it doubles as evaluation, cannot be finally satisfactory. It is their importance as art, rather than as mere self-expression, that matters. Even with that caution, Reik's explanation can be used to describe the impulses behind the expression that a confessional art then transforms. The repression through which such poems as Sexton's "The Double Image" or Sylvia Plath's "Daddy" explode is a part of their compulsive force. In fact, the great poems of madness and loss in Sexton's early books had their deeply personal source in what she once described as "a terrible need to kill myself."[6]

To some extent, then, the poetry is therapeutic; or as D. H. Lawrence said, "One sheds one's sicknesses in books—repeats and presents again one's emotions, to be master of them." Eric Erikson underscores this aspect of the situation by reminding that "the individual's mastery over his neurosis begins where he is put in a position to accept the historical necessity which made him what he is."[7] Acceptance becomes survival. Anne Sexton: "writing, and especially having written, is evidence of survival—the books accumulate ego-strength."[8] And so confessional poets are driven back to their losses, to that alienation—from self and others, from sanity and love—which is the thematic center of their vision and work. The betrayals in childhood, the family romance, the divorces and madnesses, the suicide attempts, the self-defeat and longing—the poets pursue them in their most intimate and painful detail. The pressure of public events,

of the world outside the skin, is rarely felt, except perhaps in Robert
Lowell's work. But the lives these poets have survived in their poems
become emblems of larger forces. In answer to a question about
putting "more of the political and cultural life of the country into [his]
verse," W. D. Snodgrass once remarked on the way in which confessional poems are subjective correlatives:

> A psychoanalyst a couple of years ago said, someplace or other, that
> family trouble, troubles in your love life, have caused people a hundred
> times more real agony than all the wars, famines, oppressions and the
> other stuff that gets in the history books. If those were your only
> troubles, boy would you be lucky. No, it's the fact that you keep
> devouring the person you love, that you keep throwing people away
> and sitting there saying "Where'd everybody go?" And you can't help
> it. And you just keep doing it. These are agonies much more important,
> and it seems to me that they are the agonies out of which we create our
> other agonies: that's one of the things I try to say in my poems, that
> it is out of the pattern of the life you know, with the people you love,
> that you create these larger patterns. It seems to me that Freud would
> have seen it that way entirely, and I must say that I do, but I don't think
> I get that from him, I hope I don't.[9]

Whether or not Snodgrass got that from Freud, there is much else
that confessional poetry owes to the human science Freud inaugu-
rated. All the contemporary poets central to confessionalism have
undergone extensive psychotherapy, and while it would be foolish to
account for their poetry by this experience, it would be careless to
ignore its influence, especially given the strong similarities between
the process of therapy they have needed as individuals and the process
of poetry by which they have then sought to express the lives they
have come to explore or understand. Psychotherapy and psychoanaly-
sis, abstractly outlined, involve a process during which the patient
recounts his or her most intimate experiences, both conscious and
unconscious, memories and fantasies. Though these "spots of time"
overlap and perhaps even contradict each other, their deeper continui-
ties assume the crucial patterns by which a life was led and sense is
made. Both the experiences still painfully central and the unaccounta-

ble gaps are endlessly recircled, and those recountings—themselves depending on the same sense of experience-in-time—not only reveal the neuroses that have obscured the real experience and self, but also work toward what Freud once called a *Nacherziehung,* an after-education. We learn what we are by relearning what we have become. But what is important to note now is the essentially narrative structure of the process, of one's experiences recounted in this time as remembered in their own past time. And narrative is likewise the most distinctive structural device in confessional poetry. The importance and integrity of chronology affect both the way in which individual poems are composed and the way they are collected into sequences and volumes, and these arrangements, in turn, are of thematic importance as facts or memories, shifting desires or needs or anxieties or gratifications change the landscape of personality. Sexton's poem "The Double Image," for instance, is a closely written and carefully parted account of her hospitalization and her necessary separation from her mother's shame and her daughter's innocence. The poem opens with the specificity of the achieved present—"I am thirty this November. . . . We stand watching the yellow leaves go queer"—and then drifts back through three yeers of madness and bitter history, to Bedlam and part way back, its larger thematic concerns held in precise details—dates, objects, places, names—among which are studded still smaller stories that memory associates with the main narrative. The destructions that survival implies in the poem are given their haunting force and authenticity by the history which the narrative leads the reader through so that he himself experiences the dramatic life of events and feelings.

In the same way, the poems of the confessionalists—Sexton especially—have a kind of chronicle effect on readers, as one keeps track volume by volume. This pervasive need to follow the contours of time, as if they sanctioned the truth they contain, is most clearly exemplified by *Live or Die,* where the poems are arranged in no particular narrative chronology but rather according to the compositional chronology, with the date carefully added to each poem like a clinching last line—from "January 25, 1962" to "February the last, 1966." Such a dependence on the details of time and place becomes a rhetorical method of definition and discovery, and points finally to the essentially epistemological concern of confessional poetry: since all that can meaningfully be known is my individual self, how is that self to be known and communicated except through the honest precision of its cumulative experience?

The rhetorical importance of confessional subject matter—especially insofar as it involves a characteristically Freudian epistemology —leads, in turn, to another consideration. In his most important gloss on the mediation of art, Freud wrote: "The essential *ars poetica* lies in the technique of overcoming the feeling of repulsion in us which is undoubtedly connected with the barriers that rise between each single ego and the others."[10] Or between the single ego and its history, he might have added. And among the barriers the self constructs are the familiar defense mechanisms: repression, displacement, suppression, screen memories, condensation, projection, and so on. Such psychological techniques, in turn, have their rhetorical analogues, not surprisingly those most favored by modernist poets and their New Critics: paradox, ambiguity, ellipsis, allusion, wit, and the other "tensions" that correspond to the neurotic symptoms by which the self is obscured. And in order to write with greater directness and honesty about their own experiences, Sexton and the other confessional poets have tended to avoid the poetic strategies of modernism—to de-repress poetry, so to speak—and have sought to achieve their effects by other means. Sexton's turn toward open forms, as though in trust, is an example. In general, it can be said of Sexton's poems, as of other confessional poems, that the patterns they assume and by which they manage their meanings are those which more closely follow the actual experiences they are recreating—forms that can include and reflect direct, personal experience; a human, rather than a disembodied voice; the dramatic presentation of the flux of time and personality; and the drive toward sincerity. By this last concept is meant not an ethical imperative, but the willed and willing openness of the poet to her experience and to the character of the language by which her discoveries are revealed and shared. Not that the structures of sincerity abandon every measure of artifice. While she may have associated the imagination so strongly with memory, Sexton realized as well that the self's past experiences are neither provisional nor final, that even as they shape the art that describes them, so too they are modified by that very art. The flux of experience, rather than its absolute truth, determines which concerns or wounds are returned to in poem after poem, either because they have not yet been understood or because the understanding of them has changed. And Sexton is sharply aware, in her work, of the difference between factual truth and poetic truth —of the need to "edit" out, while trying not to distort, redundant or inessential "facts" in the service of cleaner, sharper poems. In a crucial sense, confessional art is a means of *realizing* the poet.

As the poet realizes himself, inevitably he catches up the way we live now: especially the personal life, since our marriages are more difficult than our wars, our private nightmares more terrifying than our public horrors. In addition, then, to our sense of the confessional poet as a survivor, he or she functions as a kind of witness. What may have begun as a strictly private need is transformed, once it is published, into a more inclusive focus—and here one recalls Whitman's "attempt, from first to last, to put a *Person,* a human being (myself, in the latter half of the Nineteenth Century, in America) freely, fully, and truly on record." The more naked and directly emotional nature of confessional poems heightens the integrity and force of their witness to the inner lives of both poets and readers; or, as Sexton has remarked, "poems of the inner life can reach the inner lives of readers in a way that anti-war poems can never stop a war." The final privatism of poetry itself, in other words, affords the confessional poet a certain confidence in using the details of intimate experience in ways that earlier would have been considered either arrogant or obscure. And the ends to which those details are put are not merely self-indulgent or self-therapeutic—or, in Robert Lowell's phrase, "a brave heart drowned on monologue." Of her own work, Anne Sexton once reminisced: "I began to think that if one life, somehow made into art, were recorded—not all of it, but like the testimony on an old tomb-

stone—wouldn't that be worth something? Just one life—a poor middle-class life, nothing extraordinary (except maybe madness, but
that's so common nowadays)—that seems worth putting down. It's
the thing I have to do, the thing I want to do—I'm not sure why."
And she went on to describe a reader's response to this "testimony":
"I think, I hope, a reader's response is: 'My God, this has happened.
And in some real sense it has happened to me too.' This has been my
reaction to other poems, and my readers have responded to my poems
in just this way."[11]

Perhaps the most telling evidence of this sort of response are the
countless letters that anonymous readers sent to Sexton, explaining
how her poetry revealed their own troubled lives to them and often
making impossible demands on the poet, so strong was the readers'
sense of the real, suffering person in the poetry. It is no wonder that,
with bitter wit, Sexton once described herself in a poem as "mother
of the insane." But at a deeper level, there is some dark part in any
one of us which her work illuminated, often distressingly. Like
Wordsworth, who wished to allow his audience "new compositions of
feeling," Sexton's response to her own experience becomes a model for
a reader's response to his or her own. The poems function as instruments of discovery for the reader as well as for the poet, and the
process of discovery—ongoing through poems and collections, as
through life—is as important as the products, the poems which the
poet has drawn directly out of her experience, often as isolated stays
against confusion. The immediacy of impact and response, and the
mutual intimacy between poet and reader, correspond with an observation by Ernst Kris on aesthetic distance: "When psychic distance
is maximal, the response is philistine or intellectualistic. At best, the
experience is one of passive receptivity rather than active participation
of the self. . . . [But] when distance is minimal the reaction to works
of art is pragmatic rather than aesthetic."[12] To emphasize the "pragmatic" response of readers to this poetry—even though the term
describes the response of most poets to their experience, however the
subsequent poem may inform it—may be viewed as an effort to mini-

mize the "art" of the poems. I hope my subsequent remarks will describe that art sufficiently, or at least with more attention to real questions than most critics have so far paid Sexton.

Despite the authority and abundance in *To Bedlam and Part Way Back*, Sexton was careful, perhaps compelled, to include an apologia, a poem called "For John, Who Begs Me Not to Enquire Further"— addressed to her discouraging teacher John Holmes, and so finally to the critic in herself. The poem's title echoes the book's epigraph, from a letter of Schopenhauer to Goethe concerning the courage necessary for a philosopher: "He must be like Sophocles's Oedipus, who, seeking enlightenment concerning his terrible fate, pursues his indefatigable enquiry, even when he divines that appalling horror awaits him in the answer. But most of us carry in our heart the Jocasta who begs Oedipus for God's sake not to inquire further. . . ." The sympathy she can afford for Holmes—"although your fear is anyone's fear,/ like an invisible veil between us all"—recalls Freud's sense of the repulsion with the self and others which art overcomes. Her cautious justification is modeled on her psychiatrist's plea: "that the worst of anyone/ can be, finally,/an accident of hope." And the standard she sets herself is simply making sense:

> Not that it was beautiful,
> but that, in the end, there was
> a certain sense of order there;
> something worth learning
> in that narrow diary of my mind,
> in the commonplaces of the asylum
> where the cracked mirror
> or my own selfish death
> outstared me.

Part of that order is substantive and thematic, the urge to recover and understand the past: "I have this great need somehow to keep that time of my life, that feeling. I want to imprison it in a poem, to keep it. It's almost in a way like keeping a scrapbook to make life mean something as it goes by, to rescue it from chaos—to make 'now' last."[13] But if the ability to extend the past and present into each other further depends upon the orders of art, that art cannot succeed without a prior commitment to honesty—or, to use Sexton's peculiar term, as a confessional poet she must start with a wise passivity, with being "still." That word occurs in her poem about the tradition, "Portrait of an Old Woman on the College Tavern Wall," where the poets sit "singing and lying/ around their round table/ and around me still." "Why do these poets lie?" the poem goes on to question, and leaves them with mortal irony "singing/ around their round table/ until they are still." Whether death or silence, this "stillness" is the view of experience, both prior to and beyond language, from which her ordering proceeds. The difficulty, as she knows in another poem, "Said The Poet to The Analyst," is that "My business is words":

> I must always forget how one word is able to pick
> out another, to manner another, until I have got
> something I might have said . . .
> but did not.

The business of the Analyst—again, an internal figure, a sort of artistic conscience—is "watching my words," guarding against the Jocasta who would settle for "something I might have said" instead of what must be revealed.

Sexton's business with words—the ordering of statement and instinct—is the adjustment of their demands to her experience: in her figure, to make a tree out of used furniture. Though her attitudes toward form evolved, from the beginning there was an uneasy ambivalence: the poet insisting on control, the person pleading, "Take out rules and leave the instant," as she said in one interview. Her solution was to use the metaphor of deceit, but to reverse it into a very personally inflected version of form:

> I think all form is a trick to get at the truth. Sometimes in my hardest poems, the ones that are difficult to write, I might make an impossible scheme, a syllabic count that is so involved, that it then allows me to be truthful. It works as a kind of super-ego. It says, "You may now face it, because it will be impossible ever to get out." . . . But you see how

> I say this not to deceive you, but to deceive me. I deceive myself, saying
> to myself you can't do it, and then if I can get it, then I have deceived
> myself, then I can change it and do what I want. I can even change and
> rearrange it so no one can see my trick. It won't change what's real.
> It's there on paper.[14]

Though her early work occasionally forces itself with inversions and
stolid High Style, her concern for the precisions of voice and pace
reveal her care in indulging a lyric impulse only to heighten the
dramatic. What Richard Howard has said of her use of rhyme is
indicative of her larger sense of form: "invariably it is Sexton's practice to use rhyme to bind the poem, irregularly invoked, abandoned
when inconvenient, psychologically convincing."[15] The truth-getting
tricks, in other words, serve as a method of conviction for both poet
and reader. For the poet, form functions to articulate the details and
thrust of her actual experience, while for the reader it guides his
dramatic involvement in the re-creation: both convictions converging
on authenticity, on realization. And so the voice is kept conversa-
tional, understated by plain-speech slang or homely detail—its imagery drawn from the same sources it counterpoints, its force centered
in the pressure of events it contours, the states of mind it maps. This
is clearly the case with the poems of madness in the first section of
To Bedlam and Part Way Back. Compared with Sexton's powerful
control in this group, a similar but more celebrated poem, Lowell's
"Waking in the Blue," seems faded with retrospective observation
rather than immediate involvement. True to the several experiences,
cut across time, that they describe, the poems vary the means they
take to explore the common meaning. They range from expressionistic
projections:

> It was the strangled cold of November;
> even the stars were strapped in the sky
> and that moon too bright
> forking through the bars to stick me
> with a singing in the head.
> > ("Music Swims Back to Me")

to the menacing, flat accent of life-in-death:

and this is always my bell responding
to my hand that responds to the lady
who points at me, E flat;
and although we are no better for it,
they tell you to go. And you do.
("Ringing the Bells")

Together they devise, in Michel Foucault's phrase, "the formulas of exclusion."

M. L. Rosenthal has seen in these poems "the self reduced to almost infantile regression,"[16] but more often the voice is that of an older child, which implies a consciousness that can experience the arbitrariness of authority and the sufferings of loss without understanding either chance or cause. The inferno of insanity opens, appropriately, with the poet lost in the dark wood of her "night mind":

And opening my eyes, I am afraid of course
to look—this inward look that society scorns—
Still I search in these woods and find nothing worse
than myself, caught between the grapes and the thorns.
("Kind Sir: These Woods")

The disorientation necessitates the search: here, the descent into her own underworld, as later she will ascend part way back. Likewise, the figure of the child—so important in Part Two, where it subsumes both the poet and her daughter—introduces the themes of growth and discovery, of the growth into self by discovering its extremes, as in the poem addressed to her psychiatrist:

And we are magic talking to itself,
noisy and alone. I am queen of all my sins
forgotten. Am I still lost? ↓
Once I was beautiful. Now I am myself,
counting this row and that row of moccasins
waiting on the silent shelf.
("You, Dr. Martin")

The "private institution on a hill," like Hamlet's nutshell, is finally the self in which she is confined:

> They lock me in this chair at eight a.m.
> and there are no signs to tell the way,
> just the radio beating to itself
> and the song that remembers
> more than I. Oh, la la la,
> this music swims back to me.
> That night I came I danced a circle
> and was not afraid.
> Mister?
>
> ("Music Swims Back to Me")

The struggle to find "which way is home" involves the dissociation and resumption of different personalities ("Her Kind," "The Expatriates," "What's That"), the limits of paranoia and mania ("Noon Walk on the Asylum Lawn," "Lullaby"), and the dilemma of memory that drives pain toward exorcism ("You, Dr. Martin," "Music Swims Back to Me," "The Bells," "Said the Poet to the Analyst").

Though, as she says, there is finally "no word for time," the need to restore it is the essential aspect of the ordering process:

> Today is made of yesterday, each time I steal
> toward rites I do not know, waiting for the lost
> ingredient, as if salt or money or even lust
> would keep us calm and prove us whole at last.
>
> ("The Lost Ingredient")

What has been lost, along with sanity, is the meaning of those who made her, and this first book introduces us to the cast she will reassemble and rehearse in all her subsequent work, even through "Talking to Sheep" and "Divorce, Thy Name is Woman" in *45 Mercy Street:* the hapless boozy father, the helpless cancer-swollen bitch of a mother, the daughters as both victims and purifiers, the shadowy presence of her husband, the analyst as dark daddy and muse, the clutching company of doomed poets—and most touchingly, the great-aunt whom she calls Nana. Sexton's obsession with her Nana—the "Nana-hex" she calls it later—results from both sympathy and guilt. "She was, during the years she lived with us, my best friend, my teacher, my confidante and my comforter. I never thought of her as being young. She was an extension of myself and was my world."[17] For this very reason, when her great-aunt, after a sudden deafness, had a nervous breakdown from which she never recovered, the poet could find her both an emblem of her own suffering and a source of guilt for fear she had somehow caused it. Nana is brought on tenderly in the lyrical elegy "Elizabeth Gone," but in the next poem, "Some Foreign Letters," her life is used as the focus of the poet's own anxieties as she sits reading the letters her great-aunt had sent to her family as a young woman on her Victorian Grand Tour. The poem proceeds by verse and refrain—Nana's letters of her youth, the poet's images of the same woman different—to point up the disjunction between memories: Nana's diaried ones, which have trapped her youth in an irretrievable past, and the poet's own memories of Nana trapped in age and lost to death:

> Tonight your letters reduce
> history to a guess. The Count had a wife.
> You were the old maid aunt who lived with us.
> Tonight I read how the winter howled around
> the towers of Schloss Schwöbber, how the tedious
> language grew in your jaw, how you loved the sound
> of the music of the rats tapping on the stone
> floors. When you were mine you wore an earphone.

The "guilty love" with which the poem ends is the poet's own ambivalent response to her inability to have rescued her Nana—even as she realizes she will not be able to save herself—from the facts that are fate, a life that cannot be unlived or chosen. The last stanza's pathos derives from its prediction of what has already occurred, the proof that guilt is suffered again and again:

> Tonight I will learn to love you twice;
> learn your first days, your mid-Victorian face.
> Tonight I will speak up and interrupt
> your letters, warning you that wars are coming,
> that the Count will die, that you will accept
> your America back to live like a prim thing
> on a farm in Maine. I tell you, you will come

here, to the suburbs of Boston, to see the blue-nose
world go drunk each night, to see the handsome
children jitterbug, to feel your left ear close
one Friday at Symphony. And I tell you,
you will tip your boot feet out of that hall,
rocking from its sour sound, out onto
the crowded street, letting your spectacles fall
and your hair net tangle as you stop passers-by
to mumble your guilty love while your ears die.

The poet speaks her warning here not as a suspicious Jocasta but as
a knowing Tiresias, helpless before time, that most visible scar of
mortality. And the family to which she resigns Nana is, of course, her
own as well, and the self-recovery which the volume's arrangement
of poems plots necessarily moves to recover her parents, as so much
of her later work too will do.

The book's second section is The Part Way Back, in the sense of
both return and history. The painful realizations of adjustment, the
lessons of loss and recovery weight the book's two anchor poems—
"The Double Image" and "The Division of Parts." They are long
poems, explorations lengthened to accommodate their discoveries and
unresolved dilemmas, and extended by subtle modulations of voice
and structure to dramatize their privacies. "The Double Image," the
book's strongest and most ambitious poem, is actually a sequence of
seven poems tracing the terms of Sexton's dispossession—similar to
Snodgrass's "Heart's Needle," which was its model. The other poem,
which clearly echoes Snodgrass's voice as well, is an independent
summary of her losses, and makes the subsequent poems seem to have
insisted themselves on her later. If that was the case, there is reason
for it, since the jagged lines of the first poem reflect the uncertain
hesitancy in naming the guilt that had caused her self-hatred and her
suicide attempts and breakdown. It is addressed, in retrospect, to the
daughter whose infant illness released the long-held guilt:

　　　. . . a fever rattled
in your throat and I moved like a pantomime
above your head. Ugly angels spoke to me. The blame,
I heard them say, was mine. They tattled

like green witches in my head, letting doom
leak like a broken faucet;
as if doom had flooded my belly and filled your bassinet,
an old debt I must assume.

She tries to solve her life with death—"I let the witches take away
my guilty soul"—but is forced back from the "time I did not love/
myself" to face the new life she has made in her child and the old life
she had made for herself. She assumes the old debts in the following
narrative of her recovery. If the first poem turned on her commitment
and the loss of her daughter, the second turns on her release and the
loss of her mother, to whom she returns as "an angry guest," "an
outgrown child." The poet had grown "well enough to tolerate/
myself," but her mother cannot forgive the suicide attempt and so
cannot accept her daughter: she "had my portrait/ done instead," a
line that refrains the tedium and repressed menace that punches out
each stanza. The tension of presence begins to sort the past; the
church is another Bedlam, her parents her keepers:

> There was a church where I grew up
> with its white cupboards where they locked us up,
> row by row, like puritans or shipmates
> singing together. My father passed the plate.
> Too late to be forgiven now, the witches said.
> I wasn't exactly forgiven. They had my portrait
> done instead.

The third poem opens up the deaths in and of relationships. Sexton's distance from her own daughter gains its double reference: "as
if it were normal/ to be a mother and be gone." As the poet gathers
her strength, her mother sickens, and madness, love-loss, and death
are drawn into a single figure which points again at guilt. Her mother's cancer—"as if my dying had eaten inside of her"—accuses Sexton
with questions that "still I couldn't answer." The fourth poem is
centered as an interlude of partial return and acceptance: Sexton back
from Bedlam, her mother from the hospital, her daughter from the
exile of innocence. The fact of survival converts its sterility into
patience: the blank, facing portraits mirror the reversal of concern:

> During the sea blizzards
> she had her
> own portrait painted.
> A cave of a mirror
> placed on the south wall;
> matching smile, matching contour.
> And you resembled me; unacquainted
> with my face, you wore it. But you were mine
> after all.

The fifth poem begins to draw the women together into a chorus, their roles merging into a new knowledge:

> ... And I had to learn
> why I would rather
> die than love, how your innocence
> would hurt and how I gather
> guilt like a young intern
> his symptoms, his certain evidence....
>
> We drove past the hatchery,
> the hut that sells bait,
> past Pigeon Cove, past the Yacht Club, past Squall's
> Hill, to the house that waits
> still, on the top of the sea,
> and two portraits hang on opposite walls.

The sixth is a self-study, the poet finding herself in the distanced image of her mother, as in the next poem she discovers how selfish are the maternal motives of love. But in this poem, it is the process of life that learns from *la nature morte:*

> And this was the cave of the mirror,
> that double woman who stares
> at herself, as if she were petrified
> in time—two ladies sitting in umber chairs.
> You kissed your grandmother
> and she cried.

The final poem, again addressed to the poet's daughter, summarizes her learning:

You learn my name,
wobbling up the sidewalk, calling and crying.
You call me *mother* and I remember my mother again,
somewhere in greater Boston, dying.

But the last stanza unwinds into a tentative resumption of guilt—its last line speaking, with an odd irony, the voice of Jocasta: "And this was my worst guilt; you could not cure/ nor soothe it. I made you to find me."

In "The Division of Parts," Sexton carries the account past her mother's death, which has left her, on Good Friday, with "gifts I did not choose." The last hospital days are retold, and the numbness with which they stun her implies the larger truth of the poem:

> But you turned old,
> all your fifty-eight years sliding
> like masks from your skull;
> and at the end
> I packed your nightgowns in suitcases,
> paid the nurses, came riding
> home as if I'd been told
> I could pretend
> people live in places.

But people live not in space or places, but in time and in others, and their demands puzzle the poet's guilt: "Time, that rearranger/ of estates, equips/ me with your garments, but not with grief." Her inheritance steals on her "like a debt," and she cannot expiate her loss: "I planned to suffer/ and I cannot." Unlike "Jesus, *my stranger,*" who assumed "old debts" and knew how and why to suffer, Sexton is emptied of belief by need:

> ... Fool! I fumble my lost childhood
> for a mother and lounge in sad stuff
> with love to catch and catch as catch can.
>
> And Christ still waits. I have tried
> to exorcise the memory of each event
> and remain still, a mixed child,
> heavy with cloths of you.
> Sweet witch, you are my worried guide.

And she realizes the motive of her subsequent books: "For all the way I've come/ I'll have to go again." Only ever part way back, she tries her art against her mind—"I would still curse/ you in my rhyming words/ and bring you flapping back, old love"—but her litany of incantatory adjectives cannot lose loss, and if she cannot love it, she has learned to live it.

The religious note introduced at the end of *To Bedlam and Part Way Back,* evoked by the death which aligns it with other needs and losses, is even more apparent in her next book, *All My Pretty Ones* (1962). Two of its best-known poems—"For God While Sleeping" and "In the Deep Museum"—are really part of a much larger group that threads through all her collections, on through "The Jesus Papers" in *The Book of Folly* and into "Jesus Walking" in *The Death Notebooks* and the major poems in *The Awful Rowing Toward God,* whose title best describes the project. Though she herself referred to these poems as "mystical," they are more obviously religious since their concerns are always the human intricacies of need and belief, and their context is Sexton's need for belief and her inability to believe as that dilemma interacts with her relationships to herself and others, the dead and dying. This explains too why her religious poetry centers almost exclusively on the person of Jesus, the central figure of belief who himself despaired at the end, who brought love and found none, who gave life and was nailed to a tree. But her relationship to Jesus, as it develops through the books, is an ambivalent one. On the one hand, he serves as a sympathetic emblem of her own experience: "That ragged Christ, that sufferer, performed the greatest act of confession, and I mean with his body. And I try to do that with words."[18] This is the force of the poems in *All My Pretty Ones.* To touch a crucifix—"I touch its tender hips, its dark jawed face,/ its solid neck, its brown sleep"—is to remind herself of poetry's work for salvation:

> My friend, my friend, I was born
> doing reference work in sin, and born
> confessing it. This is what poems are:
> with mercy

> for the greedy,
> they are the tongue's wrangle,
> the world's pottage, the rat's star.
> ("With Mercy for the Greedy")

The Christ who is "somebody's fault," like the poet, is "hooked to your own weight,/ jolting toward death under your nameplate" ("For God While Sleeping"). But at the same time, Sexton is fascinated by another Jesus: "Perhaps it's because he can forgive sins."[19] Like her psychiatrist, Jesus is a man who can take on her guilt, a man who suffers with her and for her. This is the Jesus "In the Deep Museum," where gnawing rats are the "hairy angels who take my gift," as he blesses "this other death": "Far below The Cross, I correct its flaws. Her purest statement of this sense of Christ comes in *The Death Notebooks,* in "Jesus Walking": "To pray, Jesus knew,/ is to be a man carrying a man." It is the simplicity of such strength which takes the measure of weaker men in her life, especially her father, whose death brings him into the poetry of *All My Pretty Ones.*

This second book is less an extension than a completion of her first, just as its epigraph—from Kafka—describes the motive and effect of the courage invoked earlier: "the books we need are the kind that act upon us like a misfortune, that make us suffer the death of someone we love more than ourselves, that make us feel as though we were on the verge of suicide, or lost in a forest remote from all human habitation—a book should serve as the ax for the frozen sea within us." But Sexton's own evaluation is misleadingly neat: "Well, in the first book, I was giving the experience of madness; in the second book, the causes of madness."[20] That account of "causes" is not sustained, and most of this book—whose poems are more expert but less urgent than before—catches the reader up with the poet's life. That is to say, its confessions converge toward the present, and the chronicle begins to include more immediate and intimate events. Previously worked aspects of and approaches to her experience are here retried: "The Operation" clearly derives from "The Double Image," "The House" expands "Some Foreign Letters." The greater assurance of her verse likewise allows Sexton to experiment successfully with open forms and new voices. Besides the religious poems already mentioned, *All My Pretty Ones* includes several distinctive love poems, real and invented, of which "Flight" and "Letter Written on a Ferry While Crossing Long Island Sound" are most incisive, the latter poem recalling Whitman's "Crossing Brooklyn Ferry," whose "dumb, beautiful ministers" are redressed as nuns who float up in a fantasy of redemption.

But Sexton's burden remains her inward argument: "I cannot promise very much./ I give you the images I know." The effort in these early books remains to get back at herself. The dead haunt like "bad dreams," and the heart loves only "the decay we're made of." The poem addressed to her "Old Dwarf Heart," in lines that echo Roethke and fold back in their rhymes like a trap, sets the stakes for *All My Pretty Ones:*

> Good God, the things she knows!
> And worse, the sores she holds
> in her hands, gathered in like a nest
> from an abandoned field. At her best
> she is all red muscle, humming in and out, cajoled
> by time. Where I go, she goes.
>
> Oh now I lay me down to love,
> how awkwardly her arms undo,
> how patiently I untangle her wrists
> like knots. Old ornament, old naked fist,
> even if I put on seventy coats I could not cover you . . .
> mother, father, I'm made of.

The book opens on "The Truth the Dead Know," which is their absolute isolation, against which the poet fights to save both herself and her dead parents. Her father's death, three months after her mother's, intervened not only between the different concerns of these first two books but also between the completed realization of her inheritance: in the fine print of their wills, the poet fears to find her father's alcoholism and her mother's cancer, which would at the same time prove her their daughter and destroy her. The sins of the father are revisited in the title poem, which blends memories and objects like snapshots out of order to invoke the man's loss and, again, her guilt:

> This year, solvent but sick, you meant
> to marry that pretty widow in a one-month rush.
> But before you had that second chance, I cried
> on your fat shoulder. Three days later you died.

The fear that she has somehow killed her father is the familiar origin of guilt for which she seeks both the retribution of punishment and the reconciliation of a forced forgiveness:

> I hold a five-year diary that my mother kept
> for three years, telling all she does not say
> of your alcoholic tendency. You overslept,
> she writes. My God, father, each Christmas Day
> with your blood, will I drink down your glass
> of wine? The diary of your hurly-burly years
> goes to my shelf to wait for my age to pass.
> Only in this hoarded span will love persevere.
> Whether you are pretty or not, I outlive you,
> bend down my strange face to yours and forgive you.

The volume's most striking poem, "The Operation," returns to her mother's death, which the poet must now have cut out of herself: "the historic thief/ is loose in my house/ and must be set upon." Unconscious under the surgeries of survival, her experience is another madness:

> Next, I am hung up like a saddle and they begin.
> Pale as an angel I float out over my own skin.
>
> I soar in hostile air
> over the pure women in labor,
> over the crowning heads of babies being born.
> I plunge down the backstair
> calling *mother* at the dying door,
> to rush back to my own skin, tied where it was torn.
> Its nerves pull like wires
> snapping from the leg to the rib.
> Strangers, their faces rolling like hoops, require
> my arm. I am lifted into my aluminum crib.

Reborn from death, as in "The Double Image" she was from insanity, her scarred, scared response to life is inadequate to its new demands, and the poem ends understated, with a child's diction, a deflecting image:

> Time now to pack this humpty-dumpty
> back the frightened way she came
> and run along, Anne, and run along now,
> my stomach laced up like a football
> for the game.

Much more is faced in "The House," which loosens its regard and drifts back over her childhood, dream-distorted and so clarified. Reruns of "the same bad dream . . . the same dreadful set,/ the same family of orange and pink faces" are set spinning to portray the atmosphere in which death was first preferred. These three album photographs, each a collage of hurt and menace—in ways that oddly prefigure *Transformations*—are sufficient example of the poem's force:

> Father,
> an exact likeness,
> his face bloated and pink
> with black market scotch,
> sits out his monthly bender
> in his custom-made pajamas
> and shouts, his tongue as quick as galloping horses,
> shouts into the long distance telephone call.
> His mouth is as wide as his kiss.
>
> Mother,
> with just the right gesture,
> kicks her shoes off,
> but is made all wrong,
> impossibly frumpy as she sits there
> in her alabaster dressing room
> sorting her diamonds like a bank teller
> to see if they add up.
>
> The maid
> as thin as a popsicle stick,
> holds dinner as usual,

rubs her angry knuckles over the porcelain sink
and grumbles at the gun-shy dog.
She knows something is going on.
She pricks a baked potato.

The poet then walks into her own dream, "up another flight into the penthouse,/ to slam the door on all the years/ she'll have to live through . . ." until she wakes in italics: *"Father, father, I wish I were dead."* She wakes as well into the self she has become, caught between neurosis and nostalgia: "At thirty-five/ she'll dream she's dead/ or else she'll dream she's back." In the death that poses desire as dream nothing has changed, and it merges in her awareness with history— again, facts are fate, the infernal machine: "All day long the machine waits: rooms,/ stairs, carpets, furniture, people—/ those people who stand at the open windows like objects/ waiting to topple." What the past has lost cannot be salvaged in the future, and her poem "The Fortress," a meditation over her sleeping daughter Linda, submits to a life other than hers:

> Darling, life is not in my hands;
> life with its terrible changes
> will take you, bombs or glands,
> your own child at your
> breast, your own house on your own land.
> Outside the bittersweet turns orange.
> Before she died, my mother and I picked those fat
> branches, finding orange nipples
> on the gray wire stands.
> We weeded the forest, curing trees like cripples.

Time draws on change, and the love she leaves her child seems as fragile as innocence. That too is part of the weary acceptance of this book.

The oneiric organization of "The House" looks forward to the important changes that her next and decisive book, *Live or Die* (1966), announces. With its longer poems in open forms which more subtly accommodate a greater range of experience, and with a voice pitched higher to intensify that experience, *Live or Die* represents not a departure from her earlier strengths but the breakthrough into her distinctive style. Perhaps the most immediate aspect of that style is its more extravagant use of imagery:

> I sat all day
> stuffing my heart into a shoe box,
> avoiding the precious window
> as if it were an ugly eye
> through which birds coughed,
> chained to the heaving trees;
> avoiding the wallpaper of the room
> where tongues bloomed over and over,
> bursting from lips like sea flowers. . . .
> ("Those Times . . .")

This is the sort of imagery that will be even more exploited in later books where "like" becomes the most frequently encountered word. It is a technique that risks arbitrary excesses and embarrassing crudities, that at its best can seem but a slangy American equivalent of Apollinaire's surrealism: *Les nuages coulaient comme un flux menstruel.* But it is crucial to remember, with Gaston Bachelard, that "we live images synthetically in their initial complexity, often giving them our unreasoned allegiance."[21] And Sexton's use of images is primarily psychotropic—used less for literary effect than as a means to pry deeper into her psychic history, to float her findings and model her experience. As she said, "The poetry is often more advanced, in terms of my unconscious, than I am. Poetry, after all, milks the unconscious."[22] And so she came increasingly to identify the imagination less with her memory than with her unconscious: "Images are the heart of poetry. And this is not tricks. Images come from the unconscious. Imagination and the unconscious are one and the same."[23] Sexton's commitment to honest realization is thus only carried to a deeper level. And if Rimbaud was right to demand of such associative poetry a *"dérèglement de tous les sens,"* it can be seen as Sexton's necessary road of excess through her experiences of madness and the disorientation of her past, so that her metaphors are a method not to display similarities but to discover identities.

Although *Live or Die* shows, for this reason, the influence of her readings in Roethke and Neruda, a more important factor was the new analyst she began seeing while at work on this book. He was more interested in dreams than her earlier doctors had been, and Sexton found herself dealing more directly with her unconscious: "You taught me/to believe in dreams;/ thus I was the dredger" ("Flee on Your Donkey"). Several poems in *Live or Die* are direct dream-songs —"Three Green Windows," "Imitations of Drowning," "Consorting with Angels," "In the Beach House," and "To Lose the Earth." The latent content in these poems—such as the primal scene of "the royal strapping" in "In the Beach House"—is expressive but abandoned to its own independence, unlike more conscious fantasies such as "Menstruation at Forty," in which themes of death and incest are projected onto the imagined birth of a son. The insistence of the unconscious also draws up the poems of her childhood—"Love Song," "Protestant Easter," and especially "Those Times . . .," one of the book's triumphs. Robert Boyers has described *Live or Die* as "a poetry of victimization, in which she is at once victim and tormentor,"[24] and "Those Times . . ." torments the poet with her earliest memories of victimization: "being the unwanted, the mistake/that Mother used to keep Father/ from his divorce." Her suffering was as silent as her envy of a doll's perfection: "I did not question the bedtime ritual/ where, on the cold bathroom tiles,/ I was spread out daily/ and examined for flaws." But her felt exclusion was assumed and rehearsed in a closet's dark escape, where she sat with her hurts and dreams, as later she would sit in madness and poetry:

> I did not know that my life, in the end,
> would run over my mother's like a truck
> and all that would remain
> from the year I was six
> was a small hole in my heart, a deaf spot,
> so that I might hear
> the unsaid more clearly.

The other crucial influence on *Live or Die* is the play she wrote at the time—first titled *Tell Me Your Answer True* and eventually produced in 1969 as *Mercy Street*—sections of which were carried over as poems into *Live or Die* and lend the book its character of psycho-drama. Sexton's description of herself during a poetry reading could apply to her presence in this book as well: "I am an actress in my own autobiographical play."[25] The vitality, even the violence, of the book's drama of adaptation recall Emily Dickinson's sly lines: "Men die—externally—/ It is a truth—of Blood—/ But we—are dying in Drama—/ And Drama—is never dead." To match the expansive forms and intense imagery of these poems, the voice that speaks them grows more various in its effects, matching a strident aggression or hovering tenderness with the mood and matter evoked. Above all, there is energy, whether of mania or nostalgia. And it is more expressly vocative here, as her cast is introduced separately and her relationship to each is reworked: her father ("And One for My Dame"), mother ("Christmas Eve"), daughters ("Little Girl, My Stringbean, My Lovely Woman," "A Little Uncomplicated Hymn," "Pain for a Daughter"), husband ("And One for My Dame," "Man and Wife," "Your Face on the Dog's Neck"), and Nana ("Crossing the Atlantic," "Walking in Paris"). There is a very conscious sense about these poems of the times since her first book that she has spent with her living and her dead. "A Little Uncomplicated Hymn," for instance, alludes directly to "The Double Image" to catch at a perspective for the interval; the new poem, according to Sexton, was the "attempt to master that experience in light of the new experience of her life and how it might have affected her and how it affects me still; she wasn't just an emblem for me any longer. Every book, every poem, is an attempt to master things that aren't ever quite mastered."[26] And so one watches her recircling her experiences to define and refine her understanding of them. Her parents are written of more sharply, and her regret is less for what she has lost than for what she never had. Her great-aunt's account of her youth in Europe, which structures "Some Foreign Letters," was the motive for Sexton's attempt to re-trace in person Nana's journey—"I'd peel your life back to its start" —both to solve the riddle of Other People ("I come back to your youth, my Nana,/ as if I might clean off/ the mad woman you became,/ withered and constipated,/ howling into your own earphone"), and so to solve her own origins ("You are my history (that stealer of children)/ and I have entered you"). But the attempt is not only abandoned, it is impossible; she cannot walk off her history, the past cannot be toured, only endured: where I am is hell.

The hell in her head is the subject of "Flee on Your Donkey," whose title and other details are taken from Rimbaud's *"Fêtes de la faim."* Begun in a mental hospital and worked over four years, the poem draws the past into the present to realign the poet's perspective on both:

> Recently I noticed in "Flee on Your Donkey" that I had used some of the same facts in *To Bedlam and Part Way Back*, but I hadn't realized them in their total ugliness. I'd hidden from them. This time was really raw and really ugly and it was all involved with my own madness. It was all like a great involuted web, and I presented it the way it really was.[27]

The madness that in "The Double Image" had been an escape from guilt has become a "hunger": "Six years of shuttling in and out of this place!/ O my hunger! My hunger!" The hospital scene this time resembles a sort of religious retreat—"Because there was no other place/ to flee to,/ I came back to the scene of the disordered senses" —and the poet inventories her time, fingers the black beads of loss. Like Rimbaud, she has been "a stranger,/ damned and in trance" during the years huddled in her analyst's office. Another poem, "Cripples and Other Stories," makes explicit the connection implied here: this ambivalent love song to her doctor is the pleas to her father, and the self he helps her deliver describes a birth:

> O my hunger! My hunger!
> I was the one
> who opened the war eyelid
> like a surgeon
> and brought forth young girls
> to grunt like fish.
> I told you,
> I said—

but I was lying—
that the knife was for my mother . . .
and then I delivered her.

Similarly, "For the Year of the Insane" invokes "Mary, fragile mother," the name of both the Virgin and Sexton's own mother. And again, her prayer for rebirth fantasizes a return: "A beginner, I feel your mouth touch mine." But more striking still is the repetition of the image of the eye as vagina in the call for delivery into light:

> O Mary, open your eyelids.
> I am in the domain of silence,
> the kingdom of the crazy and the sleeper.
> There is blood here
> and I have eaten it.
> O mother of the womb,
> did I come for blood alone?
> O little mother,
> I am in my own mind.
> I am locked in the wrong house.

This demand for release into life, as the title *Live or Die* balances her options, is the counterweight to the measure of death in the book, scaled from suicide attempts ("Wanting To Die," "The Addict") to the deaths of past figures who were part of her—John Holmes ("Somewhere in Africa") and Sylvia Plath ("Sylvia's Death"). "Flee on Your Donkey" struggles with the ambiguous impatience, introducing it first as weariness with "allowing myself the wasted life": "I have come back/ but disorder is not what it was./ I have lost the trick of it!/ The innocence of it!" Her desire for communion—"In this place everyone talks to his own mouth"—reverses her earlier escape inward: "Anne, Anne,/ flee on your donkey,/ flee this sad hotel." And by the time she can write the simple title "Live" over the book's last poem, the "mutilation" that previous poems had struck off is renounced. The evidence of survival is enough: "Even so,/ I kept right on going,/ a sort of human statement" that says finally: "I am not what I expected." If her guilt has not been solved, it has at least been soothed by her acceptance of and by her "dearest three"—her husband and daughters. And if the resolution of "Live" sounds unconvinced, unconvincing, it is because of Sexton's dependence on others, lulling the self into a passive tense.

The survival achieved, the rebirth delivered, is then praised in *Love Poems* (1969), in many ways her weakest collection since most of it is sustained by language alone. Its self-celebration tends either to avoid or to invent the experience behind it, or revolves on minimal events: a hip-fracture, a summer safari. Secure in her use of free verse, Sexton crafts these poems with equivalents: litanies of images which are more often additional than accumulative. As before, the book's epigraph—this time from Yeats—defines its intention, and here the concern is with roles: "One should say before sleeping, 'I have lived many lives. I have been a slave and a prince. Many a beloved has sat on my knees and I have sat on the knees of many a beloved. Everything that has been shall be again.' " And so she explores her womanhood ("The Breast," "In Celebration of My Uterus"), and her roles as woman, wife and lover. Not surprisingly, she is best when describing how lovers swim "the identical river called Mine": "we are a pair of scissors/ who come together to cut, without towels saying His. Hers" ("December 10th"). The poem to her husband, "Loving the Killer," speaks of the selfishness carved out by the past:

> Though the house is full of
> candy bars the wasted ghost
> of my parents is poking
> the keyhole, rubbing the bedpost.
> Also the ghost of your father,
> who was killed outright.
> Tonight we will argue and shout,
> "My loss is greater than yours!
> My pain is more valuable!"

The masks she wears in *Love Poems* don't hide Sexton's confessional impulse, they avoid it. Her motive may well have been to search out new voices. Certainly this is the case with her next work, *Transformations* (1971). She began these versions of Grimms' tales on the

advice of her daughter after an extended dry spell in her work, and
when, five poems later, she had written "Snow White and the Seven
Dwarfs," she felt she should continue the experiment into a book
which would release a more playful aspect of her personality that her
earlier books had neglected.[28] The result—considering its cloyingly
"cute" Kurt Vonnegut introduction, its illustrations, and commercial
success—seems at most a divertissement and surely a conscious effort
to avoid her confessional voice. Like *Love Poems,* it seems content to
present women in their roles, from princess to witch, with the poet
merely presiding as "Dame Sexton," as the introductory poem, "The
Gold Key," explains:

> The speaker in this case
> is a middle-aged witch, me—
> tangled on my two great arms,
> my face in a book
> and my mouth wide,
> ready to tell you a story or two.

And the poem goes on to offer a key to her technique here:

> It opens this book of odd tales
> which transform the Brothers Grimm.
> Transform?
> As if an enlarged paper clip
> could be a piece of sculpture.
> (And it could.)

That is to say, her "transformations" exaggerate and so distort the
originals to create contemporary camp. And indeed the tales are
blown up like pop-art posters by means of an irreverently zippy style,
slangy allusions, and a strongly Freudian slant to her stories. But what
draws *Transformations* more centrally into this discussion is Sexton's
inability to keep her characteristic concerns from seeping into what
would otherwise seem her most distanced work.

The book's Ovidian title points to Sexton's first fascination with
Grimm—one which Randall Jarrell spoke of in his poem "The Mär-
chen":

Had you not learned—have we not learned, from tales
Neither of beasts nor kingdoms nor their Lord,
But of our own hearts, the realm of death—
Neither to rule nor die? to change, to change!

The power of fairy tales has always resided in their "changed" dream-landscapes, and Freud discussed them as "screen memories," survivals of persistent human conflicts and desires, narratives whose characters and situations are symbolic of the unconscious dramas in any individual's psyche.[29] With this in mind, the psychoanalytical uses of the word "transformations" bear on Sexton's work. It can refer both to the variations of the same thematic material represented in a patient's dreams of experience and to the process by which unconscious material is brought to consciousness. So too Sexton's poems are variations on themes familiar from her earlier work—at one point she says, "My guilts are what/ we catalogue"—transformed into fantasies or dreams discovered in the Grimm tales, which are anyone's first "literature" and become bound up with the child's psyche. The introductions that precede each story—replacing the analogous moral-pointing in the fairy tale—usually isolate her more private concern in each, and the tales which elaborate them include subjects ranging from adultery ("The Little Peasant") to despair ("Rumpelstiltskin") to deception ("Red Riding Hood") to parents' devouring their children ("Hansel and Gretel"). Other poems are even more explicit in that their subjects allude directly to earlier poems: "The Operation" is recalled in "The Maiden Without Hands" with its lines "If they have cut out your uterus/ I will give you a laurel wreath/ to put in its place." "Rapunzel" fantasizes on her "Nana-hex," and "The Frog Prince" is a daring exploration of her father-feelings: "Frog is my father's genitals. . . . He says: Kiss me. Kiss me./ And the ground soils itself." But a majority of these poems link their dreams with those of madness and with Sexton's strong poem on its asylum. "The White Snake," "Iron Hans," "One-Eye, Two-Eyes, Three-Eyes," "The Wonderful Musician," "The Twelve Dancing Princesses," and "Briar Rose (Sleeping Beauty)"—each is set at an outpost of psychosis, the often bizarre details creating a narrative of insanity from the inside.

"Briar Rose (Sleeping Beauty)," the final and most intense poem in the book, was actually written while Sexton was hospitalized, and loosens its disguise into an identity. Once awake, Briar Rose cannot bear to sleep again, to imprison herself in the dreams that are Sexton's:

> There was a theft.
> That much I am told.
> I was abandoned.
> That much I know.
> I was forced backward.
> I was forced forward.
> I was passed hand to hand
> like a bowl of fruit.
> Each night I am nailed into place
> and I forget who I am.
> Daddy?
> That's another kind of prison.
> It's not the prince at all,
> but my father
> drunkenly bent over my bed,
> circling the abyss like a shark,
> my father thick upon me
> like some sleeping jellyfish.
> What voyage this, little girl?
> This coming out of prison?
> God help—
> this life after death?

The fabular impulse behind *Transformations* is resumed in *The Book of Folly* (1972), both in the three short stories included among the poems and in "The Jesus Papers" sequence, which is a taunting, Black-mass transformation of the salvation story. The entire book, in fact, has a summary quality to it. The forged stylization of *Love Poems* returns in "Angels of the Love Affair," six sonnets on love's seasons. The angel in each is the "gull that grows out of my back in the dreams I prefer," and those dreams are hushed, flamboyant, touching memories of certain sheets, bits of dried blood, lemony woodwork, a peace march—all the abstracted details of moments that are warm only in her darknesses. But what is more important is her return to the fully confessional mode: "I struck out memory with an X/ but it came back./ I tied down time with a rope/ but it came back" ("Killing the Spring"). On the simplest level, the detritus of time has clustered new collisions or crises: the death of her sister—"her slim neck/ snapped like a piece of celery" in a car crash—or the national disasters ("The Firebombers," "The Assassin"). Generally, the subjects she recircles are familiar, but her angle of attack and attitude is new: more self-conscious, often more strident and defiant, more searching. Like the later Lowell, Sexton's self-consciousness results from the ironies of exposure, the logistics of fame. These permit her both a guilty longing:

> I would like a simple life
> yet all night I am laying
> poems away in a long box.
>
> It is my immortality box,
> my lay-away plan,
> my coffin.
> > ("The Ambition Bird")

and an empty pride:

> Now Sweeney phones from London, W. 2,
> saying *Martyr, my religion is love, is you.*
> Be seated, my Sweeney, my invisible fan.
> Surely the words will continue, for that's
> what's left that's true.
> > ("Sweeney")[30]

Both her art and her audience, her fans and family exist beyond their ability to help her, as a poem to her now-grown daughter Linda laments:

> Question you about this
> and you will sew me a shroud
> and hold up Monday's broiler
> and thumb out the chicken gut.
> Question you about this
> and you will see my death

> drooling at these gray lips
> while you, my burglar, will eat
> fruit and pass the time of day.
>   ("Mother and Daughter")

It is this sense of what still remains to be lost that occasions the tonal shift. In contrast with "You, Dr. Martin" or "Cripples and Other Stories," a new poem to her psychiatrist, "The Doctor of the Heart," is scornfully reductive, resentful of the soothing instead of solving, challenging the doctor with her history and her art:

> But take away my mother's carcinoma
> for I have only one cup of fetus tears.
>
> Take away my father's cerebral hemorrhage
> for I have only a jigger of blood in my hand.
>
> Take away my sister's broken neck
> for I have only my schoolroom ruler for a cure.
>
> Is there such a device for my heart?
> I have only a gimmick called magic fingers.

Whether the mind is too strong or not strong enough to adjust to the violent changes that death forces on us no longer seems to matter to the poem's manic finale:

> I am at the ship's prow.
> I am no longer the suicide
>
> with her raft and paddle.
> Herr Doktor! I'll no longer die
>
> to spite you, you wallowing
> seasick grounded man.

This defiance of death demands, first of all, that the tyranny of her own impulse toward suicide be fully evoked: she must "lie down/ with them and lift my madness/ off like a wig," since "Death is here. There is no/ other settlement" ("Oh"). And for this reason she returns, in "The Other," to what has always terrified her poetry: the alien self she cannot escape, who insanely possesses her and can keep her from the self that makes poems and love and children:

> When the child is soothed and resting on the breast
> it is my other who swallows Lysol.
> When someone kisses someone or flushes the toilet
> it is my other who sits in a ball and cries.
> My other beats a tin drum in my heart.
> My other hangs up laundry as I try to sleep.
> My other cries and cries and cries
> when I put on a cocktail dress.
> It cries when I prick a potato.
> It cries when I kiss someone hello.
> It cries and cries and cries
> until I put on a painted mask
> and leer at Jesus in His passion.

As in *Live or Die,* these are the dreams that confront endurance. Reformulated, death and madness, which had once seemed her only innocence, come to the silence she is writing against:

> The silence is death.
> It comes each day with its shock
> to sit on my shoulder, a white bird,
> and peck at the black eyes
> and the vibrating muscle
> of my mouth.
>
> ("The Silence")

The *Book of Folly*'s remembrance of things past is likewise more direct when it turns to her family. "Anna Who Was Mad"—Anna, the anagram for the Nana whose namesake Sexton is—alternates interrogative and imperative lines to force the guilt of cause and effect: "Am I some sort of infection?/ Did I make you go insane?" This paralyzing guilt, itself a form of self-hatred, is "all a matter of history" in "The Hex," a poem which links her relationship with this same great-aunt to that with The Other: "Every time I get happy/ the Nana-hex comes through." This strong poem on how "The dead take aim" to leave her "still the criminal" is an angry pacing off of the past's cage:

> Sitting on the stairs at thirteen,
> hands fixed over my ears,
> the Hitler-mouth psychiatrist climbing
> past me like an undertaker,
> and the old woman's shriek of fear:
> You did it. You are the evil.
> It was the day meant for me.
> Thirteen for your whole life,
> just the masks keep changing.

But this is a prelude to the book's centering six-poem sequence, "The Death of the Fathers"—surely one of Sexton's triumphs, daring in its explorations and revelations, its verse superbly controlled as the voice of each poem is modulated to its experience, now shifting to the declaratives of a child, now heightening to involved regrets and prayers. While watching Sexton trace memories of her father mixed with sexual fantasies, one must recall Freud's sense of the origin of childhood memories:

> Quite unlike conscious memories from the time of maturity, they are not fixed at the moment of being experienced and afterwards repeated, but are only elicited at a later age when childhood is already past; in the process they are altered and falsified, and are put into the service of later trends, so that generally speaking they cannot be sharply distinguished from phantasies.[31]

Similarly, since fantasies become memories, it becomes impossible and useless beyond a certain point to distinguish between "events" that happened and fears or desires imagined so strongly that they might as well have happened. And further, Freud writes that the "screen memories" made of childhood traumas "relate to impressions of a sexual and aggressive nature, and no doubt also to early injuries to the ego (narcissistic mortifications). In this connection it should be remarked that such young children make no sharp distinction between sexual and aggressive acts, as they do later."[32]

Sexton's sequence divides naturally into two parts of three poems each, the first set in childhood to evoke her father, and the second set in the present to focus his double death and the "later trends" that have occasioned the fantasies in the first. The opening poem, "Oysters," is her initiation, at once a fantasy of self-begetting and a memory of desire that, once conscious, defeats innocence. She is Daddy's Girl having lunch with her father at a restaurant, and fearfully eats her oysters—"this father-food," his semen: "It was a soft medicine/ that came from the sea into my mouth,/ moist and plump./ I swallowed." Then they laugh through this "death of childhood"—"the child was defeated./ The woman won." The second poem, "How We Danced," continues the fantasy in an Oedipal round:

> The champagne breathed like a skin diver
> and the glasses were crystal and the bride
> and groom gripped each other in sleep
> like nineteen-thirty marathon dancers.
> Mother was a belle and danced with twenty men.
> You danced with me never saying a word.
> Instead the serpent spoke as you held me close.
> The serpent, that mocker, woke up and pressed against me
> like a great god and we bent together
> like two lonely swans.

And the third poem, "The Boat," though it reverts to an earlier time, is a kind of coital coda to her subconscious victory. This time Leda's swan is her godlike captain, out in the same sea from which the oysters came, "out past Cuckold's Light," where "the three of us" ride through a storm that her father masters, but at its height there is the moment which both resolves her fantasies and predicts their destruction, in a memory of violence both sexual and aggressive:

> Now the waves are higher;
> they are round buildings.
> We start to go through them
> and the boat shudders.
> Father is going faster.
> I am wet.

> I am tumbling on my seat
> like a loose kumquat.
> Suddenly
> a wave that we go under.
> Under. Under. Under.
> We are daring the sea.
> We have parted it.
> We are scissors.
> Here in the green room
> the dead are very close.

The second part narrates the death of the fathers. In "Santa," the child's mythic sense of her father is killed: "Father,/ the Santa Claus suit/ you bought from Wolff Fording Theatrical Supplies,/ back before I was born,/ is dead." After describing how her father dressed up her childhood—when "Mother would kiss you/ for she was that tall"—she comes to liquor's reality principle: "The year I ceased to believe in you/ is the year you were drunk." And by the time her father, in turn, dressed up for her own children, the emptiness of having replaced her mother is apparent: "We were conspirators,/ secret actors,/ and I kissed you/ because I was tall enough./ But that is over." "Friends" details another death, as her father is distanced by doubt. The Stranger in her childhood could have been any of the men who would come to steal her from her father, but this family friend is more ominous:

> He was bald as a hump.
> His ears stuck out like teacups
> and his tongue, my God, his tongue,
> like a red worm and when he kissed
> it crawled right in.
>
> Oh Father, Father,
> who was that stranger
> who knew Mother too well?

The question this poem ends on—"Oh God,/ he was a stranger,/ was he not?"—is answered brutally in the last poem, "Begat," a kind of family romance in reverse:

> Today someone else lurks in the wings
> with your dear lines in his mouth
> and your crown on his head.
> Oh Father, Father-sorrow,
> where has time brought us?
>
> Today someone called.
> "Merry Christmas," said the stranger.
> "I am your real father."
> That was a knife.
> That was a grave.

The father she had called hers dies again—the stranger takes "the *you* out of the *me*"—and the poems end with a pathetic elegy on the distance she has come since childhood and the first poem of this sequence, since the understood desire. The end rises to a last regret with the simple details of intimacy's allowances and sadnesses, and the memory of her father dressed as Santa turns as raw as the blood they no longer share, the "two lonely swans" who danced in fantasy are now fired by betrayal and loss:

> Those times I smelled the Vitalis on his pajamas.
> Those times I mussed his curly black hair
> and touched his ten tar-fingers
> and swallowed down his whiskey breath.
> Red. Red. Father, you are blood red.
> Father,
> we are two birds on fire.

The blend of memory and fantasy in "The Death of the Fathers," each sharpening and supporting the effect of the other, is the culmination of Sexton's confessional style. Her next book, *The Death Notebooks* (1974), develops this technique still further, but without any consistency. The reason for this is that the book collects poems she had written over many years without intending to publish them, and as meditations on her own death they tend to fantasize forward rather than remember back. But with their frequent sense of having been written from beyond death, there is a retrospective character to them that continually catches up long memories and fragments of experience. And the exercise itself—especially its eventual publication, which seems reluctant but inevitable, even in its duplication of the smaller deaths she had detailed before—adds a note of shabby self-consciousness to "this last peep show" ("Making a Living," "For Mr. Death Who Stands with His Door Open," "Faustus and I," "Clothes"). But the book's powerful confrontation with death—and even its cover schemes in black-and-blue—tries to work its way toward the accommodations of understanding: "For death comes to friends, to parents, to sisters. Death comes with its bagful of pain yet they do not curse the key they were given to hold" ("Ninth Psalm"). So Sexton sees herself "knitting her own hair into a baby shawl" because "There is a death baby/ for each of us./ We own him" ("Baby"), carried for a lifetime, delivered slowly and rocked into darkness. And as she sits "in that dark room putting bones into place" ("Seventh Psalm"), she edges "the abyss,/ the God spot" ("The Fury of Sundays")—a dilemma first raised in "The Division of Parts" back in *To Bedlam and Part Way Back* and left as ambiguous here in several religious poems. That personal paradox reflects the difficulty with the book itself, whose "summing-up" remains too immediate and unresolved.

The title of the book implies excerpts of unfinished spontaneity, and there are two long experiments which, by their very nature, could have been continued or concluded at the poet's will. "The Furies" was written while the poet was recuperating in bed from an illness and began associating at the typewriter on suggestive topics. Their antecedent is "Angels of the Love Affair" (or even the variations-form in the uneven sequence titled "Bestiary U. S. A.," later included in *45 Mercy Street*), and their energy is their own rather than the poet's. And a sequence of nine psalms called "O Ye Tongues" attempts to adapt the patterns of Smart's *Jubilato Agno* and to identify Smart with both herself and The Other, combined into "the mad poet":

> For I am an orphan with two death masks on the mantel
> and came from the grave of my mama's belly into the
> commerce of Boston.

> For there were only two windows on the city and the
> buildings ate me.
>
> For I was swaddled in grease wool from my father's
> company and could not move or ask the time.
>
> For Anne and Christopher were born in my head as I
> howled at the grave of the roses, the ninety-four rose
> crèches of my bedroom.
>
> ("Third Psalm")

Her success is variable, but when the excess is simplified the result is the genuine pathos of Smart's own verse: "For in my nature I quested for beauty, but God, God, hath sent me to sea for pearls."

But clearly the most significant and successful poem in *The Death Notebooks* is "Hurry Up Please It's Time," a sort of long, hallucinatory diary-entry: "Today is November 14th, 1972./ I live in Weston, Mass., Middlesex County,/ U.S.A., and it rains steadily/ in the pond like white puppy eyes." The style is pure pastiche, mixing dialect and dialogue, nursery rhymes and New Testament, references ranging from Goethe to Thurber, attitudes veering between arrogance and abasement. At times she is "Anne," at times "Ms. Dog"—becoming her own mock-God. She can sneer at herself ("Middle-class lady,/ you make me smile"), or shiver at what "my heart, that witness" remembers. The recaptured spots of time—say, a quiet summer interlude with her husband and friends—are run into projected blotches spread toward the death to come. And though its expansive free form dilutes all but its cumulative force, the poem is an advance on the way "The Death of the Fathers" had whispered its confessions.

Sexton's two posthumously published collections—*The Awful Rowing Toward God* (1975) and *45 Mercy Street* (1976)—are largely disappointing and anticlimactic, except when isolated poems in either book echo earlier successes. The last volume is particularly flat—because, one presumes, the poet did not revise the poems or arrange the selection. Its dominating section is a painful sequence called "The Divorce Papers," an entirely unresolved series of reactions to "the dead city of my marriage" and to the ways in which divorce exhumes it. The ambivalence that informs these seventeen poems—alternating relief and regret, guilt, despair, and exhilaration—is less enriching than enervating. One reason for that is the very immediacy of the work, which is not grounded in an adequate perspective on the history of her marriage, the evolution of her feelings, or the complication of two lives lived together. It is as if the poet—and her poetry—simply resigned themselves to necessary conditions. And that aspect of autopsy is also apparent elsewhere in *45 Mercy Street,* for instance in the title poem, the book's best. Here we are given glimpses of a dream-vision whose burden is the inability to recover what has been lost in and to the past, whose own character shifts from history to hallucination. This can result in bursts of self-disgust or helpless bewilderment, which are combined in the poem's final lines and testify to the blind end these last poems embody:

> Next I pull the dream off
> and slam into the cement wall
> of the clumsy calendar
> I live in,
> my life,
> and its hauled up
> notebooks.

The stronger and more fluent book is *The Awful Rowing Toward God,* which consolidates her experiments in *The Book of Folly* and *The Death Notebooks.* Like the latter, it is thematically organized into a series of variations on a religious doubt that swerves between exorcism and exultation. What she calls "my ignorance of God" is figured as a cancerous crab "clutching fast to my heart" ("The Poet of Ignorance"), while on the other hand there is an ecstatic, almost murderous release of desire:

> I am on the amphetamine of the soul.
> I am, each day,
> typing out the God
> my typewriter believes in.

Very quick. Very intense,
like a wolf at a live heart.
("Frenzy")

Within such a dialectic, "You have a thousand prayers/ but God has one," and she repeats her poems as if hoping they accumulate into *His* prayer. But though this may be a God a typewriter can believe in, it seems questionable that Sexton does. At the very least, He is an abstracted presence—perhaps merely an obvious displacement of the father with whom she is attempting to effect a reconciliation. This may be one reason why the religious experience she records in this book is transposed into an almost mythic mode—one which, for instance, projects a version of her asylum life into a vision of an afterlife. As if to underscore this mode, both her voice and her line have the poise and concision of proverbs. There is little interest in elaborate exposition or explanation; instead there is a dialogue with herself, private and associative. The surrealistic and domestic imagery employed have considerable authority, and the book's long—and usually successful—poem "Is It True?" is a continuation of the diaristic "Hurry Up Please It's Time," though the later poem has a quiet control that strengthens the free form's urgent sprawl. Though still intensely personal, the book's privatism is of the peculiar variety that renders it accessible, undoubtedly because its subject is one in which the individual personality is less prominent than the character of the quest itself. At its best moments, Sexton's voice swells to assume that character, her rhetoric purified to austere grandeur. The conclusion of "The Big Heart," a poem addressed to her intimate companions, is one such moment:

> They hear how
> the artery of my soul has been severed
> and soul is spurting out upon them,
> bleeding on them,
> messing up their clothes,
> dirtying their shoes.
> And God is filling me,
> though there are times of doubt

as hollow as the Grand Canyon,
He is giving me the thoughts of dogs,
the spider in its intricate web,
the sun
in all its amazement,
and a slain ram
that is the glory,
the mystery of great cost,
and my heart,
which is very big,
I promise it is very large,
a monster of sorts,
takes it all in—
all in comes the fury of love.

That very fury of love, occasionally so moving in the posthumous books, does tend to distort or diffuse their force. Still, they remain as flawed evidence of Sexton's steady boldness, her readiness to risk new experiments in verse to record renewed perceptions of her experience in life, in the manner Emerson claimed that art is the effort to indemnify ourselves for the wrongs of our condition. There is, as one critic has said of her, "something awesome, even sublime in a woman who is not afraid to sound crude or shrill so long as she is honest, who in her best work sounds neither shrill nor crude precisely because she is honest."[33] Her courage in coming true not only made Sexton one of the most distinctive voices in this generation's literature, and a figure of permanent importance to the development of American poetry, but has revealed in its art and its honesty a life in which we can discover our own.

SELECTED BIBLIOGRAPHY

I. Work by Anne Sexton

A. Poetry Collections

To Bedlam and Part Way Back. Boston: Houghton Mifflin, 1960.
All My Pretty Ones. Boston: Houghton Mifflin, 1962.
Selected Poems. London: Oxford University Press, 1964.
Live or Die. Boston: Houghton Mifflin, 1966; London: Oxford University Press, 1967.
Poems (with Thomas Kinsella and Douglas Livingstone). London: Oxford University Press, 1968.
Love Poems. Boston: Houghton Mifflin, 1969; London: Oxford University Press, 1969.
Transformations. Boston: Houghton Mifflin, 1971; London: Oxford University Press, 1972.
The Book of Folly. Boston: Houghton Mifflin, 1972; London: Chatto and Windus, 1974.
The Death Notebooks. Boston: Houghton Mifflin, 1974; London: Chatto and Windus, 1975.
The Awful Rowing Toward God. Boston: Houghton Mifflin, 1975; London: Chatto and Windus, 1977.
45 Mercy Street. Edited by Linda Gray Sexton. Boston: Houghton Mifflin, 1976; London: Martin Secker & Warburg, 1977.

B. Children's Books (all coauthored with Maxine Kumin)

Eggs of Things. New York: Putnam, 1963.
More Eggs of Things. New York: Putnam, 1964.
Joey and the Birthday Present. New York: McGraw-Hill, 1971.
The Wizard's Tears. New York: McGraw-Hill, 1975.

C. Uncollected Prose

"Anne Sexton: Worksheets." *Malahat Review,* VI (1968), pp. 105–14.

"The Barfly Ought To Sing." *TriQuarterly,* 7 (Fall 1966), pp. 89–94. Reprinted in *The Art of Sylvia Plath,* ed. Charles Newman. Bloomington: Indiana University Press, 1970, pp. 174–81.

"Classroom At Boston University." *Harvard Advocate,* CXLV, Special Supplement (November 1961), pp. 13–14.

Foreword to *The Real Tin Flower* by Aliki Barnstone. New York: Crowell-Collier, 1968, pp. v–vi.

"The Freak Show." *American Poetry Review,* 2.3 (May/June 1973), pp. 38, 40.

"The Last Believer." *Vogue,* CXII (November 15, 1963), pp. 76, 78.

["On 'Some Foreign Letters' "]. *Poet's Choice,* ed. Paul Engle and Joseph Langland. New York: Dial Press, 1962, pp. 276–77.

"A Small Journal." *Ms.,* II.5 (November 1973), pp. 60–63, 107. Reprinted in *The Poet's Story,* ed. Howard Moss. New York: Macmillan, 1973, pp. 214–22.

A recording by the poet of twenty-four poems—recorded on June 1, 1974—is available as *Anne Sexton Reads Her Poetry,* Caedmon TC 1441.

II. Work about Anne Sexton (not including work reprinted in this volume)

A. Interviews

Ames, Lois. "Anne Sexton: From 'Bedlam' to Broadway." *Boston Sunday Herald Traveler Book Guide,* October 12, 1969, pp. 1–2, 16.

"Anne Sexton." *Talks With Authors,* ed. Charles F. Madden. Carbondale: Southern Illinois University Press, 1968, pp. 151–79.

Balliro, Charles. "Interview with Anne Sexton." *Fiction,* 1.6 (1974), pp. 12–13, 5.

Berg, Beatrice. " 'Oh, I Was Very Sick.' " *New York Times,* November 9, 1969, pp. D1, D7.

Green, Carol. "A Writer Is Essentially a Spy." *Boston Review of the Arts,* 2.5 (August 1972), pp. 30–37.

Heyen, William. "From 1928 to Whenever: A Conversation with Anne Sexton." *American Poets in 1976,* ed. William Heyen. Indianapolis: Bobbs-Merrill, 1976, pp. 304–28.

Showalter, Elaine and Carol Smith. "A Nurturing Relationship: A Conversation with Anne Sexton and Maxine Kumin, April 15, 1974." *Women's Studies,* IV.1 (1976), pp. 115–36.

Weeks, Brigitte. "The Excitable Gift: The Art of Anne Sexton." *Boston,*
August 1968, pp. 30–32.

B. Essays

Alvarez, A. *Beyond All This Fiddle: Essays 1955–1967.* New York: Random
House, 1969.
Axelrod, Rise B. "The Transforming Art of Anne Sexton." *Concerning Po-
etry,* 7.1 (Spring 1974), pp. 6–13.
Fein, Richard J. "The Demon of Anne Sexton." *English Record,* 18.1 (Octo-
ber 1967), pp. 16–21.
Fields, Beverly. "The Poetry of Anne Sexton." *Poets In Progress,* ed. Edward
Hungerford. Evanston: Northwestern University Press, 1967, pp. 251–85.
Hoffman, Nancy Jo. "Reading Women's Poetry: The Meaning and Our
Lives." *College English,* 34.1 (October 1972), pp. 48–62.
Jones, A. R. "Necessity and Freedom: The Poetry of Robert Lowell, Sylvia
Plath and Anne Sexton." *Critical Quarterly,* 7.1 (Spring 1965), pp. 11–30.
Juhasz, Suzanne. *Naked and Fiery Forms: Modern American Poetry by
Women, A New Tradition.* New York: Harper Colophon, 1976.
Mills, Ralph J., Jr. *Contemporary American Poetry.* New York: Random
House, 1965.
———. "Creation's Very Self: On the Personal Element in Recent American
Poetry." *Cry of the Human: Essays on Contemporary American Poetry.*
Urbana: University of Illinois Press, 1975, pp. 1–47.
Mizejewski, Linda. "Sappho to Sexton: Woman Uncontained." *College En-
glish,* 35.3 (December 1973), pp. 340–45.
Molesworth, Charles. " 'With Your Own Face On': The Origins and Conse-
quences of Confessional Poetry." *Twentieth Century Literature,* 22.2 (May
1976), pp. 163–78.
Mood, John J. " 'A Bird Full of Bones': Anne Sexton—A Visit and A Read-
ing." *Chicago Review,* 23.4/24.1 (1972), pp. 107–23.
Newlin, Margaret. "The Suicide Bandwagon." *Critical Quarterly,* 14.4 (Winter 1972), pp. 367–78.
Northouse, Cameron and Thomas P. Walsh. *Sylvia Plath and Anne Sexton:
A Reference Guide.* Boston: G. K. Hall, 1974. Includes a chronological
listing of original appearances of poems, occasionally uncollected, through
1971.
Phillips, Robert. *The Confessional Poets.* Carbondale: Southern Illinois University Press, 1973.
Poulin, A., Jr., ed. "A Memorial for Anne Sexton." *American Poetry Review,*
4.3 (1975), pp. 15–20. Contributions by John Malcolm Brinnin, Maxine

Kumin, Kathleen Spivack, Susan Fromberg Schaeffer, C. K. Williams, and others.

Rosenthal, M. L. *The New Poets: American and British Poetry Since World War II.* New York: Oxford University Press, 1967.

Shor, Ira. "Anne Sexton's 'For My Lover . . .': Feminism in the Classroom." *College English,* 34.8 (May 1973), pp. 1082–93.

Zollman, Sol. "Criticism, Self-Criticism, No Transformation: The Poetry of Robert Lowell and Anne Sexton." *Literature and Ideology,* 9 (1971), pp. 29–36.

NOTES

Jane McCabe,
" 'A Woman Who Writes': A Feminist Approach
to the Early Poetry of Anne Sexton"

1. References to Sexton's work will be incorporated into my text, with page numbers to the appropriate volume, and the following abbreviations will be observed: *To Bedlam and Part Way Back (BPWB), All My Pretty Ones (AMPO), Live or Die (LD), Love Poems (LP), Transformations (Trans), The Book of Folly (BF), The Death Notebooks (DN), The Awful Rowing Toward God (ARTG).*

2. Barbara Kevles, "The Art of Poetry XV: Anne Sexton," *Paris Review,* 52 (1971), p. 160.

3. Suzanne Juhasz, *Naked and Fiery Forms: Modern American Poetry By Women, A New Tradition* (New York: Harper Colophon, 1976), p. 1.

4. Barbara Segnitz and Carol Rainey, eds., *Psyche: The Feminine Poetic Consciousness* (New York: Dell, 1973), pp. 16–17.

5. Ibid., p. 22.

6. Juhasz, p. 58.

7. Ibid., p. 118.

8. Adrienne Rich, "After Twenty Years," *Diving Into The Wreck* (New York: Norton, 1973), p. 13.

9. Diane Wakoski, *Dancing on the Grave of a Son of a Bitch* (Los Angeles: Black Sparrow, 1973), pp. 57–58.

10. Linda Bamber, *Comic Women, Tragic Men,* unpubl. Ph.D. diss., Tufts University, 1974.

11. Juhasz, p. 2.

12. Adrienne Rich, "A Marriage in the 'Sixties," *Snapshots of a Daughter-in-Law* (New York: Norton, 1967), pp. 45–46.

J. D. McClatchy,
"Anne Sexton: Somehow To Endure"

1. A. Alvarez, *Beyond All This Fiddle* (New York: Random House, 1969), pp. 14–15. It is important to add that Sexton herself conceded the point:

"There is some very bad writing in some of my best poems, and yet those flaws seem to me to make them even better. They are with all their flaws, a little more human, you might say" (Patricia Marx, "Interview with Anne Sexton," *Hudson Review,* XVIII.4 [Winter 1965–66], p. 569).

2. AS to JDMcC, recorded conversation, September 23, 1973.

3. "Classroom at Boston University," *Harvard Advocate,* CXLV, Special Supplement (November 1961), p. 14.

4. AS to JDMcC, recorded conversation, July 3, 1973.

5. Theodor Reik, *The Compulsion to Confess* [1925] (New York: Farrar, Straus and Cudahy, 1959), pp. 195–99, 206–207, 347.

6. AS to JDMcC, recorded conversation, September 23, 1973.

7. Erik H. Erikson, *Identity: Youth and Crisis* (New York: Norton, 1968), p. 74.

8. AS to JDMcC, recorded conversation, September 23, 1973.

9. "W.D. Snodgrass: An Interview," *Salmagundi,* 22–23 (Spring–Summer 1973), p. 150.

10. "Creative Writers and Day-Dreaming" (1907), *Standard Edition of the Complete Psychological Works of Sigmund Freud,* ed. James Strachey (London: Hogarth Press, 1953–   ), IX, p. 153.

11. AS to JDMcC, recorded conversations, July 3 and September 23, 1973. This sense of witness is shared by poets with very different approaches. For instance, in the preface to a collection of her work, Denise Levertov writes of her hope that the book will be seen "as having some value not as mere 'confessional' autobiography, but as a document of some historical value, a record of one person's inner/outer experience in America during the '60s and the beginning of the '70s, an experience which is shared by so many and transcends the peculiar details of each life, though it can only be expressed in and through such details" (*To Stay Alive,* New York: New Directions, 1971, p. ix).

12. Ernst Kris, *Psychoanalytic Explorations in Art* (New York: International Universities Press, 1952), p. 256.

13. Marx, p. 563.

14. Ibid., p. 568.

15. Richard Howard, *Alone with America* (New York: Atheneum, 1971), p. 445.

16. M. L. Rosenthal, *The New Poets: American and British Poetry Since World War II* (New York: Oxford University Press, 1967), p. 134.

17. *Poet's Choice,* ed. Paul Engle and Joseph Langland (New York: Dial Press, 1962), p. 227.

18. Barbara Kevles, "The Art of Poetry XV: Anne Sexton," *Paris Review,* 52 (Summer 1971), p. 187.

19. Beatrice Berg, " 'Oh, I Was Very Sick,' " *New York Times,* November 19, 1969, p. D7.

20. Kevles, pp. 171–72.

21. Gaston Bachelard, *L'Eau et les Rêves* (Paris: J. Corti, 1942), p. 10. See also, Kris, p. 258.

22. Kevles, p. 162.

23. William Packard, "Craft Interview with Anne Sexton," *New York Quarterly,* 3 (Summer 1970), p. 11.

24. Robert Boyers, *"Live or Die:* The Achievement of Anne Sexton," *Salmagundi,* II.i (Spring 1967), p. 64.

25. Kevles, p. 189.

26. AS to JDMcC, recorded conversation, September 23, 1973.

27. Kevles, p. 180.

28. AS to JDMcC, recorded conversation, September 23, 1973.

29. Sigmund Freud, "The Occurrence in Dreams of Material from Fairy Tales" (1913), *Standard Edition,* XII, pp. 279–87. Also, Freud and D. E. Oppenheim, "Dreams in Folklore" (1911), *Standard Edition,* XII, pp. 175–203; Emanuel K. Schwartz, "A Psychoanalytic Study of the Fairy Tale," *American Journal of Psychotherapy,* X.4 (October 1956), pp. 740–62; Ernest Jones, "Psycho-analysis and Folklore," *Essays in Applied Psycho-analysis* (London, 1951), II, pp. 1–21. For a more general discussion of the unconscious motives and strategies of fairy tales, see also Bruno Bettelheim, *The Uses of Enchantment: The Meaning and Importance of Fairy Tales* (New York: Knopf, 1976), a book which singles out Sexton's *Transformations* for their powerful insights.

30. For an interesting example of the continuity between her life, poetry, and fiction, see the reappearance of Sweeney (an Australian businessman and fan) in "A Small Journal," *Ms.,* II.5 (November 1973), pp. 60–63, 107. This journal in the form of a confessional story is reprinted with the title the poet herself preferred, "All God's Children Need Radios," *The Poet's Story,* ed. Howard Moss (New York: Macmillan, 1973), pp. 214–22.

31. Sigmund Freud, "Leonardo da Vinci and a Memory of His Childhood" (1910), *Standard Edition,* XI, p. 83.

32. Sigmund Freud, "Moses and Monotheism: Three Essays" (1934–38), *Standard Edition,* XXIII, p. 74.

33. Boyers, p. 71.